Edited by ANDRÉ PRATTE
and JONATHAN KAY

LEGACY

HOW FRENCH CANADIANS SHAPED NORTH AMERICA

SIGNAL
McClelland & Stewart

Hardcover edition published 2016

Signal is an imprint of McClelland & Stewart, a division of Penguin Random House Canada Limited

Signal and colophon are registered trademarks of McClelland & Stewart

Library and Archives Canada Cataloguing in Publication is available upon request

ISBN: 978-0-7710-7239-0
ebook ISBN: 978-0-7710-7241-3

Library of Congress Control Number is available upon request

French Language edition published simultaneously by Les Éditions La Presse

Typeset in Quadraat by M&S, Toronto
Printed and bound in the USA

Published by Signal,
an imprint of McClelland & Stewart,
a division of Penguin Random House Canada Limited,
a Penguin Random House Company

www.penguinrandomhouse.ca

1 2 3 4 5 20 19 18 17 16

SIGNAL | Penguin Random House

CONTENTS

ANDRÉ PRATTE

FOREWORD

ON FEBRUARY 16, 1913, schoolchildren playing on bluffs near Fort Pierre, South Dakota, made a remarkable discovery. Protruding from the ground, under a fine dusting of snow, was a very old piece of metal. It had words engraved on either side. Words that they couldn't understand.

For nearly two hundred years, the work of the early-eighteenth-century explorer Pierre Gaultier de Varennes et de La Vérendrye and his sons had remained unknown to historians. Many doubted the claims that their travels west of Lake Superior had taken them as far as the Rocky Mountains. And besides, the explorers had failed in their mission, since they never found the passage leading to the fabled Western Sea.

Some, though, were convinced that the La Vérendryes deserved recognition as the first white men to have seen the great plains of central North America—and indeed they had dedicated a dozen years of their lives to exploring the region and forging relationships with the Indigenous peoples who had lived there for centuries. One such historian, Doane Robinson, wrote in his 1904 *History of South Dakota* that one of La Vérendrye's sons, Louis-Joseph, made a journal entry noting that in 1743 he had placed a lead plaque engraved with the name of King Louis XV in a spot that in all likelihood was located in South Dakota.

The youngsters playing at Fort Pierre 170 years later knew nothing of the La Vérendryes. But the adults with whom they shared their discovery decided to contact the local historian—none other than Robinson. He immediately grasped that the hunk of metal the children had found might be the plaque left by Louis-Joseph de La Vérendrye. Once he saw the inscriptions, there was no doubt. Engraved in Latin on the obverse side, before the party had set out from Quebec City, were the words

Anno XXVI *regni Ludovici* XV *Prorege*
Illustrissimo Domino Domino Marchione
De Beauharnois M D CC XXXXI
Petrus Gaultier de Lavérendrie Posvit

("In the twenty-sixth year of the reign of Louis XV, Pierre Gaultier de la Vérendrye, acting on behalf of the Marquis de Beauharnois, deposited this plate in 1741 in the name of our most illustrious sovereign, the King")

On the reverse, added on site in French, were the names of the members of that leg of the expedition, which had led them to the foothills of the Rockies.

There was no longer any question as to the routes that the La Vérendryes claimed to have taken. And since 1913, their names have been celebrated along with those of the other great explorers of the Americas.

As with any science, so it is with history: our knowledge must evolve as new discoveries come to light. In the case of Pierre Gaultier de La Vérendrye, though, some confusion persists. He is often spoken of as a "French explorer." For example, the U.S. National Parks Service's webpage dedicated to the historic site where the plaque was found reads in part: "The Verendrye Site . . . is one of only a few verifiable sites associated with the first *Europeans* to explore the northern Great Plains region. *Frenchman* Pierre Gaultier De La Verendrye and his sons explored the interior of North America in the 18th century" (emphasis mine). Except that La Vérendrye and his sons were not Frenchmen. They were Canadians. French Canadians.

Yes, Pierre de La Vérendrye considered himself a subject of King Louis XV, and explored North America for the glory of France. But, like his mother before him, he was born in New France and had chosen to make his life there. At the time, these French residents of northeastern North America were named *Canadiens*, and had been for a number of decades. They were viewed as distinct in their mores and characterized by an independent spirit, a certain indiscipline, a taste for liberty, and a contempt for social constraints, among other things.* La Vérendrye himself, in his writings, discriminated between those men who had been born in Canada and his "*François*," or Frenchmen.

Who knows whether the expeditions of La Vérendrye and his sons would have turned out the same way had these explorers been born in France. Would the Crown, which refused them financial backing, have been more supportive? Was La Vérendrye's skill in dealing with the First Nations a hallmark of his "Canadian" culture? And what about the disorderly aspect of his explorations, which had so displeased the Comte de Maurepas, France's minister of the marine, and cost La Vérendrye valuable time?

In any case, the story of the French-Canadian explorer La Vérendrye remains little known. And he is far from being the only member of his "race" consigned to the hazy plains of oblivion. A great many French Canadians, in all eras, left their mark on the history of North America, and notably that of Canada, yet we know relatively little about most of them.

---

* Gérard Bouchard, *Genèse des nations et cultures du nouveau monde—Essai d'histoire comparée*, Montreal: Les Éditions du Boréal, 2000, p. 88.

There are probably several explanations for this phenomenon. I offer one here. For years, the history learned by the majority of francophones in North America—namely, those who live in Quebec—hewed to the following narrative.

In the beginning there was paradise: New France.

Then, disaster: *La Conquête.* French Canadians are cut off from their motherland, crushed under the heel of new masters who seek to obliterate their language and religion.

The Rebellions of 1837–1838 are bloodily suppressed. The Durham Report confirms the intent of the English: assimilation. This design finds concrete expression in the 1867 Act of Confederation.

French Canadians are relegated to working infertile land and, in the cities, low-paying jobs. They are poorly educated and in servitude to an ultra-conservative, abusive clergy. Francophone Quebec remains a backward place until 1960 and the advent of the Quiet Revolution.

"Liberation" would have been complete were it not for the defeat of the *indépendantistes* in the 1980 and 1995 referendums on the political future of Quebec.

THE END.

You may say this is caricature. And it is, but barely so. Historians have of course painted a much more nuanced picture—but their work has had relatively little impact on public knowledge. In Quebec's schools, history classes skim the surface. In popular culture—cinema, journalism, comedy—the "canonical" version of our history prevails. Especially entrenched is the notion that before the Quiet Revolution, French Canadians were a minor people of illiterates, isolated from the rest of the world. This was the time of the *Grande Noirceur*, the "long Québécois winter."*

Historian Éric Bédard, among many others, has more subtly shaded this narrative:

---

* Marcel Rioux, cited in Claude Couture, *Le Mythe de la modernisation du Québec: Des années 1930 à la Révolution tranquille*, Montreal: Éditions du Méridien, 1991, p. 13.

> It is true that in 1960, Quebec lagged behind in certain areas; the French-Canadian majority was economically inferior; there was little state intervention in health and social services; married women were legally minors per the Civil Code; some *curés* exerted often unbearable moral pressure on women; the Church was omnipresent (for example in education); and a few fascistic intellectuals were influential to a degree. It is also true, however—as historical research in recent decades has shown—that Quebec prior to 1960 became urbanized and unionized at the same pace as Ontario; that a French-Canadian bourgeoisie considered economic recovery to be an essential condition of "national recovery"; that Duplessis instituted a first-class system of technical colleges and had several hundred schools built in compliance with the Compulsory Education Act (which he had opposed); that heads of female religious congregations administered huge institutions; that *Action Catholique* activists of the 1940s and 1950s were in many instances the catalysts for reforms introduced during the Quiet Revolution; that a dynamic arts and culture scene had flourished well before the *Osstidcho*; and that there were probably fewer right-wing extremists in the years prior to 1960 than there were Maoists in the 1970s.*

Bédard may well be among the most influential of Quebec historians, but the "gospel truth" dies hard.

This book pays tribute to the contributions of several great French Canadians to the building of Canada, and the United States, in various spheres. Many readers will immediately point to some glaring absences: Joseph-Armand Bombardier, Alphonse Desjardins, René Lévesque, Maurice Richard, or Pierre Elliott Trudeau, for instance. We have deliberately chosen to exclude them: what use would there be in repeating what little everyone already knows? We have decided to tell

---

* Éric Bédard, *Recours aux sources—Essais sur notre rapport au passé*, Montreal: Les Éditions du Boréal, 2011, pp. 12–13. [Freely translated.]

the stories of several people who did important things, but who are often less well known to the general public. Our choice is founded on the firm belief that these French-Canadian contributions to the building of a continent were not the work of a tiny elite but of a great many people—dare we say, an entire people.

Only the La Vérendryes saw fit to leave a lead plaque in the ground testifying to their exploits for future generations. But if one takes the time to dig deeper, as the authors of this book have, one discovers that many other French Canadians left traces of themselves—traces that describe their enduring legacy. Starting with **Pierre de La Vérendrye** himself. In the first chapter, Philip Marchand, a Canadian journalist with a Franco-American background, describes La Vérendrye as a man who "put his stamp on the land that would become Canada, and indeed on the whole of North America," forged "genuine ties with First Nations," and was "the guiding spirit and the genius" behind the expedition to the Canadian Rockies by two of his sons.

In the same region, in what is now North Dakota, Father **Albert Lacombe** missioned among the Indigenous peoples of the West. In his essay on this "[p]riest, Oblate missionary, polyglot, linguist, diplomat, peacemaker, [and] pioneer," novelist Daniel Poliquin explains that Lacombe's main objective was, of course, to convert the First Nations peoples to Catholicism. It was a goal for which he was prepared to endure the harshest conditions, and one that he achieved only rarely, as Poliquin explains: "Those he did succeed in baptizing were often sick or dying. . . . One of Lacombe's great qualities, though, was that he never became discouraged, and he never upbraided the more stubborn among his flock." Among Lacombe's many accomplishments, Poliquin emphasizes his role in the negotiation of treaties between First Nations and the federal government, which "came to constitute, and indeed still constitute, the legal basis for Native identity and the principal foundation for Indigenous rights in Canada . . ."

While Father Lacombe devoted himself body and soul to his mission in western Canada, **George-Étienne Cartier** strove to bring Confederation into being while safeguarding the essential interests of

French Canadians. When John A. Macdonald attempted a last-minute stratagem to grant more powers to the central government, Cartier wielded his full influence to oppose it. In the words of former Quebec premier Jean Charest, who penned this chapter with his son, Antoine, Cartier believed that "the existence of French-Canadian political, social, and cultural institutions could not be subjected to any political compromise." Though he was conservative both in party affiliation and mentality, the authors write, Cartier introduced reforms that proved decisive for the future of the province of Quebec: abolition of the seigneurial regime, adoption of the Civil Code, and creation of the Council of Public Instruction. As Charest *père et fils* conclude, "There are two great thrusts of George-Étienne Cartier's career that ensured his legacy as a pre-eminent figure in Canadian history: the notion of duality, and economic development. These lines of force intertwine to describe the singular journey of a man as well as a people whose future he helped shape in durable fashion."

As a man of power, George-Étienne Cartier was generally, and of necessity, a man of compromise. **Henri Bourassa** was very much the opposite—so much so that Lucien Bouchard, another former premier of Quebec, ponders how he "tolerate[d] the political arena." "The fact is," Bouchard concludes, "he always refused to play the game, and usually to his detriment. That he left his mark on the politics of his time was more a matter of his sincerity, verging on passion, and his peerless talent." Bouchard gives an emotional account of Bourassa's dramatic 1926 audience with Pope Pius XI, who urged him to put his religious beliefs ahead of his nationalism: "His faith in the Gospel message was accompanied by complete obedience toward the authority of the Roman Catholic Church. In 1930 he admitted that, after his first political disappointments, he had taken 'the resolution . . . in all matters . . . to obey the Pope.'" In 1935, Bourassa disavowed "everything in his career that 'had not clearly respected the primacy of the rights of the Church over race, over language and over any human interest.'" He went further still in 1943: "'[From] this decisive hour of my life, I resolved, to the very end, to do everything to combat the evil signalled by the Pope.' The evil, of course, was the nationalism the Pope had denounced as 'extreme.'" Imagine how painful it must have been for the greatest nationalist leader of his time to have to sacrifice one ideal on the altar of another that he believed was greater still. These statements left Henri Bourassa's supporters disappointed and bewildered, as Lucien Bouchard describes. Yet Bourassa's influence, in his day and in ours, has been no less immense.

Bourassa had many reservations about Canada's engagement in the First World War, and he opposed Conscription when it was enacted in 1917. While politicians debated the issue on this side of the Atlantic, **Thomas-Louis Tremblay**, like tens of thousands of other Canadians—including some fifteen thousand French Canadians—enlisted. He went on to become the commander of the 22nd Battalion, the first French-speaking unit in Canada's armed forces. In their essay, Lieutenant-General Roméo Dallaire and military historian Serge Bernier explain Tremblay's conviction that, by demonstrating their prowess in battle, the "Van Doos" could undo Anglo-Canadians' prejudices with regard to their francophone compatriots. Accordingly, Tremblay was a harsh disciplinarian—yet at the same time, his war diary reveals how close he felt to his men. In September 1916, after the 22nd Battalion took the French village of Courcelette from the Germans, Tremblay lamented the loss of hundreds of Canadian lives in the battle, writing, "We have paid dearly for our success; our consolation is that those sacrifices were not made in vain, that one day our nationality will benefit from them." Tremblay's belief was well founded: as Dallaire and Bernier write, "the impact of that vision on the sociology and configuration of Canada's armed forces as well as those of the federal public service was felt over both the medium and the long term," paving the way for a more prominent role for francophones.

One of the men under Thomas-Louis Tremblay's command in the 22nd Battalion was Lieutenant **Georges Vanier**, a machine-gun officer. Despite the grave wounds he suffered during the Battle of Chérisy in August 1918, Vanier chose to continue his military career after the war ended. Then, in the mid-1920s, his career shifted to diplomacy. Before and after the Second World War, he spent fifteen years as Canada's envoy extraordinaire, and later ambassador, to France. He urged the government of William Lyon Mackenzie King to open Canada's doors to refugees, including Jews, fleeing Europe. He also pressed Ottawa to recognize the Free French under Charles de Gaulle, with whom he had been in contact since 1940. As Jeremy Kinsman, himself a former member of the Canadian foreign service, writes, Vanier's "whole life epitomized the values that are now seen as lying at the core of the Canadian identity: humane internationalism, tolerance, pluralism, including a rejection of anti-Semitism and other forms of bigotry, multiculturalism (as we now would call it), enlightened monarchism, and a powerful faith in a national project founded on the union between French and English peoples."

When Vanier took up his position as head of the Canadian legation in Paris in 1938, a young Quebecker, **Paul David**, was completing his secondary studies in the same city, at Collège Stanislas. The following year, David returned to Montreal to attend medical school. He became a cardiologist and later founded the Montreal Heart Institute, "a jewel in Quebec's health care crown, shining in the rest of Canada, in North America, and across the planet," in the words of physician and novelist Vania Jimenez. But, she adds, Dr. David's legacy encompasses much more than a medical facility, even one as prestigious as the MHI: "the life of Paul David endures—in the lives of so many who owe their lives to his pioneering work." It was at the MHI that Canada's first human heart transplant was performed. More important still, "[c]onfronted with the dismal reality that, worldwide, cardiac transplant patients' survival times were so brief, [David] was the first to recommend a moratorium on the procedure until immunosuppressive drugs could be developed. . . . And the world followed suit, beginning in 1969." Dr. Jimenez points to a paradox of the pioneering cardiologist's career: "in spite of his insistence that the Institute remain a distinct entity, Paul David had foreseen a new type of global, or holistic, medicine—one emphasizing prevention and a humanist approach."

Some will be surprised to find, among the names celebrated in these pages, that of **Jehane Benoît**. They no doubt recall that Madame Benoît was the author of many cookbooks. And? Well, the fact is, few people have had as great an impact on the everyday lives of Canadian women, and in particular Québécoises, as she did, over a span of four decades. Novelist and avowed foodie Chrystine Brouillet reminds us that Madame Benoît's *Encyclopedia of Canadian Cuisine* sold more than a million copies, and "was the go-to culinary bible for homemakers of the time." And Benoît was more than just a great cook: she was a visionary, a devotee of science, and a businesswoman. Brouillet fondly quotes Benoît's definition of Canadian (and especially Quebec) cuisine: "*La cuisine d'un pays témoigne de sa géographie, de son histoire, de l'ingéniosité gourmande de son peuple et de ses atavismes. S'y ajoute une longue période de tâtonnements et d'expériences.*" More than fifty years after those words were written, Brouillet says, "it is amazing to consider the enduring relevance of Jehane Benoît's definition of Québécois gastronomy. It can be encapsulated in one word: *métissage*, or hybridization."

If Madame Benoît was a pioneer, so was **Thérèse Casgrain**, in quite a different way and with a considerably larger sphere of action. "Born into *exceptional* privilege," Samantha Nutt explains, Casgrain became "one of the most important leftists Canada has ever produced, critically contributing to many of the public policy ideas, rights, and freedoms Canadians have cherished since her time." The tenacious Casgrain and her Ligue des droigts de la femme tried on fourteen occasions to have a bill tabled that would grant women the right to vote in provincial elections in Quebec. Unfortunately, they failed. Casgrain gradually broadened her activism to come to the aid of other victims of injustice, including workers, teachers, immigrants, and First Peoples. In 1951, she was elected leader of the Quebec wing of the CCF (ancestor of the NDP), thus becoming the first woman to head a Canadian political party. Despite those achievements, Nutt says, Casgrain remains little known outside Quebec: "This is in part because she was a more prolific political organizer and activist than essayist, and so she produced little in the way of first-person grist for biographers. Nevertheless, there emerges from her historical docket a woman who was ahead of even prime ministers Lester B. Pearson and Pierre Elliott Trudeau in seeding the modern, humanist Canadian sensibility."

While Thérèse Casgrain denounced injustice, **Gabrielle Roy** painted a striking portrait of it that ensured the phenomenal success of her debut novel, *Bonheur d'occasion*, not only in Canada but in the United States as well. "The scale of her success was unprecedented for a Canadian writer," remarks the great Canadian author Margaret Atwood, who recalls that Roy's second book, *La Petite Poule d'Eau*, was part of the curriculum at her suburban Toronto high school in 1956, a curriculum "otherwise dominated by European authors"—most of whom were male and deceased. How was this possible? "The short answer is that Gabrielle Roy was very famous," Atwood explains. None of Roy's subsequent books duplicated the success of *Bonheur d'occasion*. But many are important works. In them, writes Margaret Atwood, Gabrielle "opens the curtains on windows people did not suspect were there—a remote corner of Manitoba, the ordinary life of an ordinary man, the lost but teeming past of her natal province, the many journeys of an artist—and asks readers to look through. Then—whatever the smallness, harshness, or oddness of the view—to understand, and then to empathize." Atwood concludes that in today's society, "Roy's vision has more relevance . . . than ever."

Still, how many Canadians today know who Gabrielle Roy was? With hockey occupying a larger space in the public imagination than does literature, **Jacques Plante** remains famous thirty years after his death: everyone knows him as the first goaltender in pro hockey to don a mask. What they may not realize is that by making that decision to shield his face—which was prompted not by fear but, on the contrary, by a great deal of courage—Plante radically transformed our national game. As explained by Ken Dryden, one of Plante's illustrious successors in the Montreal Canadiens' netminder role, "It took several years, but goalies eventually came to realize the tactical implications of this new technology. The long-dominant stand-up style had been a compromise between (a) the goalie's mission to keep pucks out of his net and (b) his biologically rooted desire to keep pucks away from his head. With the new mask, no compromise was necessary. A goalie could bring his head and shoulders below the bar and cover more net. He could crouch lower—spreading his feet to each corner in a permanent butterfly style."

Dryden writes that Plante, like many other great players from the 1950s to the 1970s, "was part of the golden age of hockey in Quebec," but adds that those years are long gone: these days, the best Canadian players in the NHL hail from outside Quebec, and Montreal's roster includes only two or three players born in the province. What has happened? he asks. "What is Quebec's next great hockey act? Who is the next Jacques Plante?"

Besides Pierre de La Vérendrye, two other subjects of this book had significant impact beyond Canada's borders.

The author of the iconic *On the Road*, **Jack Kerouac**, is one of the world's most-read American novelists. Very little is known, however, about the "French Jack Kerouac." Deni Béchard provides an introduction, revealing the extent to which the apostle of the Beat Generation felt torn between his French-Canadian roots and his American identity. "*Je suis Canadien Francais*—I am French Canadian, born in New England," Kerouac wrote. "When I am angry I often curse in French. When I dream I often dream in French. When I cry I always cry in French, and I say: 'I don't like it, I don't like it!' It's my life in the world that I don't want."

Kerouac's writings in French, recently published after sitting in oblivion for years, "are of tremendous historical value," Béchard says. "Virtually no other enduring texts from that time show us the cultural collision then taking place in New England, nor the Franco-Americans' contribution to America in a voice that was authentically theirs. In the way Kerouac merges the two languages, in the phonetic renderings of French words he knew by sound but struggled to reproduce on paper, the ebbing of the French-Canadian experience in New England is powerfully felt."

Prudent Beaudry was born in Mascouche in 1818, and elected mayor of Los Angeles six decades later. How did he get that far? Quebec businessman Gaétan Frigon tells the unlikely story of this real estate magnate who, journeying from Montreal to San Francisco, with stops in New York and New Orleans, tried his hand at just about everything: import-export, the ice business, general trade, and mining. Successive ventures left him practically ruined on four separate occasions; each time, he started again from scratch and rebuilt his fortune. In Los Angeles, Beaudry hatched a scheme to convey water to the parched bluffs overlooking the city, and converted land he'd bought there into a lush residential neighbourhood; his keen sense of urban planning and marketing made him a rich man. Frigon goes on to retrace the lives of other French-Canadian businessmen in the years before 1960 who defied the prevailing, and stereotyped, view of Quebeckers as insular, noting that "decades before what came to be known as 'Quebec Inc.,' French Canadians were doing business, building and managing factories, and creating banks."

The fact that Kerouac, Beaudry, and so many others left their marks in the United States is not the only reason why Americans should be interested in French Canadians and their history. This book provides a much more expansive argument, as does the remarkable *The French Canadians*, written in 1955 by the U.S. historian Mason Wade. In his preface, Wade explained, "The matters with which this book is concerned are not exclusively Canadian in nature. . . . There are common patterns, as well as significant differences, in the behavior of all minority groups. These are of concern to all North Americans, whether citizens of Canada or the United States, and indeed to all mankind, for only by the acceptance of diversity, through the understanding and reconciliation of cultural differences, can the great world problems of our time be solved."*

That being said, this work is aimed primarily at Canadians. It has much to offer those anglophone Canadians—whether English is their mother tongue or their adopted language—who still know too little about the debt they owe French Canadians. Were it not for the

* Mason Wade, *The French Canadians*, New York: Macmillan, 1955, ix-x.

contributions of the latter, Canada might not be the land of diversity, tolerance, respect for fundamental rights, and promotion of peace that we know and cherish today. It is a land, however, that could not have been made by francophones alone. It is what it is because we built it together, and it will keep on growing in relative harmony (nothing's perfect!) only if we continue on our journey hand in hand, reaching out with those hands to the new Canadians joining us every day, and drawing on the knowledge and wisdom of the First Nations, as La Vérendrye did so brilliantly two and a half centuries ago.

⚜ ⚜ ⚜ ⚜

AFTER THE PUBLICATION OF a short biography of Sir Wilfrid Laurier that I wrote for the series *Extraordinary Canadians*, I was dismayed to see how few francophones knew who he was. Yet Laurier, in his day, was like a god to French Canadians. His portrait hung in every family home, and for good reason: he had become prime minister of the fledgling Canadian federation at a time when many believed that a francophone would never rise to so lofty an office. He served as leader of the Liberal Party of Canada for thirty-two years, and as prime minister for fifteen. Fluently bilingual, his eloquence praised as much in London as in Paris, Wilfrid Laurier was a tremendous source of pride for French Canada. That he was not remembered less than a century after his death was simply astonishing to me.

Whenever I spoke about Laurier in the media or at public gatherings, though—never failing to underscore both his strengths and his weaknesses as a politician—I could see that my audiences were fascinated. People wanted to know all about him. And it was as if they were relieved to learn that, contrary to what they'd been taught, here was a man who, well before the Quiet Revolution years, had given French Canadians reason to be proud.

That is why, to my mind, this book is aimed above all at francophone Canadians, especially those who live in Quebec. Perhaps it will serve to convince those who do not realize, or who doubt, that their history did not begin forty or fifty years ago—that long before Jean Lesage and René Lévesque, in every field of endeavour, there were plenty of French Canadians who were open to the world, and who were successful, despite formidable opposition. And those pioneers were not exceptions. Far outside the bounds of the elites, people educated themselves, took an interest in international affairs (one need only read nineteenth-century newspapers for proof), did business, read books, went to the theatre, and showed courage, ingenuity, and tenacity in the face of obstacles.

It is not by accident that, despite extremely challenging circumstances, the French Canadians have resisted assimilation. It is because they are a proud people who showed themselves to be economically and politically enlightened—exhibiting far more discernment, for example, than those adversaries of Confederation who proposed annexation by the United States.

There are those who would have French Canadians believe that, from the defeat at the Plains of Abraham until the *Grande Noirceur*, they were on the losing end of things. The intellectuals and politicians who were the architects of the Quiet Revolution erected for us a pantheon of defeated heroes—Papineau, Dorion, Lévesque. While continuing to admire and love those figures, French Canadians have preferred the wisdom and principles of winners like LaFontaine, Cartier, and Trudeau (*père*). In a host of other fields, as we shall see in the following pages, they have simply taken their place, without necessarily waiting for help from the state of Quebec—help that, when it has arrived, however, has been no less salutary, no less essential.

Having discovered the life stories of these important but relatively unsung French Canadians, our readers may want to delve deeper into the history of their ancestors. In doing so, they will realize that the French Canadians have always been a great people. Not a greater people than any other, but not a lesser one either. A people that, given its small size and the trying circumstances it has faced, has made a remarkable contribution to the building of North America.

PHILIP MARCHAND

PIERRE DE LA VÉRENDRYE

"EVERYONE KNOWS THAT CANADA is very poor," lamented Pierre Gaultier de Varennes, sieur de La Vérendrye in a 1743 letter to the governor of New France, Charles de la Boische, marquis de Beauharnois. The memoir outlined the reasons why La Vérendrye had failed in his quest to find the Western Sea (a non-existent inland body of water that was then widely believed to offer passage to the Pacific Ocean). Several impediments blocked his way, the memoir stated—so that, in the end, his backers, the fur-trading merchants of Montreal, would have to remain unsatisfied. The sad result was not untypical for the time: in the economic environment of this period, it was hard to launch ambitious new commercial enterprises.

In his lonely fastness, in this lonely continent, virtually the only means of making money was the trade in beaver pelts and in Aboriginal slaves. But mere commerce is not what we remember La Vérendrye for: the fur and the slaves were acquired merely to finance his true enterprise, the exploration of the West and the discovery of a gateway to China. It was in service to this enterprise that he endured every sort of privation and mortal danger, thereby earning a place among the great explorers of North America. He was not the first person of European descent to lay eyes on the Canadian Rockies and to record the experience. (That honour belongs to his sons—"sons worthy of their father," in historian Francis Parkman's words.) But La Vérendrye was the guiding spirit and the genius of that moment in history, and inspired many of the triumphs that would come after his time.

This was the dawn of the Romantic era—though Europe's intellectual currents were scarcely felt in the North American hinterlands. We can still savour La Vérendrye's moment in the light of Romanticism, however: the sudden and momentous revelation of the sublime. "Then felt I like some watcher of the skies," Keats proclaimed in "On First Looking into Chapman's Homer." To eighteenth-century explorers from the east, the Canadian Rockies might as well have been a new planet.

La Vérendrye mistakenly thought that his Western Sea was just a few days' trek across these mountains. But his ignorance does not minimize his accomplishment—even if today's students of history are encouraged to find ways to disparage any heroic persona. This also goes for La Vérendrye's seventeenth-century predecessor in heroism, René-Robert Cavelier, sieur de La Salle (whom I have heard called a "poseur"). In some ways, the La Vérendrye story is a reprise of La Salle's—including the forging of genuine ties with First Nations, the pioneering of trade routes, massacres, desertion, harassment by jealous Montreal-based rivals, and a form of ultimate personal defeat. It is uncanny, in fact, the prototype set by La Salle: the great explorer who functions brilliantly in the wilderness and among the Aboriginals but is unable to deal with his own people.

But in the end, La Vérendrye put his stamp on the land that would become Canada, and indeed on the whole of North America—one that goes far beyond the theme of exploration. When anyone asks that important question, "Can't we all just get along?" they are echoing a question that, in one form or another, La Vérendrye asked many times, or many peoples.

TO OBTAIN THE FLAVOUR of La Vérendrye's heroism, the best place to start is the chapter "Search for the Pacific," in Parkman's 1892 history *A Half-Century of Conflict*. "Plans for reaching the *Mer de l'Ouest*, or Pacific Ocean, were laid before the Regent [of France] in 1716," he writes. "It was urged that the best hope was in sending an expedition across the continent, seeing that every attempt to find a westward passage by Hudson Bay had failed."

Various plans were laid for this trek, and some attempts made to launch expeditions, but the presence of the Sioux—who played the same role of formidable foe in western French Canada as the Iroquois did in eastern French Canada—posed difficulties. The Sioux were mortal enemies of the Cree and the Assiniboine nations in the lands north and west of Lake Superior, through which the French proposed to pass.

Regardless, in 1730, La Vérendrye obtained permission from the governor of New France to build a fort on Lake Winnipeg, in modern-day Manitoba, at his own expense. His recompense for the outlay would be a monopoly on the local fur trade—the characteristic form of finance at the time. The system never seemed to generate large profits for traders and explorers, but, in the absence of royal subsidies, it was the only method someone such as La Vérendrye could use for seed money.

With supplies and trade goods purchased through these funds, La Vérendrye set out from Montreal in 1731, headed for Lake Winnipeg, with his three sons, a nephew, and some fifty *engagés* (principally paddlers, servants, hunters, construction workers, and armed personnel—though, as Denis Combet, editor of the journals of La Vérendrye, notes, the word also could signify "an interpreter, a blacksmith, a tool maker, or perhaps even a doctor").

How did La Vérendrye get to this point in life? His mother was a Canadian named Marie Boucher, who married at the age of twelve and gave birth to ten children, of whom eight survived to maturity—our hero Pierre being the youngest. Her husband, René Gaultier, came to Canada as an officer in the Regiment of Carignan-Salières, famous in the history of New France. Gaultier himself was a well-known (and much mocked) type in the colony—the aristocrat endowed with a number of seigneuries who was nonetheless always strapped for cash.

Canada, he might have complained to his son, was a very poor place.

PIERRE DE LA VÉRENDRYE was born in November 17, 1685, at Trois-Rivières—roughly halfway between Quebec City and Montreal. He was well educated in the schools and seminaries of the time, but ultimately had in mind his father's career as a soldier.

This was not an unusual choice: as a younger son, his options were extremely limited (the priesthood being one of the only other attractive alternatives). And a military career would allow Pierre to roam the frontier. "Like the rest of the poor but vigorous Canadian noblesse," Parkman writes, he "seemed born to the forest and the fur trade."

La Vérendrye served as a nineteen-year-old in the War of the Spanish Succession in North America, and then left for France in search, it seems likely, of receiving greater notice in the world. The trip nearly killed him. At the Battle of Malplaquet, in 1709, he was riddled with gunshot and carved up with sabre cuts—but amazingly, he survived, and was captured by enemy forces. Released a few months later, La Vérendrye was promoted to a rank somewhat beyond his means—a lieutenant in the army of Louis XIV. (These were the days when officers were expected to finance the trappings of military office out of their own pocket.)

In 1712, he decided to return to Canada, arriving even poorer than when he had left it. This rags-to-adventure-to-rags cycle would become one of his life's great themes.

Shortly after his return, La Vérendrye married Marie-Anne Dandonneau du Sablé, the daughter of another Canadian seigneur. They had four sons and two daughters. For fourteen years, the couple lived a quiet life in the seigneury of Tremblay, inherited from her father's side. Pierre supplemented his income with army pay, and with a small-time fur-trading operation. At the age of forty, Pierre de La Vérendrye seemed destined to continue his slide into a comfortable middle age. But as Parkman notes, the man was born for more rugged pursuits.

The fateful sequence began with the appointment of Pierre's brother Jacques-René as head of the Poste du Nord, a fur-trading station north of Lake Superior, in 1726. Pierre became his assistant, and subsequently assumed command when his brother moved on. It was then that he became consumed by dreams of the Western Sea—the same dream that had exercised the wits and ambitions of innumerable North American explorers since the days of Columbus.

By the time of La Vérendrye, possibilities for the imagined location of this body of water were narrowing. Europeans had by now ruled out Hudson Bay as a convenient terminus. The Mississippi River valley seemed less and less likely. What remained, in La Vérendrye's mind, was Lake Winnipeg to the north and west. A post on that body of water would provide a strategic location for further exploration.

Which is how La Vérendrye found himself in Montreal, making a sales pitch to fur magnates. As part of the deal they struck, La Vérendrye would become the commander of the fort on Lake Winnipeg, with a monopoly on the local fur trade for a period of three years. That would allow enough time, it seemed, for La Vérendrye and his men to establish trading posts, create alliances with First Nations, organize a logistical network to compete with the English traders on Hudson Bay, and, ultimately, locate the fabled Western Sea.

Geography was not on the man's side. "This vast and remote country was held by tribes who were doubtful friends of the French and perpetual enemies of each other," Parkman writes. "Forts must be built, provisioned, and stocked with goods brought through two thousand miles of difficult and perilous wilderness."

It was easy to lose critical capital in this environment. La Salle's great catastrophe was the disappearance of his ship, *Griffon*, somewhere in the Great Lakes—a vessel loaded with furs and trade goods. In the case of La Vérendrye, a major setback occurred when persons unknown stole crucial trade goods from inventory being kept at a Mandan village in present-day North Dakota. Reports suggest that the *engagé* looking after the goods was negligent. La Vérendrye, who had intended to distribute the items in order to cement crucial alliances, was dismayed. His Aboriginal friends searched the village to no avail. The area, as they explained, was full of caves where it was easy to hide things.

Desertion had been a major factor for La Salle, who was known as a hard taskmaster. One particularly grievous loss of men occurred at Fort Crèvecoeur, in what is now Illinois. Not only did the desertion result in a labour shortage; it put La Salle and his few remaining men in grave danger from surrounding Aboriginals—who never attacked but might have if they'd taken true measure of the diminished size of La Salle's contingent. (This was a dark period all around. One deserter famously carved a sentence on a piece of wood left in the forest: *Nous sommes tout sauvages*. It resonates like a cry from the heart of darkness.)

The desertions suffered by La Vérendrye were not quite as cataclysmic, but they nonetheless came as a major blow to his fortunes. Less than three months after he left Montreal, many of his *engagés*, having made the trek to Grand Portage on the southeast shore of Lake Superior, refused to go farther. This was the gateway to densely forested country, riven with mosquitoes—a dark wilderness. These *engagés* had not yet become the fabled voyageurs, travellers par excellence. La Vérendrye was forced to accommodate the deserters, and shelter was provided them while a small, more intrepid band, led by La Vérendrye's son Jean-Baptiste, pushed forward, erecting the first of the Winnipeg forts, Fort Saint-Pierre, on the shores of Rainy Lake, halfway to Lake Winnipeg.

In the spring, the two groups reunited and pressed on. Ahead lay the site of forts that would settle this territory for the French and their Aboriginal allies—Fort Saint-Charles, southeast of Lake of the Woods; Fort Maurepas, on the banks of the Red River; the first fort on the prairies, Fort la Reine, on the site of what is now the town of

Portage la Prairie, west of Winnipeg; and five others. These explorations proved to be hugely important historical achievements that helped establish a route to Lake Winnipeg for future explorers.

La Vérendrye's challenges were less straightforward in the domain of diplomacy. He had to discourage Aboriginals from trading with the English posts on Hudson Bay, downriver to the northwest, and maintain peaceful relations among First Nations groups that, as Parkman put it, were "perpetual enemies of each other."

His situation was similar to that faced by the French in Louisiana and Mississippi, where members of the powerful Chickasaw Nation were steadfast allies of the English. The French tried to turn things to their advantage by arranging peace conferences between the Chickasaw and their own Aboriginal allies, the Choctaw—but with no success.

The deeper problem here was that the Chickasaw had become deeply attached to English trade goods, which almost always were of superior quality to those of the French. And so the French failures in diplomacy reflected their failure to keep up with the march of British industrialization. During this historical period, wars were increasingly being won by superior artillery, logistics, and manufacturing rather than by old-fashioned rifle or sabre.

From the Carolinas, a steady stream of pack trains loaded with blankets, tobacco, brass kettles, rum, needles and thread, hatchets and knives, and above all British muskets, came climbing over the Appalachian trails to Chickasaw country. English traders came back, not with furs but with deer hides and Aboriginal slaves bound for the West Indies. As the eighteenth century wore on, this trade became essential to the Chickasaw, who became less attached to traditional hunting and farming, and more so to slaving.

The French could not survive this economic competition. As the march of industrialization gained steam, the old warfare of woodcraft and ambuscade became obsolete. Military codes of honour, developed over centuries on the battlefields of Europe, fell away. And there was nothing La Vérendrye could do about it.

The Cree and the Assiniboine professed every good intention to the French, but they still traded with Hudson Bay because its goods were cheaper and better. "Father, when you came to our land you provided for our needs, you promised to continue doing so and we lacked nothing for two years, but now we lack everything because of the traders," one chief complained to La Vérendrye. "You have forbidden us to go to the English. We have obeyed you, and if today we are forced to go there to obtain muskets, gunpowder, pots, tobacco, and so on, you have only your own people to blame."

La Vérendrye did not have much luck with keeping the peace, either. The Sioux were considered by their neighbours to be especially ferocious—but the Cree and the Assiniboine, both French allies, were quick to take revenge against them if they felt they could get away with it. Combet writes, "La Vérendrye failed to take into account the attitudes of these nations, hereditary enemies of long standing, and who, masters in their own home, did not take kindly to advice from the newcomers."

For their part, the Cree asked La Vérendrye to give them his son Jean-Baptiste as both a symbol of their alliance and an eyewitness of their courage. With great misgivings, La Vérendrye acceded to their wish. To refuse would have indicated a lack of trust. "Who knows if my son will come back," he lamented. "On the other hand, if I refuse, I am afraid, and rightly so, that they will think all the French are cowards." (According to historical accounts, Jean-Baptiste himself seemed eager to go.)

La Vérendrye also attempted to supply his Aboriginal clients when their wild rice crop suffered from heavy rains. French men, equipped with fishing nets, supplied abundant fish, while La Vérendrye encouraged the growing of corn and wheat. "I saw to it that all were given gunpowder, musket balls, and flints, knives, awls, tobacco," he reported. "They gave long speeches of thanks, as is their custom, and let out great cries of joy." In the same breath, he also mentioned "the order I had given to prevent them from going to the English."

These diplomatic efforts would eventually be overshadowed by tragedy, however. In June 1736, La Vérendrye sent a party of twenty-one

Frenchmen to retrieve supplies held at Michilimackinac and other eastern posts. The party consisted of his son Jean-Baptiste and the requisite Jesuit missionary—in this case, one Jean-Pierre Aulneau, a well-liked and respected cleric whose fondest wish was to learn Aboriginal languages.

Unfortunately, a war party of 130 Prairie Sioux happened to be in the area—perhaps on a vengeance raid following some lethal wilderness encounter. A letter written by La Vérendrye describes the subsequent events. The Sioux, he writes, "found Father Aulneau's canoe with [a] man called Bourassa at its helm. They took all the French as prisoners and attached the leader to the stake in order to burn him. Luckily for him, he had with him a slave woman of the same nation that he had bought from the Monsonis. She told the Sioux: 'My people, what are you about to do? I owe my life to this Frenchman, he has always been good to me. If you wish to take vengeance for the attack against our people, you need only to go a little further, you will find 21 Frenchmen." They let Bourassa and his *engagés* go, and went off to track the larger convoy. At Lake of the Woods, they massacred their victims where they found them. Governor General Beauharnois writes about the scene that greeted a reconnaissance party later travelling through the area. "The heads were all placed upon beaver robes, most of them having been scalped," Beaharnois wrote. "[Jean Baptiste] de La Vérendrye was lying faced down, with his back covered in knife wounds, a hoe driven into his ribs, headless, his torso decorated with garters and bracelets made of porcupine quills."

Even as he mourned his son's death, La Vérendrye knew he had to prevent his Cree and Assiniboine allies from going to war. In that unsettled climate, everybody was suspicious of everyone else. The Assiniboine were afraid of being killed (and eaten) by the Sioux, and by the French as well. In the dwellings of both Cree and Assiniboine, the women applied steady pressure, crying over the deaths of men who died in skirmishes, and urging warriors to go to war to avenge them.

The Cree told La Vérendrye they were grieving night and day over the death of his son, whom they had adopted as their own chief. La

Vérendrye replied that they could not go to war without word from the governor of New France. He also reminded them that they lacked gunpowder and musket balls, because of interruptions in their supply chain.

La Vérendrye succeeded in putting off the initiation of out-and-out war, and made some remarkable friends in the process. In his journal, he mentioned a particular chief named Marte Blanche (White Marten), "more than one hundred years old, of very sound judgement and still vigorous. So that I could have his support and work more assuredly on improving our affairs, I personally gave him presents. . . . I clothed his women, or rather his slaves, of which there were five, and three of his children."

The explorer also recorded his meeting with an aged voyageur, seventy-seven years old, named Griguierre. The man had spent a good portion of his life among the Sioux, hunting with them, going to war with them, travelling with them. La Vérendrye was impressed with his sprightliness—he could still snowshoe and hunt—and might have thought the man a real treasure trove of information.

But in general, La Vérendrye rarely sought after the reports of voyageurs. Though they have become lionized in modern myth, La Vérendrye dismissed them at the time as men "who for the most part can hardly tell east from west."

Slavery was common in this world, and the subject appears often in La Vérendrye's journals, where it is discussed casually as a fact of commerce. "In exchange for [a] slave [from a Cree Chief], I gave a cloak, a shirt, leggings and breeches, a knife and an awl, gunpowder and musket balls," La Vérendrye wrote. Later, he reported that "everything useful for my personal needs was carried by my servant and my slave." Another chief, who supposedly knew well the mystical sea that La Vérendrye was seeking—and its inhabitants—told the French explorer that these people had many slaves, each with a separate apartment. They married each other, the chief said, and are not bothered by their lot: "The slaves are happy, and don't try to escape."

For his part, La Vérendrye entertained his hosts with stories about warfare in Europe. They didn't shoot from behind trees, he told them, as they did in America, but rather in open countryside. "I showed them the wounds I had received in the battle of Malplaquet," he wrote. "They couldn't get over their astonishment."

These First Nations companions seemed to be polite listeners, by La Vérendrye's account—although how much they actually believed is hard to say. (From their own experiences, Aboriginals presumably knew their way around campfire bullshit.) "I gave them news from Canada and from France," La Vérendrye wrote. "I spoke to them of the victories that the King had won, of the cities taken from his enemies, and so on. That seemed to give them pleasure and they listened to me attentively."

La Vérendrye, in his journals, refers briefly to the dreaded smallpox, attributing the outbreak among the Cree to their having traded with the English: "I made a point of telling them that the Master of Life had punished them for not having come to Fort Saint-Charles as they had promised." He concludes his report with cheerful news: "In the ten lodges which were with my son not one person has died, because of the medicines he gave them and the good care that he took of them, all of which increased the friendship and the confidence they had in him and in the French." (Less happy is the report that the Aboriginals threw contaminated furs in the river. Henceforward, no one would dare touch them. The associated loss may well have erased an entire year's worth of profit.)

While La Vérendrye immersed himself in the business of exploration, he never completely forgot the world of titles and honours he had left behind. In 1737, he wrote to a man he regarded as his nemesis—Jean-Frédéric Phélypeaux, comte de Maurepas, then acting as France's minister of the marine—asking for a promotion. "I beg your highness to have the goodness to thank me for my long service by giving me command of a company, given that there are many vacant ones in this country, and to reward me with a Cross of Saint-Louis for my wounds." The request was refused.

The following year, La Vérendrye set out on an expedition to the country of the Mandan Aboriginal tribe, south and west of Lake Winnipeg, along the banks of the Missouri River. Accompanying him were two of his three surviving sons, a band of voyageurs, and a few hundred Assiniboine. He had high hopes that on this trip the Aboriginals would finally get him to the great Western Sea—a hope that La Vérendrye connected in some way to the rumour that the Mandan were descendants of white men. The stakes were high. Combet writes, "Beauharnois let La Vérendrye know that his future in the west depended on the success of the expedition to the Mandans." In the background, meanwhile, stood Maurepas in the French court, ever complaining of La Vérendrye's "*manque d'efficacité*."

La Vérendrye duly met the Mandan, who he immediately saw were not descendants of Europeans. "I must admit that I was surprised, since I had expected to see people different from the other Indians, especially in view of the accounts that we had been given," he later recalled. "There is no difference between them and the Assiniboines; they go naked, covered only by a robe of bison worn loosely with no loincloth. I knew then that we would have to disregard everything that we had been told."

Nonetheless, La Vérendrye found much to admire in the Mandan—particularly, according to his view, in comparison with the Assiniboine. The Mandan were shrewd traders, for one thing. La Vérendrye noted that they "trade grains, tobacco, quills and painted feathers which they know the Assiniboine hold in high esteem. The latter brought to trade muskets, axes, pots, gunpowder, musket balls, knives and awls. The Mandans are much more clever than the Assiniboine, in their trading as everything else; the latter are always taken in by them." Combet notes that La Vérendrye also claimed the Assiniboine were unreliable and cowardly—but also justly known for their hospitality.

La Vérendrye and his party made a tour of the Mandan forts. On leaving one village, they proceeded in due order. "I had one of my sons take the flag painted with the French coat of arms to lead us and ordered the French to follow in order," he writes. "The Mandans didn't want to let me walk and offered to carry me; I had to let them do this, being begged to do so."

On arrival at a village, La Vérendrye recalls, "I received their compliments, which simply conveyed the joy they felt at my arrival. . . . I ordered my son the Chevalier to have all our Frenchmen form an honour guard with the flag four paces in front. All the Assiniboine who had muskets formed a line with our Frenchmen. After the compliments, I had the fort saluted with three salvoes." As guests, the French had free run of the house. "I was to make use of the provisions as I pleased, being master," La Vérendrye recalls. (It was in one of these houses, where a crowd of Mandan and Assiniboine jostled one another, that La Vérendrye had his trove of offerings stolen, as described above.)

An Assiniboine elder took leave of this expedition with the following words, addressed to the Mandan: "We are leaving our Father [by which he meant La Vérendrye] with you; take good care of him and of all the Frenchmen; learn to know them; he is a spirit and they know how to do everything. We love him and fear him; do as we do."

If there was any component of irony in this address, we shall never know. According to La Vérendrye, writing in his journal, "I put an end to this speech, seeing that the old man was starting to get worked up."

It was uncertain when, in fact, the Assiniboine were intending to leave. They had spent their wealth in exchange for what goods they wanted—painted bison robes, deer hides adorned with painted quills and feathers, garters, trinkets, headbands, belts—all the finery that the Mandan were so skilled at manufacturing and that the Assiniboine weren't. But now that the Mandan had finished fleecing their guests, they began to feel uneasy about their continued presence. To prompt their departure, the Mandan reported that some of their hunters had spotted Sioux warriors in the region. The Assiniboine fell for the ploy. Not looking forward to any bloodshed, they struck camp. As La Vérendrye recalled, "They all left in a great hurry, believing that the Sioux were near and might cut off their route."

La Vérendrye at this point had pressing reasons—the importunities of his creditors foremost among them—to attend to business matters elsewhere. And so he left the party in the charge of his two sons, François and Louis-Joseph, while he returned to Montreal toward the end of August 1740. There, he found that his wife, who was not only a beloved companion but also his business manager, had died. The blow to the widower was severe.

La Vérendrye returned to the West in June 1741, where, as Combet puts it, he "applied himself to consolidating the French presence in the West." The forts that he and his sons built in strategic locations around the Manitoba lakes and rivers had already become instrumental in that respect (though, sadly, few have survived to the current day).

It was his two sons, François and Louis-Joseph, who became the first white men to see the Rockies. But they did not scale them. "I was quite mortified to be unable to scale the mountains, as I had wished to do," Louis-Joseph wrote in his journal. His Aboriginal companions had become panic-stricken at the presence of their enemies, the Gens du Serpent, or Shoshonis, a nation said to be even more bloodthirsty than the Sioux, and fled from the scene.

Needless to say, none of this impressed Maurepas. But Governor General Beauharnois, always the champion of La Vérendrye, wrote a letter to France in 1744, defending the explorer: "I cannot deny him what it seems to me to be his due, that he has only, through his discoveries, benefited the colony through the number of posts he has established in places where no one had yet penetrated and which produce today quantities of beavers and furs which would otherwise only profit the English, without him having caused any expense to His Majesty through the establishment of these posts. The idea that some have entertained of the fortune he has amassed in these places is absurd given the poverty in which he finds himself."

Not long after this letter was sent, La Vérendrye finally received his rank of captain from the French court. His fortunes were lifted as well, with the replacement of Maurepas as minister of the marine by Antoine-Louis Rouillé in April 1749. The new appointee awarded La

Vérendrye the Cross of Saint-Louis, France's highest military decoration. In December of that same year, La Vérendrye died, virtually a pauper. It was the story of his life.

LA VÉRENDRYE'S LEGACY remains ambiguous. He was a brave, ground-breaking adventurer—but also, many would say, a colonist and an imperialist. Such epithets are freely bestowed these days, especially within academe. But I believe the reputation of La Vérendrye should—and will—survive ideological fashions.

I see in my mind's eye two contrasting protagonists of the European invasion of North America. On the one hand, we have the expedition of Hernando de Soto and his soldiers roaming through the hinterlands of what is now the American South, searching for gold and leaving behind them a trail of blood and fire. (At a 1540 battle in the village of Mabila alone, de Soto's troops killed thousands of Mississippian fighters while losing only twenty of his own.) By contrast, we have La Vérendrye and his expedition arduously making their way across the prairies and the foothills of the Rockies, not as masters and conquerors, but as commercial partners—interfering with long-established Aboriginal feuds, to be sure, but on the whole anxious to keep the peace with the natives they encountered.

In general, the French were clumsy at the project of settling North America—especially when compared to the British, who created substantial coastal enclaves from the moment of their first arrival. (Fortunately, the portion of New France devoted to settlement—the fertile areas of the St. Lawrence Valley—was uncontested terrain when Champlain arrived. Cartier had encountered Aboriginals in this region when he sailed up the river a half-century previously. But for reasons unknown to history—perhaps plague or warfare—they had disappeared during the interim.) As a result, the French treated their expansion more as an act of give and take with the Aboriginals they met. During this period, there would be no large-scale wars in New

France like those in New England, where Aboriginals were destroyed wholesale by English settlers hungry for land. La Vérendrye was not a harbinger of doom to the Aboriginals he encountered. His presence did not signal the end of days.

For the most part, everybody benefited from the fur trade (except the beaver, of course). If there was a threat to the Aboriginals' way of life, it was their growing dependence on European trade goods for survival. (Aboriginals traded with the English, too, when they had to—largely because they knew they couldn't defeat a people who had muskets when they didn't.) And of course the newcomers from Europe also brought brandy and rum—which also became seen as necessities, though ultimately ruinous ones.

La Vérendrye could not be held responsible for the trade in alcohol, which he abhorred. Nor for the spread of contagious diseases through European-borne pathogens. Within the scope of his dealings with the Aboriginals, he acted ethically. And so he is that rare specimen: a figure who can be honoured without the usual caveats that attend many great men from this period of history.

Even today's First Nations might be inclined to treat La Vérendrye as someone worthy of respect (though not reverence). In a moment such as the present, when history is often used as a tool of identity politics, and when goodwill between groups is desperately needed, La Vérendrye is one of those men who could be made the subject of a statue in a public space.

Perhaps the greatest legacy of La Vérendrye is racial. Jean-Baptiste Colbert, who served as minister of marine during the reign of Louis XIV in the seventeenth century, urged a "fusion" of the French and Aboriginal—which he imagined would help to make up for the disparity in numbers between English and French settlers. It would help bring Aboriginals into the "civilized" modes of European civilization (as he saw them) and would perhaps assist the French in acquiring natural graces (a theme that would appear in Voltaire's 1767 novella *L'Ingénu* [The Innocent], in which the hero is a white man raised by Hurons).

Of course, as in any marriage, both partners had to be Catholic. In part because of such conditions, there were relatively few such actual marriages in the settlements along the St. Lawrence Valley. But the prospect of "fusion" on a metaphorical level had real currency in the West. In spite of, or perhaps even because of, the fall of New France, mixed communities of French and Aboriginals flourished in the hinterlands of North America, and a genuine Métis civilization arose in the early nineteenth century—not just in La Vérendrye's old Manitoba stomping grounds but in states such as Illinois and Missouri.

As a second-generation *Canadien*—and what the Americans would have called a frontiersman—La Vérendrye dealt with *les sauvages* in a manner galvanized by his own humane personal instincts. This same benign spirit surely overshadowed the institution of "country wives" and their fur trader husbands.

"Aboriginal women's economic skills and kinship ties, as well as the complete absence of white women, became a powerful incentive for fur traders to pursue them as wives," writes Carolyn Podruchny in *Making the Voyageur World: Travelers and Traders in the North American Fur Trade*. "Aboriginal women played key economic and social roles in the emerging fur trade society by teaching their husbands to live off the land, by serving as diplomatic emissaries between the European and Aboriginal traders, and by incorporating traders into Aboriginal kin networks."

Métis couples would face their share of discrimination in French Canada, where miscegenation was frowned upon. But in the Quebec of today, as in North America more generally, it is the spirit of multiculturalism that is ascendant—including among those who proudly boast bloodlines that can be traced to new world and old world alike.

One gets the strong impression upon reading La Vérendrye that he would be greatly pleased by this outcome. Though he never could have realized it at the time, the great explorer played a crucial role in bringing English, French, and First Nations people into the messy but necessary project of sharing this continent.

DANIEL POLIQUIN

⚜ ⚜ ⚜ ⚜

ALBERT LACOMBE

PIONEER PRIEST

LACOMBE LIES IN THE CENTRE of Alberta, 25 kilometres north of Red Deer and 125 kilometres south of Edmonton. It's a tidy, prosperous town of around twelve thousand. The name was originally given to a Canadian Pacific railway station—quite an honour in itself at the time. Today it is home to the Lacombe Research and Development Centre, an Agriculture and Agri-Food Canada laboratory known for, among other things, developing the country's first hybrid breed of pig: the Lacombe hog (a form of posterity that may not be to everyone's taste, but such is perhaps the price of fame). Three schools bear the same name: Lacombe Upper Elementary, École secondaire Lacombe, and Lacombe Junior High. If you're passing through, you can lodge at the Lacombe Hotel, and grab sushi at the adjacent Tokyo Joe Lacombe Japanese Restaurant. If you'd like an after-dinner drink in your hotel room, the Lacombe Liquor Shoppe is just a three-minute drive away. You get the idea: the name is everywhere. To the point that you'll eventually wonder: "Just who was this Lacombe guy?"

And the question is bound to come up again, considering that the man formed the subject of at least two biographies,* published his memoirs during his lifetime,† and rated favourable mention in countless articles on the history of the Canadian west. In the former hamlet of Midnapore, today a neighbourhood of Calgary, you will find the Father Lacombe Care Centre (finally, a glimpse into the churchman behind the name). Albert Lacombe himself founded this facility as the Lacombe Home, in 1910. It took in orphans, the disabled, and the elderly, white and Native alike, in an authentic spirit of racial ecumenism—an all-too-rare initiative for the time. Within those walls the good father himself passed away in 1916, a few weeks shy of his ninetieth birthday. He was buried in St. Albert, north of Edmonton, which was named after him and where you will find, not surprisingly, Lacombe Drive and Lacombe Park. All of which goes to show that not only did his patronymic lend itself to many place names in the province, but his first name, too, has flourished in Alberta's toponymy, despite its already being crowded with similar denominations. For the province itself was christened in honour of HRH Princess Louise Caroline Alberta, the fourth daughter of Queen Victoria and her prince consort—whose name, as you've already guessed, was Albert.

If you'll allow me one final proof of Albert Lacombe's gift for posthumous ubiquity: you have no doubt heard of the Château Frontenac in Quebec City and the Château Laurier in Ottawa, those palatial hotels that enfold the memories of countless political intrigues and romantic honeymoons. Well, one of the grander hotels in the provincial capital, Edmonton, is named the Château Lacombe. And when you learn the price of a room there, any remaining restraint you may have will melt away and you'll demand, out loud: "Would someone please tell me who this fine fellow was, and what is his claim to fame?!"

* Two of which, it must be said, are fairly dated: Katherine Hughes, *Father Lacombe, the Black-Robe Voyageur*, Toronto: William Briggs, 1911; J.G. MacGregor, *Father Lacombe*, Edmonton: Hurtig, 1975.

† *Le Père Lacombe: "l'homme au bon cœur" d'après ses mémoires et souvenirs, recueillis par une sœur de la Providence*, Montreal: Le Devoir, 1916.

Albert Lacombe was neither a political giant nor an oil baron in his adopted province. He was above all an impoverished benefactor who succeeded in opening the hearts and wallets of philanthropists to ensure the posterity of his good works. You could say he had a fairly ordinary name for a man of such reputation, and you would be right. The toponymic root of his surname, *combe*, comes from Gaulish, and means "valley" or "hollow" (compare the English *coomb/combe*, the Welsh *cwm*, and the Dutch *kom*). He might just as well have been called Duval or Lavallée, other common names. His first name was Albert, only underscoring his everyman-ness. And he was surely not ashamed of his name: those who knew him said that he was modesty incarnate. The typically descriptive names that Native Canadians gave him are also telling: the Cree called him *Kamiyoatchakwêt*, "Noble Soul," and to the Blackfoot (Siksikáwa) he was *Aahsosskitsipahpiwa*, "Good Heart." It must have been enjoyable to go through life with those sobriquets in addition to plain old Albert.

Priest, Oblate missionary, polyglot, linguist, diplomat, peacemaker, pioneer . . . Lacombe's life could also be summed up in the words "Albert Lacombe, profession: founder." He built Edmonton's first Catholic school; the first flour mill in St. Albert and the first bridge over the Sturgeon River, which runs through that community; and the first hospital on the Blood Reserve, in southern Alberta. And there were many other initiatives that remained unrealized.

In the end, though, and like any of us, this relentless builder was not without his failings: while he accomplished great things and merits his place among the men and women who shaped the history of western Canada, there were times when he stumbled along his path—horribly botched things, even, causing harm to his Aboriginal flock despite having their best interests at heart. Fear not: we shall hear the whole story, good and bad.

ALBERT LACOMBE'S LIFE BEGAN on February 28, 1827, in Saint-Sulpice, in what was then Lower Canada. To imagine the country into which he was born—Confederation was still a half-century in the future—one need only recall paintings by Cornelius Krieghoff: a wintry world whose denizens wore fur coats and hats, were shod in bull-hide *souliers de beu*, and travelled by snowshoe or horse-drawn sleigh. The *habitants* of this bucolic environment worked the land to feed their large families, went to Mass on Sundays, and knew their prayers and hymns by heart—if only because they were incapable of reading them in the pious books of the time. The migration of French-Canadian workers to the mills and factories of New England had just begun, and a few Patriotes were preparing to take up arms against an unjust colonial regime (an episode that was to leave few traces in the mind of the young Albert).

Perhaps his mind was already elsewhere. In this setting where church took precedence over school, the eldest son of Albert Lacombe and Agathe Duhamel, both farmers, dreamed of becoming a priest. The parish curé, a man named Viau, believed in the boy's calling and paid for his studies at Collège de l'Assomption. Albert then completed his training for the priesthood at the Episcopal Palace in Montreal, which was the bastion of Bishop Ignace Bourget, a man to be reckoned with. There the twenty-year-old Albert heard the preachings of an intrepid apostle named Georges-Antoine Bellecourt, who had come from Red River, Manitoba, to raise funds for the Catholic missions out west. Albert immediately glimpsed his destiny: to minister in the Canadian west for the greater glory of God.

The impetus to venture to the West was all the stronger because he had "Indian blood in his veins." The popular saying had long been taken literally in the Lacombe family. In 1690, an Ojibwa party had come to trade in the St. Lawrence River Valley. On their return trip, they abducted a young woman, Marie-Louise Beaupré, at Saint-Sulpice, taking her to their camp near Sault Ste. Marie. Five years later, a fur trader uncle of hers found her there and brought her back home—along with her two Métis children, a boy and a girl. A year after that,

Marie-Louise married a man from the parish, who adopted the children. The daughter, it is said, was Albert Lacombe's grandmother. The young Albert was known as "the little Indian"* to all the villagers, starting with Father Viau, who presumably did not share the prejudices of certain of his contemporaries when it came to Catholics with Native ancestry. Lacombe himself took pride in those origins, seeing them as validation of his calling as a missionary in the West.

Lacombe was ordained on June 13, 1849, and sent to Pembina, in what is now North Dakota, to assist his hero, Father Bellecourt. There he grew fascinated by the culture of the Métis and, beginning in 1851, travelled as a chaplain with their caravans engaged in the twice-yearly bison hunt. It was a world in which the military hierarchy inherited from the white man blended with the traditions of community and sharing specific to the First Nations. The adventurous life thrilled the young priest, but those first heady days in the West came to an abrupt end when Bishop Bourget called him back to Lower Canada, assigning him to a tranquil vicarage at Berthier-en-Haut. Fortunately, in 1852 Bourget gave permission for him to head west again, this time accompanied by Monsignor Alexandre Taché, a young Oblate bishop who was also destined for great things. For Lacombe, after the first flush of romance three years earlier, the great love of his life had begun. He was in thrall to the wide-open West, then almost untouched. The Great Plains were populated by perhaps sixty thousand First Nations people: Assiniboine (Asinaan), Cree, Chipewyan (Denesuline), Inuit, and Blackfoot; a little more than twelve thousand Métis, descendants of French-Canadian and Scottish voyageurs and trappers and the Indigenous women they married; and barely over four thousand white colonists. It was a land in which the Native warrior's code condoned scalping, horse theft, and enslavement of prisoners of war. These masters of the Plains had their customs, their songs, their dances, their legends. The earth did not belong to them, but they to the earth; they

---

* "*Le petit sauvage.*" See Serge Bouchard and Marie-Christine Lévesque, *Ils ont couru l'Amérique: De remarquables oubliés*, Tome 2, Montreal: Lux Éditeur, 2014.

were one with it. Unbeknownst to them, though, their heyday had reached its twilight: the decline of the bison population, disease brought by the Europeans, and white colonization would soon spell the end of this golden age. Late in his own life, Lacombe, who had spent nearly seventy years alongside them, would see the Natives and Métis reduced to the status of "beggar chieftains" in their own land.

LACOMBE JOINED THE OBLATE ORDER on September 28, 1856, after completing his novitiate year at the mission in Lac Sainte-Anne, seventy-five kilometres west of Edmonton, under the guidance of Father René Rémas of France. It was a young congregation, founded in 1816 by Msgr. Eugène de Mazenod, the bishop of Marseille. De Mazenod, who came from a family of minor nobility that had been stripped of its wealth after 1789, sought to renew the apostolic foundations of the French clergy, undermined by the turmoil of the Revolution and the Napoleonic Wars. Well before he founded the order, de Mazenod had actively ministered to the poor, going so far as to preach in the Provençal language to win their hearts. He wanted to surround himself with a new breed of Jesuits—absent their reputation for deceit—following a motto that paraphrased the prophet Isaiah, and which had already been taken up by the Lazarites, among others: *Evangelizare pauperibus misit me* ("He hath sent me to preach the Gospel to the poor"). The new order received papal approval from Leo XII in 1826 and took the name Oblats de Marie-Immaculée: the Missionary Oblates of Mary Immaculate.

The Oblates were infused with a spirit that recalled the Counter-Reformation—the very movement that, in the seventeenth century, had been a driving force in the founding of New France. Its ideology was very much of the time (these were the years of the Restoration in England) insofar as it aimed to counter the revolutionary ideal. The first Oblates sent to Canada were therefore French. Among those who missioned in Ontario, the Abitibi, and the West—all places where one had to be made of stern stuff to spread the Word—was Father Émile Legal, a contemporary of Albert Lacombe, who wrote in the introduction to his *Short Sketches of the History of the Catholic Churches and Missions in Central Alberta*, "Then came the French Revolution which sowed broadcast in the world those pernicious principles from which it still suffers and will continue to suffer until it has repudiated them. It proclaimed the rights of man to the contempt of the rights of God."* Which goes to show who they were dealing with: compared to the affairs of men, God was everything.

Oblate missionaries were chosen to minister in the West because the first bishop who went there, Msgr. Joseph-Norbert Provencher, wanted to entrust the evangelization of "Indians" and colonists alike to a well-structured order rather than to secular priests, whose zeal he found too tepid. Msgr. Bourget—who led the opposition of the French-Canadian clergy to the liberal ideals of Louis-Joseph Papineau's Patriotes and those who would soon become the Rouges (Liberals) of Canadian politics—conveyed Msgr. Provencher's invitation to Bishop de Mazenod during a trip to France in 1841. De Mazenod accepted enthusiastically. Given what we know about their complementary ideals, it is not surprising that the two prelates got on well.

It would be inaccurate to infer, however, that the Oblates were all reactionaries; they had a concern for conservation, but also for construction, in keeping with the spirit of the times. It was only later that they were said to have a conservative ideology. Indeed, at the time, the word *conservateur* was a neologism, coined—as claimed in his *Mémoires d'outre-tombe*—by François de Chateaubriand, who wanted to restore France's monarchy while conserving the gains of the Revolution, such as human rights and freedom of the press. Conservatism with a human face, in short.

* Émile Legal, *Short Sketches of the History of the Catholic Churches and Missions in Central Alberta*, Winnipeg: West Canada Publishing Co., 1914, p. 7.

AMONG THAT GROUP OF FRENCH missionaries who came to Canada to found an order that was at once old and new, Albert Lacombe was one of the few Canadians, along with Bishop Taché. Doubtless he was forced to adhere to the militant ideology of his brothers, although he never addressed this in his writings, despite their prolixity. He was a priest, and moreover, a member of an order, and as such he remained obeisant, true to the Jesuit motto *Perinde ac cadaver*: "Be as disciplined as a corpse."

It is also safe to assume, however, that the difficulties of his apostolate gave him plenty of opportunities for reflections more pressing and less cerebral. When he returned to Red River in 1852, what awaited him may not have been glorious martyrdom, à la the "Black Robes" of Huronia two hundred years earlier, but it was guaranteed suffering. It took an iron constitution, like his, to endure the bone-chilling winters, when snowshoeing or dog-sledding were the main modes of travel. Summer wasn't much better, with stifling heat waves and swarms of voracious mosquitoes. Only makeshift roads crossed the prairie, passable on foot or horseback, beset by snow squalls in winter and dust storms in summer. The priests slept in tents in all seasons, with all the discomfort that implies. Hunger was unremitting, and what little there was to eat was spartan fare that would put off almost anyone. From hardships to extreme weather to close quarters that were often uncomfortable for one who had taken a vow of chastity, not to mention hair-raising trips down whitewater rivers in small boats or canoes, the missionary life was nothing like later cinematic depictions of frontier days, where the weather is always fine and insect life non-existent. Lacombe became inured to all this, and his courage in the face of adversity was enough to enshrine his name in posterity. One who did find the words to complain was Vital Grandin, a French Oblate and eventually bishop of St. Albert, who wrote to Louis Veuillot, the champion of militant ultramontanism of the time: "My mission is not poetic. Prose, a horrible prose, abounds here, as you can see. I cannot promise martyrdom, but I do promise unrelenting fatigue, unending snows, prolonged nights, marshes, mires, and finally lice."* The works.

Not to mention, the Canadian West was still a land of violence. Not the Wild West of the American frontier, with outlaws robbing stagecoaches and Bluecoats charging, swords drawn, at Native warriors, but a land in which First Nations waged ruthless war upon each other. Oblate priest or not, you were risking your life. Like Brother Alexis Raynard, "killed and eaten by his Iroquois guide in defence of an orphan girl who had been committed to his care,"† near Lac La Biche in 1875, not to mention all the other Oblates who died from cold or drowning in the rigorous years of their mission, from the middle of the nineteenth century to the dawn of the twentieth.

Lacombe himself witnessed unspeakable atrocities and nearly paid the ultimate price. In February 1857, called to help the Blackfoot, who were decimated by fever, he came across three mutilated bodies, their feet and hands severed and hanging from trees. The macabre deed was the work of the Cree, the hereditary enemies of the Blackfoot. In 1865, Lacombe was again camped with the Blackfoot, having risked his life to care for them during an outbreak of measles, when a party of Cree and their Assiniboine allies attacked. Realizing the battle was one-sided, Lacombe left his tent, crucifix in hand, to negotiate a truce. A bullet struck him in the shoulder, ricocheted, and grazed his skull. He lost consciousness, but luckily the wound was only superficial. A hard life, indeed.

Disease was another manifestation of violence in the region. Hygiene was but an illusion, and the illnesses imported involuntarily by the European colonists spread easily. The smallpox epidemic of 1870 wiped out 50 per cent of the Canadian Plains Indians. On numerous

---

* Cited in Donat Levasseur, *Les oblats de Marie-Immaculée dans l'Ouest et le Nord du Canada*, 1845–1967, University of Alberta Press, 1995. [Freely translated.]

† So reads Raynard's tombstone. *Oblate Communications, Historical Dictionary*, Vol. 2, accessed April 4, 2016, http://www.omiworld.org/en/dictionary/historical-dictionary_vol-2_r/1906/reynard-alexis.

occasions, Lacombe again went to the aid of his stricken brothers and sisters, Blackfoot and Cree alike. Like many other priests, Lacombe was tolerated, even loved, by the First Nations, because he played the useful role of healer. With smallpox devastating the Blackfoot, Lacombe worked tirelessly to save them. He had to: they were dying in large numbers, their bodies quickly buried in shallow graves; in the night, dogs would dig up and devour the bodies of the youngest. Lacombe kept a feather dipped in camphor between his teeth to guard against infection. He occasionally had to play the role of surgeon—for example, amputating the gangrenous arm of a young warrior, the son of the Cree chief named Sweet-Grass. In short, things one is hardly accustomed to doing every day.

He himself might well have succumbed to measles in 1865, had he not been saved in time by a certain Jean L'Heureux, a somewhat mysterious character who was a shadow figure of sorts to Lacombe. He is mentioned in Lacombe's letters as early as 1861. L'Heureux, born in Lower Canada in 1837, lived among First Nations people and claimed to be a missionary. He wore the cassock and Roman collar of the Oblate order; the problem was, he wasn't quite a priest. He had the calling at one time, and studied at a seminary, but was expelled after being caught either stealing or engaging in a homosexual act—accounts vary.* Undeterred, L'Heureux tried to minister with the Oblates in western Canada, staying at the St. Albert Mission near Fort Edmonton, but was permanently removed from the order for practising sodomy. He decided to settle permanently in the West, and continued his unauthorized ministering. He was especially devoted to the Blackfoot, who were tolerant of homosexuality; he learned their language and took the name Nio'kskatapi, or "Three Persons," no doubt a reference to the Holy Trinity. Much to the Oblates' annoyance, he did not hesitate to perform baptisms and marriages. Such were his talents

* Hugh A. Dempsey, "Jean L'Heureux," in *Dictionary of Canadian Biography*, Vol. 14, University of Toronto/Université Laval, 2003–, accessed April 4, 2016, http://www.biographi.ca/en/bio/l_heureux_jean_14E.html.

as an interpreter of Native languages, though, that the Hudson's Bay Company and even the clergy retained his services. He also rendered great services to the nascent state of Canada at the time of the 1885 North-West Resistance when, jointly with Lacombe, he persuaded the Blackfoot not to enter into an alliance with Louis Riel. He played an active role in the Treaty 7 negotiations, defending the interests of the Blackfoot Confederacy, and was hired as an interpreter by the Department of Indian Affairs. In the end, he was another "good heart," to whom Lacombe owed his life, and whose generous actions made amends for behaviour deemed immoral at the time, and for his fraudulent ways.

Lacombe was a fine interpreter himself. Upon his arrival in Pembina, he began studying Saulteaux, a dialect of the Ojibwa language, which his Indigenous ancestor probably spoke. He later learned the Plains Cree and Blackfoot languages. From 1853 to 1861, he ministered mostly at Lac Ste. Anne, but took advantage of his extensive travels elsewhere in the region—to Jasper House, Fort Edmonton, Lac La Biche, Lesser Slave Lake, and Fort Dunvegan, for example—to gather notes for the Cree–French dictionary and grammar that he would eventually write.

In 1861, Lacombe settled at a site north of Fort Edmonton where Bishop Taché wanted to establish a central mission. In honour of his resident priest, Taché named the spot St. Albert (it is today a town of sixty thousand). There Lacombe found plenty of ways to expend his excess energy; besides the aforementioned flour mill and bridge over the Sturgeon River, he oversaw construction of a cart trail as far as Lac La Biche, the better to organize provisioning of goods from the Red River. This marked the birth of Lacombe the builder, at the same time as Lacombe the converter of souls.

In 1865, Taché tasked Lacombe with establishing an itinerant ministry among the Cree and Blackfoot, which led to his founding the mission at Saint-Paul-des-Cris, on the North Saskatchewan River, in what is now Alberta. There he introduced the Cree to agricultural methods, but they were not about to abandon their lifestyle of far-ranging hunting. Lacombe accompanied them to their camps, instructing them. Since he would not let his parishioners out of his sight, his ministry made him an "occasional nomad"—an apt summation of his whole life. To paraphrase Salman Rushdie, "A man does not have roots, he has feet." In all, Father Albert Lacombe would spend seven years of his life travelling in the First Nations of western Canada.

Just over the horizon were the 1867 proclamation of Canadian Confederation and Canada's purchase in 1869 of the territory known as Rupert's Land, encompassing the area where Lacombe travelled. The stage was also being set for the first clash between Ottawa and the Métis. These were fruitful times, but troubled ones as well.

⚜ ⚜ ⚜ ⚜

THOUGH HE WAS ALMOST always on the move, Lacombe also watched events unfolding: the Dominion of Canada taking shape, First Nations claiming their rightful place under the sun, and the Métis under Louis Riel taking a stand against an unjust order—all of which led to the founding of the province of Manitoba in 1870. During those years, Lacombe was active in the territories that would later comprise Saskatchewan and Alberta. But he was well aware of the accelerating events all over the region and well acquainted with all of their major players, including Riel and Bishop Taché. And after the Red River insurrection, he was among those who put pressure on Ottawa to grant the Métis leaders amnesty and protect them from vindictive Orangeist factions in Ontario.

Among the Catholic priests looking for souls to convert, few roamed a "hunting ground" as vast as Lacombe's. But success was limited. He did his best to spread the Christian message and dispense his blessings among the Blackfoot, but they were seldom eager to receive them—among other reasons because they refused to accept the principle of monogamy. Those he did succeed in baptizing were often sick or dying. The Cree were less averse, but converting a healthy adult member of the Blackfoot was nigh on impossible. When the great chief Issapóómahksika (Crowfoot) of the Siksika Nation converted, he was on his deathbed, and, like more than one elderly Amerindian of the time, decided to accept Pascal's Wager. Suffice to say that history has seen more sincere professions of faith in the Trinity. One of Lacombe's great qualities, though, was that he never became discouraged, and he never upbraided the more stubborn among his flock. "Good Heart" remained their steadfast friend, supporting them unreservedly. His blessings cost him nothing and he expected nothing in return, and it is perhaps that unconditional respect for others' morals that earned him such universal affection. When he did succeed in converting, it was because, as Raymond Huel has written (invoking the ideas of John Webster Grant), an Indian who was accepting of a priest's words believed he would acquire some new shamanic power from these missionary healers and builders, and from the whites' superior technology.* Those conversions were thus self-serving, something Lacombe both understood and rued. He no doubt knew that King Clovis and his Franks, along with so many other later monarchs and their peoples, had had the same reasoning.

After these years spent travelling and doing God's work, Lacombe turned to writing, and published his version of the *Échelle*, or Catholic Ladder, a sort of visual aid to the catechism for Native people, which highlighted episodes in the Bible and the history of the Church. In 1873, he completed his Cree–French dictionary.

In the 1870s, he was forced to close the mission at Saint-Paul-des-Cris; the graft, it seemed, had failed. Tenacious as ever, in 1895 he attempted to sedentarize the Métis in Alberta and convert them to a farming existence, dedicating eleven years of his life to the project. Again he was met with failure. He then sought to open up the West to colonization by French Canadians; in this he was similarly unsuccessful. He described himself as a "man with plans," which is accurate

* Raymond J.A. Huel, *Proclaiming the Gospel to the Indians and the Metis: The Missionary Oblates of Mary Immaculate in Western Canada, 1845–1945*, Edmonton: University of Alberta Press, 1999, p. 76.

when one considers his many attempts—but his hopes were not always crowned with success.

The year 1874 saw him back in Manitoba, as curé of St. Mary's parish in Winnipeg, where, for once, he didn't have to build a church and presbytery himself, as in the adventurous days of his *missions ambulantes*. His true duties were to act as Bishop Taché's personal assistant. Besides being the parish priest, he was the prison chaplain and superior of St. Mary's Residence. He also worked to bring French-Canadian and Franco-American settlers, especially farmers, to Manitoba.

But times were changing, and not always for the better. The Plains bison had been all but exterminated by new hunters armed with repeating rifles. The Métis had lost their livelihood; many, feeling mistreated by English-speaking colonists from Ontario, sought refuge farther west, in what was to become Saskatchewan. The First Nations, already decimated by disease brought by the whites, were but shadows of themselves, "poor wretches" reduced to eating their dogs lest they die of starvation. Lacombe and his Christian brothers, Catholic and Protestant alike, worked to bring relief to the tribes amid what they felt was a white invasion, so that they might at least have places to call home, where they could retreat and regain their strength.

Some consolations and comforts could yet be found here and there, on trips to more hospitable regions, for example. Lacombe travelled eastward to Quebec often, as part of his good works. In 1879, he represented his western Oblate brothers at the order's general chapter in France, from there continuing on to Rome, where he had the pleasure of an audience with the Pope—and the misfortune of having his wallet stolen during Mass at St. Peter's Basilica (he would mostly smile about this episode, though, in recounting it later). Taking advantage of the pomp and circumstance of the Roman liturgy, the Italian pickpockets wouldn't have cared that they'd prised their latest booty from a Canadian missionary who was as poor as the proverbial church mouse.

Before long, the transcontinental railway was pushing through the prairies, and in 1880, Lacombe was assigned to minister to the construction gangs. It was a bleak mission that took him to Rat Portage (present-day Kenora, Ontario), where he had to live with the tough, hard-working navvies, who could have given lessons in impiety to those street thieves in Rome. Lacombe complained about these trying times and confessed to his diary, "My God, send me back again to my old Indian missions."* When he was finally called back to Alberta, he shed no tears.

For Lacombe, there was one benefit to the years spent with the reprobate workers in the Canadian Pacific camps: he got to know the top executives of the railway, including William Cornelius Van Horne. In 1883, when the railhead had reached southern Alberta, Lacombe was ministering among the Kainai Nation (or Blood tribe, as it was known in English) when the CPR contacted him, asking for his services as a mediator. The Blackfoot, eager to ensure respect of their rights under the treaties they had negotiated in good faith with Ottawa, refused to allow the railway surveyors to pass. The white teams cared not a whit about the Indians' land rights; they wanted to get on with their work. The looming confrontation near Blackfoot Crossing recalled another clash: that which had pitted Louis Riel and his Métis against the Canadian government surveyors at Red River. Lacombe sought out his old friend, Chief Crowfoot; negotiations took place, and a compromise was reached. Bloodshed had been averted, and Aboriginal rights respected.

Father Lacombe's favourable intercession led to an episode a year later that helped cement his legendary status. In 1884, on a ceremonial train journey through the region, Lacombe was symbolically appointed president of Canadian Pacific for one hour, and given a lifetime pass for free travel on the railway. His fruitful mediation was also the reason his name would later grace hotels and train stations. That glory mattered little, however, compared to the influence Lacombe gained with the railway capitalists, who eventually opened their wallets to support his good works and ensure their sustainability.

---

* Hughes, *Father Lacombe*, p. 258.

His talents as a diplomat and peacemaker would soon be required in a far more serious conflict: the Northwest Rebellion of 1885. Louis Riel, sympathetic to the grievances of his Aboriginal brothers, had returned to the West from exile in the United States. The poor man was now in the throes of mental illness, but the Métis and Indians' objections were, more than ever, well founded and reasonable. Ottawa, though, was not prepared to listen. The Métis armed themselves, the Cree rose up, and blood flowed. In the Frog Lake Massacre, Oblate fathers Léon Fafard and Félix Marchand were killed by a Cree party. Meanwhile, Lacombe convinced Crowfoot to stop the Blackfoot from siding with the Métis and the Cree; this provided Ottawa with greater latitude to quell the rebellion. Lacombe's laudable skills notwithstanding, it is important to recall that he did not act alone: the interpreter Jean L'Heureux also spoke out in favour of Blackfoot neutrality, and it was Crowfoot who wielded the greatest pacifying influence. The aging warrior had gauged better than anyone the belligerents' mismatched firepower, and grasped that if his people got involved, they would be courting disaster. Negotiation was infinitely preferable to confrontation, and Crowfoot had the wisdom to understand this himself. To sing the praises of Lacombe alone is to detract in the same measure from the Blackfoot chief's achievement and to unjustly favour the white version of history. We must, however, grant Lacombe his courage in later blaming Prime Minister John A. Macdonald for the legalized assassination of Louis Riel, and in leading the campaign to grant amnesty to the Cree chief Big Bear (Mistahi-maskwa) and other Native leaders. Albert Lacombe was above all a man of peace and pardon, virtues that were all too often flouted in those parlous times.

⚜ ⚜ ⚜ ⚜

THE TIME HAS COME TO address a less glorious aspect of Father Lacombe's life and work: the sinister saga of Canada's residential schools. It was not he who had the idea of institutionalizing Indigenous children; stripping them of their culture, language, and lifestyle; and making them into good little Christians who would then melt into the sociopolitical fabric of Canada. But he was engaged in that project for a time, and resolutely so, in fact. In fairness to him, his enthusiasm for that new mission was short-lived, as it brought more than its share of frustrations. But he was complicit all the same.

It was N.F. Davin, a journalist with an acerbic pen, and a soon-to-be member of Parliament, who in 1879 recommended that the Canadian government set up industrial schools, inspired by the American boarding school model, to prepare young Native children for white colonization and, essentially, make them white. The colonizers' position was that Indians would remain unchanged—that is, nomads living hand to mouth in a bountiful country—as long as they were not sedentarized. And if Indians were to be Canadianized, they first had to be Christianized: values other than those they had known forever had to be imposed upon them. For the adults, it was believed, it was too late: they would remain nomadic, polygamous, and indigent; few would bother to learn English or French, as their mother tongues were entirely sufficient; they would not willingly become farmers or landowners, as they were children of the land, not its masters; and they would only timidly embrace the Christian faith, because the sacrifices that it demanded were too onerous. The key was to address the children: if this worked, they might win over their parents, and their descendants would become "good Canadians." There was a further putative benefit: if the Indians were assimilated in this way, they would no longer exercise collective ownership of extensive territories, a troublesome impediment to white colonization.

The missionary churches of western Canada—Anglican, Catholic, and Methodist, among others—were quick to espouse the movement. In 1884, Lacombe agreed to be the head of St. Joseph's Industrial School in Dunbow. It was not a pleasant experience. His twenty-five students, who until then had known nothing but life in the freedom of the great outdoors, tolerated neither forced teaching nor a walled-in existence. They missed their families and were in constant revolt.

"These children showed themselves to be ungrateful, malcontent and undisciplined. They deserted, came back, left again; in short, stubbornly asserted their national independence,"* Lacombe wrote in his memoirs. (The choice of the last two words, "national independence," is astonishing.) By the end of the school year in spring, not one boy remained; they had left of their own accord or gone with their parents who had come to claim them.

Today it is easier to understand the children's feelings of helplessness; they had been suddenly deprived of freedom—dragged kicking and screaming from their natural environment and culture. Young Dan Kennedy, later chief of the Assiniboine Nation, was to recall how he had his hair forcibly shorn after arriving at an industrial school: "his long braids were cut and [he] wondered whether his mother had died since the cutting of hair was a sign of mourning in the Assiniboine culture."† This is to say nothing of corporal punishment, forced labour, insults, prohibition from speaking Indigenous languages, violence between students of First Nations that had always been enemies, or the severity of ignorant, contemptuous teachers with no regard for human difference. In the poisoned atmosphere of the time, the perceived superiority of Western civilization was tantamount to dogma, and if one accepted the idea of educating "little Indians," it was strictly because Christian charity dictated that this was just. This view was paternalistic, and patently unfounded.

Despite his failure, Lacombe was unwavering in his conviction:

> We believed some of these young Indians to be as gifted as other children. And yes, there are some who are brilliant and filled with talent. But that is only the beginning of the problem. The real problem comes once they have left school. Unfortunately, when these children return to their parents, they are no longer

* *Le Père Lacombe*, p. 340. [Freely translated.]

† Huel, *Proclaiming the Gospel to the Indians and the Metis: The Missionary Oblates of Mary Immaculate in Western Canada, 1845–1945*, p. 144.

> either whites or Indians. They have no need of the good manners that have been instilled in them, especially if they go back to their blankets and their huts. Little by little they return to their old habits and shortly lose what they have been taught with so much sacrifice. It is quite likely that things will be so as long as the older generation has not died.*

Having failed in his educational mission with the Indians—something to which he would never admit—Lacombe tried again, in 1901, with Métis children, who thanked him for his "kindnesses" by burning down the St. Paul des Métis school four years later.

FORTUNATELY FOR HIM and others, Father Lacombe had other talents, not least for diplomacy. In 1900, his Oblate superiors dispatched him to Europe, to recruit Ruthenian clergymen familiar with the Eastern rite, who could serve the many settlers who had come from Galicia (part of present-day Poland and Ukraine). During his mission, he was summoned to an audience with the man who ruled over that land: Emperor Franz Joseph of Austria. Lacombe played his role as a diplomat well, even if the proud descendant of the House of Habsburg appeared less than impressed with the zeal of the poor, half-wild Canadian priest.

He was less successful in his efforts to defend the rights of French Canadians as part of the so-called Manitoba Schools Question. Those rights had been guaranteed in the province's founding legislation and enshrined in the Canadian Constitution, but successive provincial governments, attuned to the prejudices of the day, had ignored them. In 1894, Lacombe left his parish in Edmonton for St. Boniface, determined to secure restitution of educational privileges for Manitoba's francophone Catholics. In late 1895, Archbishop Adélard Langevin,

* *Le Père Lacombe*, p. 507. [Freely translated.]

successor to Taché, dispatched him to Ottawa to negotiate remedial legislation with Prime Minister Mackenzie Bowell, who was a man of hardened Orangeist convictions. Msgr. Langevin was left wanting, as was Lacombe, when the House of Commons took too long to vote on a bill. A year later, Wilfrid Laurier, despite his strategy of *bon-ententisme*, quashed the idea of reparations for the Franco-Manitobans. Indeed, since the onset of the crisis, he had advocated for the creation of a task force on the issue—which, in Canadian political parlance, means giving lawmakers carte blanche to do nothing. Lacombe was distressed, but didn't say so too loudly. As a good conciliatory priest, he preferred to exercise that other virtue, patience, and not raise the government's hackles. A pity.

IN 1890, WITH HIS sixty-third birthday approaching, Lacombe declared he was weary of his endless travels across the Plains, and decided to retire to his sanctuary at Pincher Creek, near Calgary. The Ermitage Saint-Michel was a magnificent retreat, where the missionary now dreamt only of meditations and walks with his dog on the hilltop—in hindsight, a bemusing prospect, for many more travels and missions still awaited our restless hermit.

In 1895, he secured from the federal government a grant of four townships to establish a colony for Métis from Montana and western Canada: this would become St. Paul des Métis. His dream of a "Métis Utopia" ran afoul of too many obstacles, however, forcing him to eventually alter his plans: the community would house French-Canadian settlers instead. But the results were no more conclusive. In 1899, Lacombe was on the road again, taking part in the negotiations for Treaty 8, which covered northern Alberta and regions to the west, north, and east. This is noteworthy: while the numbered treaties were to be violated and ignored time and again both by governments and private enterprises, the fact remains that they came to constitute, and indeed still constitute, the legal basis for Native identity and the principal foundation for Indigenous rights in Canada, later confirmed by the Constitution and upheld by a number of Supreme Court rulings. Lacombe at least accomplished that for "his Indians."

He returned to serve as curé of St. Mary's parish in Calgary in 1903. He also continued his linguistic work, collaborating with Bishop Legal on a Blackfoot, Blood, and Peigan (Piikáni) vocabulary and publishing a new edition of a seminal Ojibwa grammar and dictionary by Frederic Baraga. Lastly, he produced Cree translations of the New Testament along with several hymns and prayers. All in a day's work . . .

In these early years of the twentieth century, the "travelling hermit" also made several trips to Europe. As mentioned, he met Emperor Franz Joseph in 1900 to discuss the Ruthenian question, went to Lemberg, capital of Galicia, to negotiate the recruitment of local priests, had an audience with Pope Leo XIII in Rome, and visited Belgium to recruit French-language settlers. On a subsequent voyage in 1904, he was received by the Austrian emperor a second time, met Pope Pius X, and travelled to the Holy Land. That trip inspired him to make some less than charitable remarks about the Jewish people: "Alas! The blood of a God has for nineteen centuries fallen on them like a curse." Here again he was, unfortunately, a man of his times.

His final and most lasting achievement was the hospice that he founded in 1908 at Midnapore. At the Lacombe Home, anyone in dire straits could find shelter, without distinction as to race. Such generosity was exceptional for the time, but only natural in Father Lacombe's case. He even took in his old companion and antagonist from the early days, Jean L'Heureux, who would live there until his death in 1919. While there, the impenitent L'Heureux continued to wear the Oblate cassock and collar despite being officially forbidden to do so, and until his dying breath described himself as a "lay missionary," no doubt to the displeasure of many—though perhaps not to that of Lacombe, who with grateful heart unhesitatingly rescued L'Heureux from misery.

In his twilight years, the man who had seen first-hand the epic bison hunts of the Métis, and who had travelled and lived among the First Nations of the Plains in the heyday of their warrior splendour, led a life that he could not have imagined as a young man: his home had electricity and a telephone, and he even had a motor car at his disposal. Life had changed dramatically around him. The early French and Canadian missionaries had been succeeded by Ruthenian-, German-, Polish-, and English-speaking Oblates.

With war raging in Europe, Father Albert Lacombe died in the home bearing his name on December 12, 1916, a final mark of fealty to his religious community. He was buried in St. Albert, the city to which he gave his name, next to Msgr. Vital Grandin. He never received the highest honours of the ecclesiastical hierarchy, nor was he a prince of industry or a master of the state. Throughout his life, he did only his duty, and he died a man. The sort of man about whom one says simply: "He was somebody."

GAÉTAN FRIGON

PRUDENT BEAUDRY

AND OTHER PIONEERING QUEBEC BUSINESSMEN

SOME MYTHS DIE HARD. That which holds that French Canadians, especially francophones from Quebec, did not develop anything resembling business acumen until the years of the Quiet Revolution is a profoundly rooted one. The truth is that, decades before what came to be known as "Quebec Inc.," French Canadians were doing business, building and managing factories, and creating banks.

True, most did business only on a small scale. For ages, in every village, including the one where I was born—Saint-Prosper-de-Champlain, in the Mauricie region—almost every *habitant* was an entrepreneur. The farmers, the doctor, the baker, and the cheese shop owner were all entrepreneurs. Because the roads weren't open in winter, every community had to be self-sufficient. The difference from today is that back then the entrepreneurs enjoyed job security while simple employees were at the mercy of their bosses.

For my father, Jean-Baptiste Frigon, who ran the general store in Saint-Prosper, fall signalled the arrival of huge barrels of molasses, vinegar, and other staples, and cases full of Aylmer's soup took up nearly a quarter of the storage space in the basement. Those stocks had to last until spring. As a general merchant, my father had to attend to inventory, credit—and, quite often, petty feuds among villagers, which made him the "arbiter in chief" among entrepreneurs.

But that reality changed dramatically in the mid-1940s, when the government under Maurice Duplessis began subsidizing Quebec's rural villages to ensure the roads remained open year-round. This marked the beginning of a slow but inexorable exodus of villagers toward larger cities nearby, where products and services were more plentiful and more modern. Large-scale entrepreneurship waned, and a job in the city became the new guarantee of employment security.

All the same, the seeds of entrepreneurship and business had been sown in French Canada. While the bastions of high finance and large corporations in the province of Quebec were to remain in the hands of English-speaking capitalists until the 1960s, many francophones were to found and develop major businesses. Their successes left enduring marks, visible today beyond the borders of the province as well as those of Canada.

Curiously, the names of these pioneers are little known to the general public. And yet, what they were able to achieve economically and politically, often in challenging market conditions, was no mean feat. Above all, their accomplishments provide compelling evidence that not all French Canadians were imprisoned in a *grande noirceur*. Far from it . . .

PRUDENT BEAUDRY: BUILDER OF LOS ANGELES

I found it especially fascinating to explore the journey of Prudent Beaudry and his brothers Victor and Jean-Louis, a journey that led Prudent and Victor all the way to California and a small town by the name of Los Angeles.

A daring, visionary property speculator, Prudent Beaudry made a significant contribution to the development of California's future metropolis and symbol of the American dream. He even served as its mayor from 1876 to 1878. To this day, an avenue, a road, and several other sites in Los Angeles bear his name.

A born entrepreneur, Beaudry was known for his ability to see the potential of projects that others would refuse even to consider. They say that an entrepreneur gets better when he fails at least once; Prudent Beaudry was practically wiped out on four separate occasions. The estate he left behind, worth $350,000 (an enormous sum for the time), was a tour de force.

He was not possessed merely of positive qualities, however. He was described as irascible. The gossipers whispered that this confirmed bachelor was faithful to no one—not even his mistresses. And he answered to only one boss: himself.

Prudent Beaudry was born in Mascouche, some forty kilometres north of Montreal, on July 24, 1818. After studying in Montreal and New York City, he travelled across the United States. In 1840, he became a partner in a trading agency in New Orleans. Two years later, he returned to Montreal and went into business with two of his brothers, Jean-Louis and Jean-Baptiste. Together, they set up an import–export firm. This led Prudent to travel often, dividing his time among Europe, New Orleans, and Montreal, where the business was headquartered.

Though the company was commercially and financially successful, Prudent got along increasingly poorly with Jean-Louis, who he felt was narrow-minded. In 1850, he left Quebec to meet up with another of his brothers, Victor, who had gone to California the year before—the year of the Gold Rush.

Prudent and Victor settled in San Francisco. They started out supplying syrup and ice blocks to the mining camps and surrounding villages. Before long, they became general traders. Prudent sank all of his savings into the venture—the not inconsiderable sum of $26,000.

Relations between the two brothers deteriorated, however, and they agreed to part ways. Prudent bought out Victor's share in the company and, on the back of that decision, realized a profit of $33,000 in less than three months, helped by variations in prices. Victor, meanwhile, set out for Central America, hoping to gain a stake in an ambitious project: the building of the Nicaragua Canal. It never happened.

It was then that Prudent Beaudry suffered his first setback. Two fires destroyed a large part of his inventory. Matters were made worse when the arrival of wares that he had ordered created massive surpluses. Prices nosedived and he lost everything he'd gained. It was price fluctuations that had earned him his fortune; this time, they brought him to the verge of ruin.

He headed south to Los Angeles, taking what little he had left: around $200 in cash along with goods worth $1,100. The year was 1852. With the Mexican–American War ended, California had recently become a State of the Union. Los Angeles was home to just five thousand people, six hundred of whom were French speakers. They included French, Belgians, and French Canadians—among the latter, gold prospectors, trappers, guides, and their descendants.

Beaudry opened a small store on one of the main thoroughfares. He chose his merchandise judiciously and, less than a month later, found himself a few thousand dollars richer. In short order, he moved his store to Commercial Street. In 1854, he purchased a property on Aliso Street for $11,000. After investing $25,000 in leasehold improvements, he raised the rents. He was soon netting a monthly profit of $1,000.

The long working days, however, adversely affected his health; he developed problems with his eyesight, among other things. This forced him to return to Montreal in 1855 to rest, and he transferred the reins of the company to his brother Victor. Except for a stay in Europe, Prudent remained in Montreal until 1861, while Victor minded the store in California. When he finally did go back to Los Angeles, fortune smiled on him again, and he earned some $40,000 in three years. He even decided to retire, though he was not yet fifty.

Prudent Beaudry was not the type to sit idle for long, however, and he snapped up, for a good price, a mining company that owed him money. The Slate Range Gold and Silver Mining Company had gone bankrupt, and the state put it up for sale. The mine was in the Mojave

Desert. Unfortunately, it was destroyed by disgruntled Aboriginal workers shortly thereafter. Almost everything Beaudry had bought was lost; he recovered only $6,000 from the insurer. The misfortune convinced him to never again invest in the mining industry.

Beaudry then turned to real estate, predicting extraordinary growth for "his" city of Los Angeles. In 1867, for the sum of $55, he purchased a barren expanse of land on a promontory overlooking the centre of town, which had been deemed worthless. Over the next few months, he bought other plots on the promontory (later to be named Bunker Hill) and on a neighbouring hill (Angelino Heights). There he undertook to develop upscale residential neighbourhoods to meet the needs of the fast-growing city.

The subdivisions would be worthless, though, unless water could be conveyed to them—which was no small challenge. With two partners, Beaudry founded the Los Angeles City Water Company, which entered into a thirty-year lease to manage the city's waterworks. The company invested considerable sums to modernize the system and enable water to be pumped from the Los Angeles River to the hilltop tracts.

To prove that the land he was selling was fertile, Beaudry came up with an original promotional tool. He transformed two parched buttes into spectacular gardens: Bellevue Terrace and Beaudry Park. From the first, lined with fruit trees, one could admire the city below and, in the distance, the Pacific Ocean. The eight-acre Beaudry Park, meanwhile, overlooked a canyon. Neither of the two parks survived the development of California's metropolis: Beaudry himself put them up for sale once he'd sold all the lots.

Beaudry had an innate sense of marketing; he knew how to attract future customers. All over Los Angeles, residents and visitors alike began to see banners proclaiming NOW IS THE TIME! DON'T SHUT YOUR EYES AND TURN YOUR BACK! HAVE A HOME ON THE HILLS! STOP PAYING RENT IN THE VALLEYS!

The land speculator had pulled out all the stops, and he met with immediate success, selling the tracts for twenty to thirty times more than he'd paid. With such huge margins, the money poured in. Beaudry was held in high esteem by many an Angeleno for two main reasons. First of all, because he gave buyers the option of paying in affordable monthly instalments, so families with relatively modest incomes could become homeowners fairly easily. Second, because although the infrastructure he built served initially to increase the value of his land, it was also of benefit to the community, and for several years.

Prudent Beaudry was a visionary urban planner, devising neighbourhoods where landscaping and greenery had pride of place. Among the many professionals he hired was an engineer from the first graduating class of Montreal's École Polytechnique, who designed villas suited to the craggy terrain of this part of Los Angeles. Just a few years later, the results were impressive: the hilltop tracts were transformed into a grand, verdant residential district. The crowning touch came in 1886, when Beaudry and partners built a mechanical streetcar line linking the lower town to Bunker Hill: the Temple Street Cable Railway.

At the time, in Los Angeles and elsewhere, politics and business made excellent bedfellows. It was thus not unusual that Beaudry, despite his real estate hyperactivity, should find the time to enter the municipal political arena. He was first elected as a councillor in 1871. Two years later, he became the first president of the Los Angeles Board of Trade. Then, in 1876, he was elected mayor of the city.

The 1889 publication *An Illustrated History of Los Angeles County*, by J.J. Warner, a prominent citizen who knew Beaudry well, contains the following assessment of the French Canadian's time as mayor: "It was a transition period for Los Angeles, and the services of just such a clear-headed, energetic and incorruptible man as Mr. Beaudry were needed to guide the struggling young city through the difficulties of changing from a Spanish American town to the proud position of being the commercial and political rival of San Francisco. Many were the schemes projected whereby the rich resources of the town would be used for the advancement of the material interests of some of the many incipient boodlers that abounded, and who found in Mr. Beaudry a barrier to the free access to the municipal treasury box that was not at all to their liking."*

At around the same time, Beaudry partnered with four other investors to purchase six thousand acres of land in the San Gabriel Valley, which the group planned to subdivide, develop, and sell. Unfortunately, the death of one partner and the failure of the Temple and Workman Bank caused legal and financial complications. A Supreme Court of California decision went against Beaudry, and he lost control of the property, which by the time the judge's gavel fell was already worth several million dollars. "Nevertheless," wrote historian Hubert Howe Bancroft in 1890 of this latest reversal of fortune of Beaudry's, "there is no one to whose enterprise and public-spirited policy Los Angeles is more indebted for her development from a struggling village in 1852, to its present position as the metropolis of southern California."†

Beaudry decided to retire from active life, this time for good. He was said to be in excellent health, but in the late spring of 1893 he fell victim to what was known at the time as a "paralytic stroke." His condition deteriorated rapidly and he died at his home on the evening of May 29. His body was repatriated to Montreal and buried in Notre-Dame-des-Neiges Cemetery on Mount Royal on June 10.

Though he lived most of his life in California, Prudent Beaudry never forgot his roots. Among other evidence of his affection for Montreal was a $150 bursary that he established in his name in 1875, to be given annually to a student who otherwise would be unable to pursue studies at the École Polytechnique.

Following his demise, the former mayor was praised in the pages of the *Los Angeles Times*: "In his official capacity he was noted

---

* J.J. Warner, *An Illustrated History of Los Angeles County, California*, Chicago: Lewis Publishing Co., 1889, p. 374.

† Hubert Howe Bancroft, *History of the Pacific States of North America, Volume XIX: California, Vol. VII, 1860–1890*, San Francisco: The History Company, Publishers, 1890, p. 159 (Note 6).

for his fearless honesty and his active advocacy of all measures looking for the benefit of the city. Only those who have lived in Los Angeles can form an idea of how great a debt the city owes to this unobtrusive quietly energetic man. His wealth was always kept occupied in developing new enterprises, and thus was diffused among the poorer people."

⚜ ⚜ ⚜ ⚜

JEAN-LOUIS BEAUDRY: ENTREPRENEUR, PATRIOTE, AND POLITICIAN

The elder of the three Beaudry brothers, Jean-Louis (1809–1886), was certainly the most nationalist. He earned a fortune as a merchant, but that did not stop him from being involved in the Lower Canada Rebellion of 1837. After the defeat of the Patriotes by anglophone Loyalist forces, he took an interest in municipal politics and was eventually elected mayor of Montreal, holding the office for several years (coincident with the period when his brother Prudent was mayor of Los Angeles).

Jean-Louis was barely fourteen years old when he left the family nest to take a job as a store clerk in Montreal. He subsequently moved to the village of Newboro, Upper Canada (present-day Ontario), where he stayed for four years. Returning to Montreal, he was hired by an English trading house, but was fired from the position in 1832 because of his active support of the Patriote movement. Good things eventually came from bad: by 1834, the jobless Jean-Louis, along with his brothers Jean-Baptiste and Prudent, had opened a used-goods store. As the years went by, they built the business into a successful import–export firm. They were the first French-Canadian merchants to import goods from Europe without going through an English middleman.

In the words of historian Lorne Ste. Croix, Jean-Louis Beaudry had "a keen, early appreciation of popular advertising. The huge shutters of the building were painted in gaudy red, white, and blue stripes, quickly acquiring for the business a local notoriety as the 'store with the striped shutters.'"*

Jean-Louis had been sympathetic to the Patriote party since 1827. Ten years later, on the eve of the armed conflicts pitting the Patriotes against Loyalists and British troops, he was a member of the Fils de la liberté (Sons of Liberty), a movement advocating for popular sovereignty and the right of the colonies to self-determination. He was arrested during a violent brawl between members of the Fils de la liberté and members of the Doric Club, a radical anglophone association. He was quickly freed, having easily arranged bail. He took refuge in the United States following the December 1837 military defeat of the Patriotes, but by the following June, taking advantage of the amnesty decreed by the new governor general, Lord Durham, he returned to Montreal and his business.

By that time, Beaudry was already a rich man. He used his money to buy land and invest in a number of ventures, notably in the financial sector. In 1861, he was one of the founders of the Banque Jacques-Cartier, one of seven banks created by francophone businessmen at the time to compensate for the dearth of financial services available to them from the English banks.

These financial institutions, as historian Ronald Rudin reminds us, "laid the foundations for francophone presence in the field of banking, which continues to this day."† Indeed, it is difficult to imagine modern-day Quebec without the Banque Nationale du Canada, the Mouvement des caisses Desjardins, the Caisse de dépôt et placement du Québec, and other institutions such as the Fonds de solidarité. All are controlled by French Quebeckers, and their performance has always compared respectably with that of the anglophone banks.

---

* Lorne Ste. Croix, "Beaudry, Jean-Louis," in *Dictionary of Canadian Biography*, Vol. 11, University of Toronto/Université Laval, 2003–, accessed March 4, 2016, http://www.biographi.ca/en/bio/beaudry_jean_louis_11E.html.

† *Banking en français: The French Banks of Quebec 1835–1925*, Toronto: University of Toronto Press, 1985. [Freely translated.]

Jean-Louis remained keenly interested in politics. He had always been a nationalist, but in later life he tempered his ideas and came to approve of the LaFontaine–Baldwin alliance. Following two unsuccessful attempts (in 1854 and 1857) to win election to the Legislative Assembly of Lower Canada, he was elected mayor of Montreal in 1862, and was re-elected almost without opposition the following three years. He decided not to run in 1866. But such was his reputation that, eleven years later, he was asked to return to the mayoralty to restore order to the city's finances. Defeated in 1879, he assumed the mayor's chair one last time, in 1881, eventually losing the 1885 race to the Liberal Honoré Beaugrand.

While there was little doubt as to Jean-Louis' determination and energy, as historian Lorne Ste. Croix notes, "A wide segment of the press . . . was quick to elaborate upon his shortcomings. He was stubborn to an extreme, hot-tempered, rude, and brutally candid."* The Beaudry brothers were clearly men of character!

On June 15, 1886, while attending a session of the Legislative Council in Quebec City, Jean-Louis Beaudry suffered a paralytic stroke (as would his brother Prudent some seven years later). He died on June 25 in Montreal, aged seventy-seven.

VICTOR BEAUDRY: MINING MAGNATE

Victor (1829–1888), the youngest of the Beaudry brothers, was born in Sainte-Anne-des-Plaines, in the Laurentians, northwest of Montreal. He emigrated to California some years before Prudent, settling in San Francisco in 1849 and profiting from the mining industry (a venture in which he was more fortunate than his elder brother). In 1855, with other investors, he founded the Santa Anita Mining Company to

---

* Lorne Ste. Croix, "Beaudry, Jean-Louis," in *Dictionary of Canadian Biography*, Vol. 11, University of Toronto/Université Laval, 2003–, accessed March 11, 2016, http://www.biographi.ca/en/bio/beaudry_jean_louis_11E.html.

exploit gold reserves in the San Gabriel River, north of Los Angeles. With another French-Canadian entrepreneur, Damien Marchesseault (who would also be mayor of Los Angeles in the 1860s), he built hydraulic works to extract the ore, which was a far more efficient (but also more destructive) method than panning.

When the Civil War broke out in 1861, Victor joined an infantry regiment of the U.S. Army. Because of his experience as a merchant, he was given the position of sutler. After the conflict, a group of officers he knew was posted to Camp Independence, in Inyo County, to repel Aboriginal raiders. Victor joined them there, where he built a general store and a hotel—the Beaudry Hotel.

After Mexican miners struck silver in the Inyo Mountains, Beaudry seized a new investment opportunity. A number of Mexican mining companies owed him money for previous purchases from his general store; in return, he acquired the rights to the most promising deposits in the Cerro Gordo region. Those mines made him a rich man.

In 1876, Victor returned to Quebec, having foreseen the coming end of the mining boom. He would return to Los Angeles between 1881 and 1886, however, to do business with his brother Prudent.

Upon his death in Montreal in 1888, he was estimated to be worth $1.5 million—more than the combined assets of his brothers Jean-Louis and Prudent at the end of their lives. Of the three brothers, Victor was the only one to never enter politics. He was known as an intelligent, discerning, and generous man.

JOSEPH MASSON: BUSINESSMAN, SEIGNEUR, POLITICIAN

The Beaudry brothers may have stood apart from the rest because of their audacity, broad range of commercial and financial interests, and—in the case of two of them—success outside Quebec, but many other French Canadians were to play significant roles in business long before the expression "Quebec Inc." was coined. While fragments of their stories are scattered here and there in various works, they remain little known to the majority of us. There were many of these pioneers of business who paved the way for such prominent dynasties as the Bombardiers, Desjardins, Desmarais, Péladeaus, and Coutus.

The "pioneering pioneer" was undoubtedly Joseph Masson (1791–1847), said to have been "the first French-Canadian millionaire." He was born January 5, 1791, in Saint-Eustache, just northwest of the island of Montreal, and by age sixteen was an apprentice clerk in a store in nearby Saint-Benoît run by Duncan McGillis, a Scottish merchant. A few years later, he moved to Montreal, where he met another Scottish merchant, Hugh Robertson.

Robertson was the owner of a company that imported textiles to Lower Canada from Great Britain, in turn exporting wheat, lumber, and especially potash: large quantities of this by-product of logging were required in English industry. The company had two divisions, one headquartered in Glasgow and the other in Montreal.

Robertson couldn't abide the Canadian winters, so he offered Masson the job of managing the Montreal firm. When the Canadian insisted on being more than a mere salaried employee, however, Robertson granted him the status of partner and a share in the profits—and the Montreal company changed its name to Robertson, Masson and Company.

In August 1815, Robertson returned to Scotland for good, leaving Masson as sole steward of the Montreal firm. Gradually, the French Canadian's stake in Robertson, Masson and Co. grew to one-third, and then to half. Thus he was able to realize substantial gains without having invested so much as a penny from his own pocket.

As the money rolled in, Masson invested in several other industries, among them shipping, canal and rail construction, gas lighting, and banking. And he bought land: in 1832, he acquired the seigneury of Terrebonne, north of Montreal. As his family were its last owners before the abolition of the seigneurial system, Masson could add the title Seigneur of Terrebonne to his list of accomplishments.

Masson was close to *les Anglais* by virtue of his business ties, and is generally considered to have been a Loyalist. That did not keep him from befriending Louis-Joseph Papineau, and in 1837, when the Patriote leader had a price on his head, Masson hid him in his home. The latter's conservative yet moderate positions would earn him the respect of both sides in the conflict.

When the Frères chasseurs (Hunter Brothers—a paramilitary secret society created by Patriotes exiled in the U.S.) attempted a new uprising in November 1838, Terrebonne was one of their bases. Law enforcement intervened. After exchanges of gunfire, Masson stepped in and offered to negotiate a truce. A "treaty" was signed: the Patriotes agreed to lay down their guns, in return for which Masson and other local Loyalists pledged not to testify against them.

Unfortunately, the police breached the spirit of the agreement and apprehended six of the Patriotes involved, two of whom would be exiled to Australia. No one, however, doubted Joseph Masson's honesty in the matter. His prime motivation was to spare Terrebonne and its inhabitants the same fate as the villages that had been razed by English militias the previous year.

As historian Fernand Ouellet notes, Joseph Masson was one of the first francophone Canadians to succeed in business on a scale that went beyond the colony's borders: "He was the major Canadian businessman of the period 1830–40. It was he who had the greatest success in gaining access to the suppliers in Great Britain, just as he was one of the few to have done business as far away as Toronto. His success proves that the obstacles ordinarily cited to account for the poor performance of Canadians in the economic field—favouritism, trouble obtaining credit, difficulty in establishing contacts in Britain and business connections in Upper Canada—were not as significant as is claimed, nor was any supposed incapacity due to ethnic origin. The essential obstacles lay in the social structures that determined certain choices."*

* Fernand Ouellet, "Masson, Joseph," in *Dictionary of Canadian Biography*, Vol. 7, University of Toronto/Université Laval, 2003–, accessed March 4, 2016, http://www.biographi.ca/en/bio/masson_joseph_7E.html.

JOSEPH BARSALOU: SOAP KING AND MAYOR

In their general store in Saint-Prosper-de-Champlain, I recall, my grandfather and my father sold Barsalou soap; it was Quebeckers' favourite brand until the 1950s. And when I hear the name of the man who founded Montreal's famed soap factory, Joseph Barsalou (1822–1897), it stirs another memory: that of the Jacques Cartier Bridge, the "crooked" span that has linked the city to its South Shore since 1930. It was built that way because one of Barsalou's sons, Hector, stubbornly resisted expropriation of the De Lorimier Avenue factory that stood in its planned path. So a curve was added to the bridge, leading to many accidents.

Born in Montreal on December 5, 1822, Joseph Barsalou was learning the ropes of the retail trade by the time he was fifteen. He then spent five years in the employ of a Montreal auctioneer by the name of Austin Cuvillier. In 1847, he went to work for Young and Benning, a merchant and auction firm; by 1853, he was a partner in the firm, which became known as Benning and Barsalou.

In 1863, with two English-Canadian partners, Barsalou acquired a rubber factory owned by one Ashley Hibbard, renaming it the Canadian Rubber Company. Three years later, Barsalou became its president. The company expanded in 1867 when a new group of investors injected substantial new capital. In the years 1870 to 1900, it captured a sizable share of the domestic market, took over several competitors, and established subsidiaries in major Canadian cities.

The Barsalou sons joined the family business in the mid-1870s. With their help, Joseph ventured into soapmaking. They acquired new technology to replace traditional manual production and built a four-storey plant at the corner of Sainte-Catherine and Durham streets. The first year, it produced a million pounds of bar and flake soap. The Imperial brand, with a horse's head as its emblem, was the most popular. Even after the family business was bought out by Procter & Gamble in 1935, production of Barsalou soaps continued for several years.

Well before Hector's obstinacy forced the builders of the Jacques Cartier Bridge to modify its configuration, the Barsalou name was linked to another bridge: one crossing the Yamaska River at Saint-Hyacinthe. In the early 1860s, Joseph Barsalou had partnered with the most powerful businessman in town, Georges-Casimir Dessaulles, in the running of a flour mill and a woollen mill. In 1864, the government authorized him to collect tolls on the bridge he had built to more efficiently supply the mills. The company enjoyed a measure of growth until 1872, when it was forced to close after a boycott led by wholesalers. Two years later, Barsalou teamed up again with Dessaulles to found the St. Hyacinthe Manufacturing Company and the Bank of Saint-Hyacinthe.

Like many businessmen of the time, Joseph Barsalou expanded his interests, branching out into oilcloth and glass bottle manufacturing, slaughterhouses, and insurance. Not all of his ventures were successful, but on balance, he did well.

In the early 1880s, Barsalou fought the City of Montreal's plan to annex the town of Hochelaga. When the annexation went ahead, he convinced the provincial government to exclude the eastern portion of Hochelaga, and Barsalou and fellow landowners founded the town of Maisonneuve. This allowed them to develop the tracts they owned there, rather than see Montreal expand at their expense. Barsalou became Maisonneuve's first mayor. The town administration swiftly implemented measures, including tax exemptions, promoting the building of factories there.

By the turn of the twentieth century, Maisonneuve was one of the leading industrial towns in the country, providing jobs to thousands of workers who moved into modest row houses erected in the new subdivisions. Impressive public buildings were also built, including the city hall, the Maisonneuve Market, a public bath, and a fire station, all of which can still be admired today.

Joseph Barsalou barely glimpsed the early growth of the town that became known as the "Pittsburgh of Canada," however: he died aged seventy-four on May 17, 1897, in Montreal.

ALPHONSE DESJARDINS: LAWYER, BANKER, AND POLITICIAN

A newspaper of the time may have deemed Joseph Barsalou the "true father" of the municipality of Maisonneuve, but another landowner, Alphonse Desjardins (1841–1912), along with his son Hubert, wielded much greater influence over the development of east-end Montreal. Desjardins (not to be confused with his contemporary of the same name, who founded the Caisses Populaires credit-union movement) and Joseph Barsalou knew each other well: Alphonse's second marriage was to one of Barsalou's two daughters, Hortense. Hubert Desjardins, meanwhile, served two terms as mayor of Maisonneuve, from 1894 to 1896 and from 1897 to 1901.

The elder Desjardins was also a good friend of Joseph Masson, seigneur of Terrebonne. The Desjardins had roots in the Terrebonne region going back to 1729, and there were several marriages between the two families.

After his studies, Alphonse Desjardins practised law for six years but also embarked on a career as a journalist. Possibly influenced by the teachings of the future bishop of Trois-Rivières, Louis-François Laflèche, at the Nicolet Seminary, Alphonse was permeated by conservative thought. His writings were a channel for his ultra-Montanist ideas, which argued that the Catholic Church should have authority in all matters, including politics.

In 1874, Desjardins ran as a candidate for the Conservative Party of John A. Macdonald, then tainted by the Pacific Scandal, involving allegations of corruption in awarding the contract to build the Canadian Pacific Railway. Desjardins was nonetheless elected as the Member of Parliament for Hochelaga, and would represent the riding for eighteen years.

The young MP wasted no time in plunging into the debate sparked by the fate of Louis Riel following the Red River Rebellion in Manitoba. To him, this was not merely a matter of principle: he had met Riel through the wife of Joseph Masson, Sophie Raymond-Masson, of whom the Métis leader was a protégé.

When Riel was hanged in 1885, Desjardins broke ranks with the Conservatives to sit as an independent. But he returned to the fold two years later to combat the Liberal Party's policies favouring free trade with the United States. The Liberal wave that swept Wilfrid Laurier to power in 1896 spelled the end of Desjardins' political career.

As a businessman, Alphonse Desjardins is known for, among other things, serving twenty years as president of the Banque Jacques-Cartier, after first joining its board of directors in 1876 to help with its reorganization. The bank had been forced to close for three months following a series of unwise investments and instances of "creative accounting" by the manager. Under Desjardins' stewardship, the Banque Jacques-Cartier regained profitability and established branches throughout the province.

On one of the plots of land he owned in Maisonneuve, Desjardins built a firebrick factory, the Montreal Terra Cotta Lumber Company, and hired his son Hubert as its manager. The factory was one of the first companies to benefit from the tax exemption offered by the newly created town's administration.

In 1899, the Banque Ville-Marie failed, sending shock waves through the community that reached all the way to the Banque Jacques-Cartier. Depositors from the fallen institution flocked to other francophone banks in Montreal. The Banque Jacques-Cartier had insufficient cash reserves to satisfy demands for withdrawals, and as a result it closed for several weeks to reorganize. When it reopened, it was known as the Banque Provinciale du Canada, retaining the name until it merged with the Banque Canadienne Nationale in 1979 to become the Banque Nationale du Canada.

During that 1899 crisis, however, Desjardins had extended personal guarantees to the bank to the tune of one hundred thousand dollars and was unable to pay back the debt. The board of directors forced him to resign as president and to surrender his properties as security.

Paul-André Linteau, who has studied Montreal and Quebec history for several years, summed up the importance of Alphonse Desjardins' role: "He was part . . . of the new wave of francophone entrepreneurs emerging in Montreal during the second half of the 19th century. He can be credited with the success of a francophone bank which, despite the difficulties of 1899, continued to develop in the next century and was one of the important financial institutions available to French Canadians."*

Alphonse Desjardins died in Terrebonne on June 4, 1912.

CHARLES-THÉODORE VIAU: COOKIE KING AND CITY BUILDER

My dad ate a lot of cookies. When I was a kid, after every meal, he would say: "Gaétan, go and get me some cookies from the store." It wasn't far: the store was right next door to our house. Dad let me choose the cookies myself: back then, they were sold in bulk, not by the bag or box. There was one condition, though: they had to be Viau cookies, even though the store also sold Charbonneau cookies (Viau eventually bought out that company).

The Viau biscuit factory, founded by Charles-Théodore Viau (1843–1898), changed hands several times after the family sold it in 1968. The facility, on Ontario Street in Montreal's Hochelaga-Maisonneuve district, closed its doors for good in 2004, marking a bittersweet end to an industrial and commercial success story that had begun in 1867. Still, Whippet, Royal, Village, and Petit Beurre cookies continue to delight connoisseurs of all ages, although they are no longer sold under the Viau brand but under the Dare Foods imprint.

Charles-Théodore Viau was born in Longueuil, on Montreal's

* Paul-André Linteau, "Desjardins, Alphonse (1841–1912)," in *Dictionary of Canadian Biography*, Vol. 14, University of Toronto/Université Laval, 2003–, accessed March 5, 2016, http://www.biographi.ca/en/bio/desjardins_alphonse_1841_1912_14E.html.

South Shore, on March 17, 1843. At age fifteen, he started work as a clerk at the Joseph Poupart grocery store in Montreal. After learning the rudiments of the trade, in 1866, aged twenty-three, he partnered with Toussaint Dufresne to buy the store. Their company, Dufresne et Viau, eventually began specializing in the flour trade, and then in baking. In 1867, they built a biscuit factory.

A true workaholic, Charles-Théodore slept little. His grandson Roger Viau recalls that he would bake bread at night, deliver it to customers in the morning, and then head to his flour-making facility in the business district.

In 1870, Viau became the sole owner of the company. Three years later, the factory added chocolate and candies to its product line. When it was destroyed by fire in 1875, Viau took the opportunity to rebuild and equip the facility with larger, more modern equipment; the owner constantly sought methods to improve production efficiency. Between 1884 and 1886, he bought large expanses of land in eastern Montreal, chiefly in Maisonneuve and Longue-Pointe. The farmland he used for, among other things, raising dairy cows, to ensure a ready supply of choice milk for Viau cookies. He took the same quality approach for another key ingredient: at the time, his biscuit factory was the only one in Canada to produce its own chocolate, using cocoa imported from Africa and the Caribbean.

We owe the existence of the brand's most beloved treat to one of Charles-Théodore's sons. It was Théophile Viau who hit upon the idea of topping a vanilla-flavoured biscuit with marshmallow and dipping the entire concoction in chocolate. The cookie was dubbed the Empire. To test their marketability, Théophile had several of them distributed to spectators at a hockey game that he was playing in at the Westmount Arena. People gobbled them up enthusiastically, and the Empire cookie went on to become one of the brand's biggest sellers. There was only one problem: making Empires was expensive. To lower the sale price without changing the taste too much, Viau replaced the vanilla cookie with a flavourless one. Thus was born the Whippet.

In the 1890s, along with Joseph Barsalou and Alphonse Desjardins, Charles-Théodore Viau was part of the group of landowners who founded the town of Maisonneuve. Viau's vision, though, stretched beyond the construction of factories and of housing for their workers. He developed a "model town," called Viauville—in the process displaying, as historian Paul-André Linteau has noted, "urban concerns then rare among francophone land developers."* He imposed strict rules on residential buildings: they were to comprise no more than two storeys, be set back from the road, have greystone façades, and so on. Viau had a riverbank park built and persuaded the archdiocese to found a parish, Saint-Clément, for the new residents.

Charles-Théodore was a great benefactor of the parish, ensuring the curé's lodgings and keep, and helping to fund construction of the church. He found an original way of getting parishioners involved as well. A spring of sulphurous water on 1st Avenue, near the corner of Notre-Dame Street, was said to have medicinal properties, and it attracted large crowds. The owner decided it would be sold at a penny per glass, with the profits going to the church building fund.

Charles-Théodore Viau wasn't known only for making food: he also had a reputation as a prodigious eater. His legendary girth no doubt contributed to his premature demise at the age of fifty-five. The family business was inherited by his brother-in-law, Jean-Baptiste Deguise, and his three sons.

In 1906, the Viau biscuit factory was forced to move from its original Notre-Dame Street location when the land was expropriated to make way for a Canadian Pacific rail line, and a new facility was built at 4945 Ontario Street East. In 1926, shares in the company began to be traded on the Montreal Stock Exchange, under the name Corporation de Biscuits Viau; it was just the second French-Canadian entity listed, after the Banque Canadienne Nationale. Théophile Viau,

* Paul-André Linteau, "Viau, Charles-Théodore," in *Dictionary of Canadian Biography*, Vol. 12, University of Toronto/Université Laval, 2003–, accessed March 6, 2016, http://www.biographi.ca/en/bio/viau_charles_theodore_12E.html.

inventor of the Whippet, became company president in 1930; ten years later, his son Roger took over.

The 1960s saw several Quebec food-industry companies, including Viau, absorbed by larger corporations. The company changed hands several times beginning in 1968: it was sold to Jacques Brillant, then to Imasco Foods (Grissol), Culinar, Placements Clairyve, Saputo, and finally Dare Foods in 2001. With that last transaction, the Viau brand was no more. Some years later, the factory on Ontario Street was converted into condominiums.

GEORGES-ÉLIE AMYOT: MANUFACTURER, BUSINESSMAN, AND PHILANTHROPIST

In the Saint-Roch neighbourhood of Quebec City's Lower Town, at the corner of Charest Boulevard and Dorchester Street, stands another factory that has been repurposed, this one into lecture theatres (Laval University) and offices (the City of Quebec). Built in 1871, it was the headquarters of the Dominion Corset Company, where workers manufactured women's undergarments for more than a century. The company, which sold its wares all over the world, was founded by Georges-Élie Amyot (1856–1930).

Until the mid-twentieth century, many women wore corsets on special occasions, to appear slimmer and achieve the coveted "hourglass figure." In my father's general store, my mother, Madeleine Cloutier, was the ultimate authority when it came to both the buying and selling of any and all "feminine" products, including corsets. She decreed that only one manufacturer was up to her standards: Dominion Corset. Every year, she made an "official" visit to the factory in Quebec City. She took me with her on one such occasion, and I still remember the huge building, impressive indeed for a young man like myself, coming from a small village.

Georges-Élie Amyot was born on January 28, 1856, in Saint-Augustin-de-Desmaures, just west of Quebec City. He grew up on a farm. When he was fourteen, he went to work in the city, where he apprenticed as a saddler. At age eighteen, he went to live with his brother Bernard in Connecticut, and then went to Springfield, Massachusetts, to ply his trade. In 1877, he returned to Canada and, two years later, was hired as a clerk in a store run by two of his cousins in Quebec City's Lower Town. In 1885, he opened his own dry goods shop, but the venture soured: by the next year, Amyot had gone bankrupt.

Undeterred, he went into business with one Léon Dyonnet, whose wife ran a corset shop. They built a corset factory under the company name Dyonnet et Amyot. Before long, the factory's pedal-powered sewing machines were supplanted by steam-driven equipment, stimulating huge productivity gains. By 1888, the company employed some sixty people, including a dozen or so girls aged from ten to fourteen.

After Dyonnet left Canada for Brazil in 1889, the partnership was wound up and Amyot reincorporated as the Dominion Corset Manufacturing Company. His sister Odile was a partner until 1890; another sister, Marie-Louise, replaced her until 1897, after which Georges-Élie became the sole shareholder.

The company prospered, and fast. Its premises in the industrial section of the Saint-Roch ward were progressively expanded. Montreal and Toronto were Dominion Corset's main markets, and wholesale offices opened there in 1889 and 1892 respectively. Sales progressed from $21,000 in 1887 to $130,000 in 1895.

Amyot gradually invested in related industry segments. In 1894, he began manufacturing cardboard boxes, needed for deliveries, followed by the steel rods required for the corset armatures. These soon generated distinct entities, the Quebec Paper Box Company and the Canada Corset Steel and Wire Corporation. Around the same time, Georges-Élie went into the beer-brewing business in the Saint-Sauveur ward, giving himself a backup option in case Dominion Corset ran into trouble.

While still in his twenties, Amyot became involved in politics. For a number of years, he was a Liberal Party organizer and fundraiser. It was not until 1906, as an established businessman aged fifty, that he stood for office. A by-election was called in the federal riding of Quebec, and Prime Minister Wilfrid Laurier offered Amyot the nomination. The riding appeared to be a Liberal stronghold, and the boss of Dominion Corset had no doubt as to his chances: "Even if I were to have serious opposition," he wrote to Laurier, "I tell you that I shall be elected." Indeed, at first glance, the opposition did not seem the slightest bit "serious": one Lorenzo Robitaille, aged twenty-four, was running as an "independent Liberal." But he had the backing of local party members who were upset that Laurier had imposed his candidate, Amyot. More important, he gained unexpected support from nationalists Henri Bourassa and Armand Lavergne, who saw the by-election as an opportunity to discredit the prime minister. Amyot's adversaries, among other things, attacked him over the poor working conditions of Dominion Corset's female employees. On voting day, the unthinkable happened: Amyot went down to defeat.

That political misfortune had little to no effect on Georges-Élie Amyot's reputation: it remained sterling enough that, in 1922, he was chosen to save the Banque Nationale, one of the leading francophone banks in the country, which was on the brink of bankruptcy. Its biggest client, Machine Agricole Nationale Limitée, was in serious financial difficulty, the country was in the midst of an economic downturn, and there was growing competition from the caisses populaires. Amyot was appointed president of the bank, and lobbied governments and the economic élites alike to win their support for the financial institution. The results were mixed, and eventually there was only one feasible solution: a merger with the Banque d'Hochelaga. In late 1923, the government of Louis-Alexandre Taschereau assigned fifteen million dollars in Province of Quebec bonds to the latter bank, to offset the burden it was about to take on. Thus was born the Banque Canadienne Nationale. Six decades later, when the BCN and the Provincial Bank of Canada merged to become the National Bank of Canada, Georges-Élie Amyot's legacy was amalgamated with that of Alphonse Desjardins to form one of the two leading francophone financial institutions in the country (the other being, of course, the

Mouvement des caisses Desjardins, founded by Alphonse Desjardins' namesake).

The phenomenal success of Dominion Corset allowed Amyot to amass a sizable fortune, a large part of which he invested in land in Quebec, as well as in Saskatchewan and British Columbia. He also devoted both money and time to philanthropic causes.

Georges-Élie Amyot died on March 28, 1930, in Palm Beach, Florida. He was laid to rest in Notre-Dame-de-Belmont Cemetery in Sainte-Foy, Quebec, in an imposing marble mausoleum that he had had built two decades earlier.

Senator Frédéric-Liguori Béique, who had been president of the Banque Canadienne Nationale since 1928, paid tribute as follows: "Underneath a sometimes stern appearance, Monsieur Amyot had a heart of gold, and few people know the number and magnitude of the donations of all kinds which he made. He owed the great fortune he had accumulated only to his energy, loyalty, business sense and excellent judgement."

THE PIONEERING FRENCH-CANADIAN businessmen whose stories I have related here had many characteristics in common. Most were born in rural villages and towns, but most settled in the city, either Montreal or Quebec, starting out as store clerks and learning the tools of the trade. And it was in the cities that they earned their fortunes. But the fact that they began as retail entrepreneurs shows the extent to which that métier is an apt training ground for acquiring all the elementary skills of business: finance, customer service, buying, negotiating, managing human resources, and the like.

These merchants rubbed shoulders with the economic, political, and cultural elites. As we have seen, the Beaudrys, Massons, Barsalous, and Desjardinses had business links and even family relationships in common. Most were well educated, and some were lawyers or journalists.

While each enjoyed success in a different field, all of them invested in convergent areas, such as real estate.

Far from restricting themselves to the province of Quebec, they travelled often to Europe or elsewhere in Canada, had a particular international outlook, and were interested in ideas and projects from elsewhere. Many tried their luck in the political arena, though not all who did were successful.

Most of these men, all francophones, had a sensitivity to the "national question" and sought to improve the lot of their compatriots—for example, by facilitating their access to credit or providing them with employment.

There can therefore be no doubt that the roots of Quebec entrepreneurship stretch back to long before the Quiet Revolution, to the hard work, ingenuity, and courage of these nineteenth-century French Canadians.

Recognition is long overdue to these pioneers for their contributions to what French Canada has become. Their example should serve to deter Quebeckers from constantly gazing at their past through a pessimist lens or clinging to the notion that their forebears were in the iron grip of a clergy that prevented French Canadians from going into business.

The new wave of entrepreneurship in Quebec, based chiefly on digital technologies, would do well to draw inspiration from that past, which is far more glorious than some have led us to believe.

JEAN CHAREST AND ANTOINE DIONNE-CHAREST

SIR GEORGE-ÉTIENNE CARTIER

NATION BUILDER

MANY A MAN LEAVES HIS MARK on history. Few can take pride in having helped build a nation. George-Étienne Cartier was one such man.

Cartier was born in 1814 into a family of shopkeepers, in the village of Saint-Antoine, on the shore of the Richelieu River, northeast of Montreal. He was likely named George-Étienne—with the English spelling, instead of Georges-Étienne—'in honour of King George III. His parents, of course, could never have known that, decades later, his political adversaries would see that missing *s* as proof of his "betrayal" of French Canadians.

Cartier left the family home when he was just ten to attend the Collège de Montréal boarding school, known for its rigorous curriculum. After completing his secondary education, he studied law under Édouard-Étienne Rodier, who would become his mentor. Rodier, a nationalist and an anticlerical who was sympathetic to the ideas of the Patriotes, considerably influenced the young Cartier's political thinking, and probably his decision to join the Rebellion of 1837. The Patriotes' principal demand was the institution of responsible government; that is, full sovereignty for the Legislative Assembly of Lower

Canada. At the time, power rested in the hands of the governor, appointed by the Crown in London: he controlled the purse strings, and wielded the power to revoke any bill passed by the Assembly.

Cartier took part in the Battle of Saint-Denis, the Patriotes' only military victory. When the rebellion was eventually crushed, he went into hiding in the countryside, and then into exile across the border in the United States. He was granted amnesty after petitioning Lord Durham's secretary, and returned to Montreal in the fall of 1838. At that moment, the young man did an about-face: he said he had joined the rebellion to combat the local Tory minority, and not the British Crown, to which he now swore his loyalty. From then on, Cartier advocated compromise with the governing authorities, a point of view opposed to that which Louis-Joseph Papineau, the leader of the Patriote movement, continued to defend. The key point here, though, is the transition from the idealistic, militant young lawyer to the man who would become Sir George-Étienne Cartier: a pragmatic lawyer, baronet, businessman, and, eventually, statesman.

THE MAN

Cartier was short in stature and elegant in bearing. His clothing, hair, and manners projected the air of a gentleman, which is perhaps explained by the fact that he was unapologetically anglophile. Like many other people of the time, he was fascinated by the English lifestyle and, in particular, by the city of London, which he visited often. He openly described himself as a "French-speaking Englishman."*

Behind the gentlemanly image, though, was a man who felt equally at home in the countryside of the St. Lawrence River Valley as at fashionable society evenings in Montreal. The Cartier men, merchants from father to son, were known to enjoy entertainment and the

* Brian J. Young, *George-Etienne Cartier: Montreal Bourgeois*, Montreal and Kingston: McGill-Queen's University Press, 1981, p. 46.

company of women. George-Étienne would not hesitate to argue with prominent public figures, even engaging in at least one duel. He never completely abandoned the irreverence of his youth. He was sociable, enjoyed singing and dancing, and, like many men of his day, was known to raise a glass or two. Luckily for him, his love of drink never approached the legendary intensity of that of his later colleague and political ally Sir John A. Macdonald.

His marriage to Hortense Fabre, the daughter of a well-to-do family of the time, was not a particularly happy one. The Cartiers would spend a good part of their conjugal life, if not the majority of it, separated from one another. Hortense lived with their two daughters in their Montreal home, while George-Étienne went wherever politics took him. Their failed relationship was due, at least in part, to Cartier's chronic womanizing. After her husband's death in London, Lady Cartier never again set foot in Canada.

"CARTIERISM"

Cartier's political philosophy is best described as healthy pragmatism: his approach to politics always considered the practical consequences, be they political, social, or economic. That philosophy aimed at achievement of concrete results with an impact on the lives of all citizens. But there was more to "Cartierism" than that. Though he was not an intellectual, and even professed to a certain form of anti-intellectualism, Cartier had his convictions. They were inextricably linked to the context of the time in which he lived, that of a French-Canadian society in the midst of significant economic and industrial change, and of an emerging country, Canada. This context, naturally, must be borne in mind in any analysis of Cartier's political career.

His convictions included adherence to the principles of responsible government and the parliamentary system. In Cartier's view, the premier or prime minister and his cabinet had to bear collective responsibility to the legislative assembly for decisions made by the executive. Furthermore, ministers were individually responsible for the affairs of their departments, or ministries. Lastly, members of Parliament were answerable to their constituents for their actions. These principles remain at the core of our political system; Cartier was one of the first politicians to defend them and put them into practice.

Cartier belonged to a group of politicians who were dubbed "Reformers." Their leader was Louis-Hippolyte La Fontaine, from whom Cartier drew much inspiration—for example, in engaging in patronage. The practice, which was common at the time, consisted of appointing people close to the governing party to governmental positions. In La Fontaine's view, this was not only about rewarding supporters; it was also "one means of entrenching the francophone bourgeoisie."*

The Reformers differed from the other political factions of the day by their constant quest for a moderate middle ground. They rejected the theses of both the Rouges and the Ultramontanists: the former hewed to radical liberalism, advocated the annexation of Canada to the United States, and were anticlerical; the latter believed that the power of the Catholic Church should take prominence over political power. The Reformers, meanwhile, sought a middle way, more likely to guarantee a stable and orderly society, with no need to resort to extreme solutions. That way consisted in allegiance to the British Crown, implementation of responsible government, and, ultimately, the co-existence of the French-Canadian and English-Canadian peoples. For these reasons, the Reformers accepted the Act of Union of 1840, despite its serious flaws, and collaborated on the project that would lead to Confederation in 1867. Clearly, to be a Reformer was above all to be pragmatic.

Property rights were another of Cartier's core convictions. He believed property was fundamental to the organization of society. To be a property owner required good judgment, as it involved the responsibility to manage and maintain that property, a concept that could

* Ibid, p. 71.

not be grasped by someone who was not an owner. Property, in Cartier's view, conferred a degree of dignity on a person. There was nothing unjust about the notion, because anybody could aspire to own property; provided that he was prepared to put in the effort required. In other words, property was accessible to all as long as those who desired it worked hard enough to earn it.

LAWYER, BUSINESSMAN, POLITICIAN

Cartier was a solicitor, a businessman, a parliamentarian, and a minister. He owed his career in law to the flourishing of Montreal's industrial and commercial centre; as he put it, he was "in the right place at the right time." The first clients of his law practice were members of his family, alumni of the Collège de Montréal, and people from his hometown. Later, his client base broadened to include entrepreneurs, manufacturers, shopkeepers, and the like. Gradually, he became part of the Montreal business community, and began to be appointed to the boards of directors of various companies. Moreover, true to his convictions, he invested part of his savings in real estate, acquiring several buildings (along Notre-Dame Street in Montreal, for example), which earned him substantial income.

Concurrently with his activities as a solicitor and landowner, Cartier took an interest in politics. He associated with former Patriotes who, like him, now favoured compromise with the political power in place, and was determined to follow in La Fontaine's footsteps. In 1848, he made his move, standing as a Conservative candidate in a by-election in the riding of Verchères. He won by a few hundred votes.

When Cartier arrived in the Legislative Assembly of the Province of Canada, the debate was dominated by two issues: reparations for victims of the 1837 and 1838 rebellions, and the proposed annexation of Canada to the United States. A discreet parliamentarian at first, Cartier tacitly supported La Fontaine, who was in favour of the

Rebellion Losses Bill. He strongly opposed the annexation movement, led by the Rouges. In historian Brian Young's view, Cartier's aversion to annexation was directly related to his multiple occupations. As a businessman, he had every reason to want to maintain the status quo, namely, preservation of a British parliamentary system, because of the guarantees it offered of economic stability and a healthy climate for business. As a politician, meanwhile, Cartier had a "lifelong distrust of American democracy," with its radicalism, and its failure to exemplify executive authority that imposed respect by everyone.* The especially bloody Civil War certainly nurtured that sense of suspicion. Cartier was adept at distinguishing economic interests from political concerns, which explains why he advocated freer trade between the Canadian and U.S. economies (following the 1846 repeal of the Corn Laws, with their preferential tariffs that favoured Canadian goods, Canada had an urgent need to find new markets).

Cartier the parliamentarian thus began to attract attention. Not because of his oratorical talents: it is said that he was not particularly charismatic, and given to long, tedious speeches. He was, however, recognized for his ability to persuade, which in politics is as valuable as charisma. He excelled in parliamentary commissions, where he won over colleagues with ease. In this way, he compensated for a lack of charisma with a good measure of intelligence and, above all, political instinct, which would serve him well in pushing through several significant reforms.

THE END OF THE SEIGNEURIAL SYSTEM

Inherited from the French colonial era, the *régime seigneurial* was the basis for the organization of social and economic life in Lower Canada, with its mostly rural populace. Under this system of land tenure, every

* Young, *George-Etienne Cartier*, p. 76.

farm was part of a *seigneurie*, or estate, which collected dues of all kinds. For example, the *censitaire** who farmed the land not only had to use implements belonging to the seigneur but had to pay to use them, despite the fact that he already paid annual tax to said seigneur.

In Cartier's view, the seigneurial system was a major hindrance to French Canadians' economic, social, and political development. He thought the rents and dues were excessive and ill suited to the economic context of the time. And he was especially opposed to this obsolete system because it prevented, or at least considerably limited, access to land ownership, a principle that he fiercely defended.

Politically, the seigneurial system was an obstacle to the establishment of a stable state and the institution of new social, commercial, and agricultural policies necessary for economic development. Cartier played a role in the adoption of the Seigniorial Act of 1854, which abolished the system by, among other ways, convincing rural residents of the benefits they would derive from the legislation.

THE COUNCIL OF PUBLIC INSTRUCTION

In 1855, Cartier was named provincial secretary for Canada East. In that capacity, he was responsible for a second major reform, that of the education system in Lower Canada. At the time, lay teachers received no professional training. Public schools were underfinanced, and there were frequent irregularities in the system. On top of this, many school principals were illiterate, and a significant number of teachers were minors. Unsurprisingly, only a small percentage of adult francophones knew how to read and write.

Cartier assigned Pierre-Joseph-Olivier Chauveau the task of assessing the situation and presenting potential solutions. After Chauveau's study confirmed the dire state of the public education system, Cartier introduced legislation in 1856 that led to the creation of the Conseil de

* The *cens* was a French land tax, and tenant farmers were known as *censitaires*.

l'instruction publique (Council of Public Instruction), the ancestor of Quebec's Ministry of Education. The Council's job was to administer the public school system, and this included regulating examinations, selecting textbooks, and establishing standards of teaching.

That a body such as the Council was created, rather than a ministry of public education, was the result of a compromise, which Cartier accepted because of opposition from the Catholic Church and its allies in the conservative bourgeoisie, who wanted to retain control over school institutions, as well as from the anglophone community, fiercely committed to autonomy for their schools. Still, implementation of the Council of Public Instruction led to more schools being built and, above all, to improved literacy.

THE CIVIL CODE

The third great reform that dates from George-Étienne Cartier's time in government is the drafting of the Civil Code of Lower Canada. During the French colonial period, Canada was subject to the *coutume de Paris*, the customary law of northern France. Under this system dating from feudal times, "property rights [were] integrated into a seigneurial, family, and religious framework."* After the 1759 Conquest of New France, however, British criminal law had been imposed, and this, combined with the later abolition of the seigneurial system, had resulted in a veritable legal hodgepodge. Cartier set up a commission tasked with codifying civil law, and chaired the parliamentary committee that studied the commission's report. He then used his parliamentary majority to enact the new civil code, in 1866.

* Young, *George-Etienne Cartier*, p. 95.

FROM RAILWAYS TO CONFEDERATION

Between 1815 and 1851, Western countries remained in the throes of a lengthy recession, and Canada was no exception.* Among possible remedies for this malaise, the idea of free trade gained increasing traction. Canadian producers no longer benefited from Britain's preferential tariffs, so the country turned to its neighbour to the south, concluding the Reciprocity Treaty with the United States in 1854. This was only a temporary panacea for the Canadian economy, though, because the agreement would only remain in force for ten years. New markets had to be found; hence the idea of a federation between the colonies of British North America to reduce barriers to trade among them.

In addition to the commercial incentive, there were political motivations. On the one hand, imperialism was becoming increasingly less popular among the British political class: they viewed the colonies, or more precisely their defence, as a financial burden. On the other, the 1840 Act of Union, which had joined Upper Canada with Lower Canada, where the majority of French Canadians lived, had become a source of chronic political instability.

Here again, a union of all the colonies of British North America seemed the ideal solution. The partnership would thus be a political one, but motivated in large part by economic imperatives, and the building of railways would be its guiding enterprise. Contrary to the opinion of some observers, in particular those who defend the principle of duality, Canada resulted not merely from a political union between two nations, French-Canadian and English-Canadian, but from an economic union of four colonies: Ontario, Quebec (formerly United Canada), New Brunswick, and Nova Scotia. George-Étienne Cartier was to play a pivotal role both in the establishment of Confederation and in the building of the great railways that would serve as the new nation's backbone.

---

* Jacques Lacoursière, Jean Provencher, and Denis Vaugeois, *Canada–Québec, 1534–2015*, Quebec City: Septentrion, 2015, p. 312.

Cartier and the railway companies had an extensive history. He had long advocated construction of a rail link between Montreal and the eastern coastal cities of the United States, to ensure year-round connections to seaports. In this, Cartier showed great foresight: winter ice brought maritime transport within Canada to a standstill six months a year, and permanent access to ports on the U.S. east coast would be a boon to the country's economy. Moreover, a modern transportation network would prevent American interests from gaining a trade monopoly in the Canadian West. So while the annexationists represented a real threat, at the same time, some sort of rapprochement with the United States was essential—at least in economic terms.

In 1848, during his earliest days as a member of the Legislative Assembly, Cartier petitioned the government to support the St. Lawrence and Atlantic Railway company, then attempting to complete its line connecting Montreal with Portland, Maine. He secured passage of a bill recognizing the principle that the government should subsidize railway construction. More specifically, the Guarantee Act stated that the government had to contribute financially to construction or extension of any line more than seventy-five miles long. Meanwhile, Montreal businessmen, sensitive to Cartier's argument that the country's political and economic destiny was dependent on railway construction, succeeded in raising enough money to build the stretch of track that would secure the government guarantee. In 1853, Cartier was invited to ride on the inaugural train between Montreal and Portland.

By the summer of 1864, the Parliament of United Canada was in the midst of a fractious session. George Brown, the leader of the Clear Grits, a group of radical liberals that held the balance of power, proposed a coalition government with the Conservatives to remedy the situation. Brown imposed a condition, however: the government must adopt a new constitution. The Conservatives, led by Macdonald and Cartier, were amenable to this, even agreeing to discuss a federal union. The idea had been around for years, but both opportunity and political will, in all likelihood, had been lacking.

The leaders of United Canada learned that the representatives of the maritime colonies—Nova Scotia, Prince Edward Island, and New Brunswick—were to meet at Charlottetown in September to discuss a possible union. They seized the opportunity and arranged to be invited to the conference as observers. Better prepared, the United Canada delegation convinced the other provinces of the advantages of federating *all* of the British North American colonies. It is likely that Cartier's persuasive skills, which he had continued to hone over the years, helped make the case for a broader union.

The representatives of United Canada and the Maritimes met for a second conference, in Quebec City in October 1864, which led to an initial agreement in principle. At this meeting, Cartier was a discreet presence. Historian Jean-Charles Bonenfant's explanation is that the delegates were busy studying Macdonald's proposals, prepared ahead of time by the cabinet of United Canada, to which Cartier belonged. He therefore focused instead on defending the measures that he believed were necessary to protect the interests of Lower Canada—that is, of French Canadians.[*]

The delegates reached agreement on a number of essential points. Representation of each province in the future House of Commons would be in proportion to its population, while in the Senate, each would have an equal number of seats. There was a commitment to build an intercolonial railway to unite Quebec and Ontario with the Maritime provinces, so that Canadian goods would no longer have to transit through the United States. There is no doubt that Cartier provided the impetus for that project. The agreement became known as the Quebec Resolutions, also referred to as the Seventy-Two Resolutions. After approval by the provincial legislatures, the text of the proposals was submitted to the British government. It served as the draft for the British North America Act.[†]

---

* J.-C. Bonenfant, "Cartier, Sir George-Étienne," in *Dictionary of Canadian Biography*, Vol. 10, Université Laval / University of Toronto, 2003–, accessed April 13, 2016.

† Lacoursière, Provencher, and Vaugeois, *Canada–Quebec, 1534–2015*, p. 317.

Though some of the colonies had misgivings as to the content of the Seventy-Two Resolutions, a Canadian delegation set sail for London in late 1866 to put the finishing touches on the legal text to be presented to the British parliament. At least one account claims that John A. Macdonald used these final negotiations to attempt to change the federative system agreed upon in Quebec City into one that would concentrate power in the hands of the central government. Cartier, proponents of this view say, opposed this, having grasped the scope of Macdonald's plan.* To him, it would have been unimaginable that the federal government should appropriate the greater share of power, including jurisdiction over education and law, which were in the hands of the future provinces, per the reforms that Cartier himself had championed. In his view, the existence of French-Canadian political, social, and cultural institutions could not be subjected to any political compromise. The French Canadians were *maîtres chez eux.* They constituted a full-fledged nation that was joining a broader economic and political union of its own volition. And that union, the Canadian federation, would ensure not only the survival of the French Canadians—including those living in the newly created province of Quebec—but also their development as a francophone people within North America.

The new Canadian constitution was submitted to the British parliament in February 1867, as a bill introduced in the House of Lords. It received royal assent in March, with a proclamation issued by Queen Victoria in May, and came into effect on July 1.

Cartier returned from London with a sense of duty fulfilled. From then on, he was among the men who would become known as the Fathers of Confederation. It was also around this time that he was made a baronet, according him the title "Sir" before his first name. In addition, he secured a twelve-million-dollar guarantee for construction of the intercolonial railroad. But rail development was no longer merely a matter of connecting Quebec and Ontario with

* Bonenfant, "Cartier, Sir George-Etienne."

the Maritimes. From then on, the federal government, and Cartier in particular, would concern itself with Canada's westward expansion, and the key, once again, would be the construction of "iron roads."

⚜ ⚜ ⚜ ⚜

ASIDE FROM HIS NEW DUTIES as minister of militia and defence, whereby he reorganized the country's system of defence, Cartier was to dedicate the remainder of his political career to extending the territory of Canada all the way to the Pacific Ocean. He travelled to London to negotiate Canada's purchase of Rupert's Land and the North-West Territory from the Hudson's Bay Company and the British government. Canada was on the way to becoming one of the world's largest countries. Cartier was the man who organized these new territories. He reached agreement with the Métis, who inhabited a significant swath of the newly acquired land, on the creation of a new province, Manitoba, in 1870. And it was largely thanks to him that British Columbia became Canada's sixth province in 1871, in return for the federal government's pledge to complete what became known as the Canadian Pacific Railway, which in 1885 at last linked the country from coast to coast.

Cartier's connections to the railway companies, including the Grand Trunk, epitomized the alliance between economic interests and the Canadian government: while the government instituted tariffs, determined the rights-of-way, defined the labour-market regulations, and so on, the railway companies financed election campaigns and provided work for politicians like Cartier. It was thus a mutually beneficial system, and common practice at the time.

In the 1872 general election, Cartier was unseated by a first-time Liberal candidate in the riding of Montreal East, after representing it for eleven years. The defeat would leave a bitter taste. He was quickly elected by acclamation in the Manitoba riding of Provencher, though, after Métis leader Louis Riel withdrew his candidacy.

BUT CARTIER WASN'T out of the woods yet. Before long, it was alleged that he and Macdonald had solicited campaign donations from a Montreal businessman in exchange for the awarding of the contract to build the transcontinental railway. Weakened by chronic nephritis (inflammation of the kidneys), Cartier left Macdonald to defend the government against the charges. The affair escalated into the so-called Pacific Scandal, which forced the Conservatives to resign. In the meantime, Cartier had left for London, hoping his health would improve. It did not: he died on May 20, 1873, in the city he had always been so fond of.

THERE ARE TWO GREAT THRUSTS of George-Étienne Cartier's career that ensured his legacy as a pre-eminent figure in Canadian history: the notion of duality, and economic development. These lines of force intertwine to describe the singular journey of a man as well as of a people whose future he helped shape in durable fashion.

Cartier embodies a certain vision of Canada: the union of the French-Canadian nation, or Quebec, and the English-Canadian nation, or the rest of Canada. Today, though, that idea of duality appears to have lost its lustre. The narrative to which many Canadians, and in particular French Canadians, choose to refer in seeking to understand their country does not seem to have the same persuasive power.

There appear to be two reasons for this. First, duality obscures the existence of other Canadian nations, not least the Acadians and the First Nations. It is thus a non-inclusive vision. Not only does it overlook those other founding nations, but it also slights populations of immigrant origin. Moreover, duality implies a Canada made up of two distinct blocs, whereas it is, in fact, anything but. One need only consider the provinces of Manitoba, Saskatchewan, and Alberta, which were initially colonized by francophones. The Métis in this region would never have identified themselves with a monolithic "French-Canadian" nation.

Although the traditional definition of Canadian duality can be called into question for these reasons, the concept has not exhausted its potential. We must, however, conceive of it differently. We therefore propose a definition based on the following fact: the French-Canadian nation, today embodied primarily in Quebec, predates the nation of Canada. In other words, its institutions, culture, and language existed before the nation of Canada. This is an important fact of history, all the more so because it nurtured the political journey of George-Étienne Cartier.

The notion of duality is evident in the Cartierist view in at least two areas. The first has to do with the reforms that he championed. For example, although Cartier campaigned in favour of its abolition, the seigneurial regime left a durable imprint on Quebec: it is the only Canadian province where farmland was divided into *rangs*, or long, narrow strips perpendicular to waterways. This is a significant indicator of difference vis-à-vis the other provinces, as the seigneurial system was one of the first methods of land-use planning in the country, if not *the* first. The difference is especially important when one considers that geography is a fundamental identifier for a people.

There was an even more important reform, though: that of the law. In addition to having had the *loi coutumière* system before the 1759 Conquest, Quebec is today the only province with a civil code—that is, a body of rules set down as general principles governing relations between persons, which differs from the British common law, under which the courts base decisions on jurisprudence. Thus there has been a system of law specific to French Canadians—at least in Quebec—both before and after the Conquest. It is significant to note that Canadian law today is characterized by a form of bijuralism—the coexistence of two distinct legal traditions—which confirms that there is at least one form of Canadian duality.

The second area in which Cartier illustrated duality was his political positions in favour of French Canadians, in particular when it came to constitutional negotiations. His opposition to Macdonald's centralist designs and his unwavering defence of French-Canadian institutions strongly suggest that he would never have agreed to Quebec's joining the Canadian Confederation without existing French-Canadian institutions being accepted by all parties. In other words, the French Canadians had to remain *maîtres chez eux*. This was non-negotiable.

Cartier's pressing for a federation less centralized than the one Macdonald sought also reminds us of two lessons about the country's origins and, concomitantly, about duality.

First, the Fathers of Confederation agreed on the creation of a federal state, not a unitary state. French Canadians in general and George-Étienne Cartier in particular would never have accepted a Canadian state that failed to take into account the existence of a historically constituted French-Canadian nation. Quebec joined the Canadian federation first of all because it obtained the guarantee that its distinct character would be respected and recognized by the other members of that federation, and second, because it also secured the right to renegotiate the conditions of its membership in the federation should it come to consider that its distinct character was no longer respected and recognized by the other provinces. In short, it would have been inconceivable for Canada to be created to the detriment of the distinct character of the French Canadians, in particular the Québécois. Let us note that this conception of duality does not cast doubt upon the explanation provided previously, that an economic union was key to the building of Canada: it is complementary to it.

Second, whether we conceive of the origin of Canada through the prism of duality, economic union, or both, one fact is incontrovertible: Canada was not a creation of the Canadian state, but of the colonies of British North America, including the French-Canadian nation. It was not the central government that decided to unite the colonies, but the colonies that united to create a federal state. In this respect, the provincial governments are subordinate neither in fact nor in law to the federal government. The two levels of government are autonomous in relation to one another, especially when it comes to their respective spheres of competence. This justifies, for example, the federal government's acknowledgement of jurisdictions—cultural, institutional, political, and so forth—specific to the provinces, in particular those specific to Quebec, by means of tools such as asymmetrical federalism. Thus it is the provinces, including Quebec, that cement Canadian unity.

Economic development is another essential aspect of the history of Canada and, as we have noted, a key path in Cartier's political journey. Consider his speeches aimed at persuading citizens of the benefits of doing away with the seigneurial system, or his activism in favour of railway construction—especially given that one of the primary motivations for the creation of Canada was the unification of a group of colonies for economic reasons.

In our opinion, economic development has a bearing on three fundamental aspects of Canadian federalism. The first is liberty: for a people to have the liberty of self-determination—and thus of making its own choices—it must first control the economic levers proper to a state, such as the provision of public finances and maintenance of a social and political environment conducive to wealth creation. That is all the more important in a country such as Canada, in which the provincial governments manage the social safety net (hospitals, education, social benefits, and so on).

That same liberty—this is the second aspect—enables a province such as Quebec to exercise its full autonomy in its own spheres of competence. We also note that it is easier for a province to negotiate a new constitutional agreement when its public finances are sound.

The final aspect involves the idea that an economy is not an end in itself, but a means to an end, which is the overall welfare of individuals and communities. It provides for what the Canadian philosopher Charles Taylor has called "the affirmation of ordinary life"—that is, family life and production. Thus economic development procures for a people the freedom to determine its future and the capacity to improve the terms of the union of which it is a part, in order for it ultimately to ensure the welfare of the greatest possible number of citizens.

GEORGE-ÉTIENNE CARTIER and the other figures whose lives are related in these pages were conveyors of a shared destiny: that of the French-Canadian nation, embodied essentially by Quebec. That shared destiny is first and foremost a shared language. French is not merely a tool for communication, an instrument for a particular purpose, but a way of existing—in other words, of being in the world. That shared destiny is also a history, stretching back to the "discovery" of a new world, America, and continuing through to the founding of the Canadian federation. That history allows us to measure the scope of everything accomplished since, including the common good that is Canada.

Our internal quarrels, in particular in Quebec, tend to cast a veil over the things that unite Quebec and Canada. That unity illustrates that our country is marked by profound diversity—cultural, linguistic, and geographical—the occasionally precarious fulcrums of which were, in many cases, erected and maintained by francophones like George-Étienne Cartier. Canada has allowed Quebec to progress from survival to development, to become a nation in its own right that—if we may be so bold—exercises sovereignty over the essential spheres of the lives of Quebeckers. A final aspect of that shared destiny is institutions. Quebec is distinguished by a British-inspired parliament that bears a French-inspired name, the National Assembly, by a tradition of civil law paired with British common law, and by a pattern of land management that is unique in North America. Each of these institutions operates in one and the same language and is the fruit of a singular history. These institutions are the culmination of the destiny common to all French Canadians, particularly Quebeckers.

There are men whose life stories overlap with a larger history, that of their country. George-Étienne Cartier's story is one such dual narrative. Through the reforms undertaken under his leadership, the building of railways, the constitutional negotiations, the addition of vast territories, and the creation of new provinces, Cartier played a pivotal role in the creation of Canada. Few people accomplish so much in the span of a lifetime. Cartier is part of the pantheon of Canada's great nation builders. We owe him a great debt. And the best way to repay it is to become acquainted with his life story.

LUCIEN BOUCHARD

HENRI BOURASSA

WHAT REMAINS OF HENRI Bourassa in Quebeckers' collective memory? Few visible traces, alas: some street names, a Montreal metro station, and the daily reminder inscribed on the masthead of *Le Devoir* by its publishers, in tribute to the newspaper's founder. He is absent from contemporary political debate and commentary in Quebec—even more so in the rest of Canada.

Not that he is the victim of some singular ostracism: any politician's endurance in the public mind is a slender thread on which the blade can quickly fall. Many others have joined Bourassa in the shadowy realm of the forgotten. Given that a recent survey found that 20 per cent of Canadians were unaware of who was currently governing their country, it should come as no surprise that such eminent figures as Lomer Gouin, Ernest Lapointe, Adélard Godbout, Joseph-Mathias Tellier, Armand Lavergne, and Olivier Asselin, to name a few, have vanished from memory. Even silhouettes that towered in their day—such as those of Wilfrid Laurier, Honoré Mercier, and (perhaps to a lesser extent) Louis-Joseph Papineau—have today receded into the mists of unfortunate unfamiliarity.

In writing this chapter on Henri Bourassa, I set out to paint a portrait of this exceptional and, in some respects, enigmatic figure. I have no pretension to a historian's view—rather, mine is that of an observer fascinated by the origins, qualities, and contradictions of this fiery, intelligent man. Everything destined him for the fierce struggles he waged on behalf of the French language, minorities, and independence for what he felt was his country. His was a life of great triumphs, but of defeats and disappointments as well. As we shall see, in his efforts he often came up against the wall that nationalist Quebeckers sooner or later confront in Ottawa—especially those who, like him, found themselves in a double bind brought on by their Catholic allegiance and the demands of the clerical authorities of the time.

THE MAN

All representations of historical figures are necessarily approximations: one can only perceive them through the layered veils spun by champions and detractors alike, not to mention the inexorable blurrings of time.

It is even more difficult to paint a picture of Henri Bourassa, so stark was the contrast between the man and the world he lived in. Francophone Quebec society of the time was essentially agrarian, poor, and bereft of education. It did comprise a petite bourgeoisie, largely made up of doctors, lawyers, judges, and, in rare instances, business people, almost all of whom had modest upbringings. So it is difficult to imagine how that society could identify with the grandson of a seigneur whose name was already written in gilded letters in the political annals of the country.

Henri Bourassa's childhood memories included the fleeting vision of that famous grandfather: Louis-Joseph Papineau, a living legend in his seigneurial manor, Montebello. Educated mostly by tutors, without ever receiving a graduate degree, young Henri was immersed in the artistic and intellectual milieux frequented by his father, the painter and sculptor Napoléon Bourassa. He read from a young age, and by his teen years was acquainted with novelists, poets, and historians both French and English. With his distinguished bearing, impeccable manners, elegant articulation in both languages, and faultless appearance, he cut an impressive figure, rather distant and severe.

He was a far cry from the typical politician spouting politicalese, and we would be hard pressed to imagine him on a modern talk-show set. It's not merely a matter of different eras, but of character. Bourassa was imperious and brooked no compromise.

The question, then, is how did he tolerate the political arena? The fact is, he always refused to play the game, and usually to his detriment. That he left his mark on the politics of his time was more a matter of his sincerity, verging on passion, and his peerless talent.

It was through words that Henri Bourassa first connected with the people. It should be remembered that this was a time of orators. Crowds could discern the best of them. In Bourassa's case, mastery of the art of speech went hand in hand with mastery of all the resources of language, leaving him fully engaged with his audiences and their emotions. History records several hundred assemblies at which he spoke, often for more than three hours at a stretch, outdoors in front of massive crowds, or in rooms packed to the rafters with fervent listeners.

Witnesses described Bourassa gesticulating and roving about the rostrum, then trying in vain to evade overexcited listeners who would accompany him home after some speeches. In the National Assembly, he was known to leave the bench, swept up by his own fiery words, and walk up and down the central aisle while continuing to speak.

Like every great orator, he had a twofold preparation process. He could always rely on a bedrock of general knowledge and deep thinking, nurtured by his wide-ranging reading. More immediately, though he would write some speeches in advance, he was most often content to draft notes, which he called his *feuilles de route*, or roadmaps. Like many speechmakers, he was a practitioner of prepared improvisation. But when confronted with consequential choices—adopting an editorial line, running for office, mapping out strategic directions—he forced himself to conduct painstaking analyses. That prudence didn't keep him from outbursts in which he unleashed the power of his passionate convictions to full effect, firing up the crowd. That ability to rouse an audience, though, made him somewhat hesitant about the virtues of oratory. After all, he had once said of his grandfather, Louis-Joseph Papineau, that he was "possessed of the fatal gift of eloquence and let the enthusiasm he created around him go to his head."*

Though his own public successes never led to disorder or agitation, Henri Bourassa would complain that they failed to produce any durable impact. He had more profound aims than to stir emotions temporarily: he had set himself the task of educating his fellow citizens and urging them to pursue the common good. This no doubt underlaid his decision to disseminate his ideas and his teaching through writing. Very early on, he began to publish texts of lectures and speeches, and his attraction to political journalism eventually led him to found *Le Devoir* in 1910. A respected editorialist and communicator, he headed the newspaper until 1932, penning countless editorials and articles. Though a proponent of *engagé* journalism, he was committed to respecting his adversaries and sought to refocus debate on ideas and principles.

To him, honesty was more than just a word. In his personal life as in his political action, he was the exemplar of integrity, relentlessly combatting corruption. Denouncing *les coquins*, or "scoundrels," was part of *Le Devoir*'s inaugural mission statement.†

Coupled with that constant concern was Bourassa's staunch independence of mind. From his very first campaign, in 1895, he told the Liberal riding leadership that, if elected, he reserved the right to follow his convictions and vote with or against the party line. And he

---

* Robert Rumilly, *Henri Bourassa : la vie publique d'un grand Canadien*, Montreal: Éditions Chantecler, 1953, p. 759. [Freely translated.]

† Editorial by the founder in the first issue of *Le Devoir*, January 10, 1910, under the title "Avant le combat," cited by Mario Cardinal in *Pourquoi j'ai fondé Le Devoir*, p. 99. [Freely translated.]

added that, to safeguard that freedom of expression, he would refuse "to allow so much as a penny of the election fund in his riding,"* paying his campaign expenses out of his own pocket.

The contemporary observer cannot help but perceive a degree of naïveté in these affirmations of independence. Though clearly sincere, they reveal—at the very least—a misunderstanding of the concessions demanded by the party line and by respect for its leader. Bourassa's struggles on behalf of the French language and national independence would provide opportunities to realize this.

THE COMBAT ON BEHALF OF FRANCOPHONE MINORITIES

From the moment he entered the House of Commons, Henri Bourassa came up against the *realpolitik* of the federal government, embodied in the debate around the fate of the French-speaking Catholic minority in Manitoba. The root of the issue dated to 1890, and the adoption of provincial legislation that abolished that minority's education rights. Such a flagrant violation of the guarantees provided in the 1867 Confederation agreement undermined the very foundations of the principle of equality between the two founding peoples, at least in the eyes of Bourassa and his supporters. The ensuing crisis was to influence Canada's political history, laying the groundwork for the debate that has pitted Quebec against the rest of Canada to this day.

Players and pundits of the time were well aware of the degree to which Manitoba's Official Language Act challenged the undergirding dynamics of Confederation. The promise of equality of the two peoples was precisely what had led Lower Canada to join the confederal partnership. Its champions had had to reassure their "rouge" opponents, who feared that "the French element would be completely

* Henri Bourassa, *Mémoires*, lecture of October 13, 1943. [Freely translated.]

crushed by the majority of English representatives."* Minorities, they were told, were protected under sections 93 and 133 of the Constitution Act. By so brutally assailing those commitments, the Manitoba statute confirmed the pessimists' worst fears.

The controversy unfolded in many twists and turns, fed by widespread indignation among not only the Quebec population but also the majority of its elected officials and clergy. After an initial round of court challenges failed, opponents demanded that the federal government intervene to re-establish the principles of duality and respect for minority rights. The government, caught between the intractable determination of English Canada and the virulence of the response from francophones, attempted in its turn to let the courts decide. In the end, the matter was brought before the Judicial Committee of the Privy Council, in London, which ruled in January 1895 that the Canadian government had authority to intervene.

Obliged to act, the federal government under Conservative prime minister Mackenzie Bowell in March 1895 passed a remedial order-in-council requiring the Manitoba government to backtrack and restore minority language rights.

Bourassa said that month that "if the remedial order-in-council were followed up by effective legislation" he "would not hesitate to approve it." By April, he had grown impatient, protesting that "hesitations, ruses, prevarication of politicians" were "poisoning the debate."† In the meantime, he announced he was running for office in the riding of Labelle, as a candidate with Wilfrid Laurier's Liberal Party.

In response to the Manitobans' refusal to accede to the order-in-council, and almost as if his Conservative government had decided to take young Bourassa at his word, in February 1896 Bowell tabled a bill in the House of Commons, intending to force the province to implement the remedial measures that had been requested. Bourassa

---

* Cited by Réal Bélanger in *Henri Bourassa : Le fascinant destin d'un homme libre*, Quebec City: Presses de l'Université Laval, 2013, p. 9. [Freely translated.]

† Cited in Ibid., p. 36. [Freely translated.]

reacted immediately, saying: "Given what we know of it today, we must say in all fairness that the bill appears acceptable to us."* He even hinted that Laurier would also welcome it.

The Liberal leader had so far refrained from expressing an opinion on the principles at issue. To buy time, however, and to delay commitment (with a federal election looming), in March 1896 he asked the House to hoist the bill for six months, much to Bourassa's dismay.

The young MP's reaction was typical of political rookies who find themselves suddenly trapped in an impasse. There is no doubt that Bourassa was an honest man, passionately engaged in upholding the rights of French Canadians and the inherent dualism of the federal system. He had entered politics with the best of intentions, with earnest early promises that he would constantly remain independent of both party and leader. He had unreservedly pledged his unwavering resolve to never stray from his convictions.

What would Bourassa do? Should he not condemn Laurier for his dithering? Would he maintain his commitment to supporting the remedial legislation, or betray it?

Laurier, too, had to take up a position. Now holding the levers of power following the June 1896 election, he could no longer duck the issue. The new Liberal prime minister was already perceived as one of the most credible of Canadian leaders. He had the support of the people of Quebec, benefited from the stature of a statesman, showed consummate skill, and spoke English so well that no one hearing him would suspect that he had French-Canadian roots. Born a quarter-century apart, Laurier and Bourassa had been sworn in at the same time; one as prime minister, the other as the Member for Labelle.

There is no space here to explore the rich, complex relationship that formed between the two men. Their mutual admiration, respect, and even affection were undeniable. The prime minister was impressed by the talent and promise of the young MP, who in turn was enthralled

---

* *Le Ralliement*, issue of February 13, 1896, cited in Bélanger, *Henri Bourassa*, p. 37. [Freely translated.]

by the elder man's charismatic personality and prestige. Laurier saw a great future for his young friend. He would later confide to him that he thought Bourassa could have become prime minister, adding that a lack of practicality was the only thing that kept him from the highest office in the land. But theirs was also a love–hate relationship, made of intense connections, separations, and reconciliations.

Laurier's temperament, and his sense of his obligations as prime minister toward the whole country, would have been good indicators of how he planned to deal with the Manitoba issue. Someone with more experience than the young Member for Labelle could have foreseen the outcome. Bourassa was about to discover the prime minister's propensity to back down any time he felt that Canadian unity was being jeopardized.

Invoking the constraints of the sociopolitical context, in July 1896 Laurier abandoned the idea of an inquiry, which he had recommended as leader of the opposition, and decided to go the route of negotiating with the Manitoba government, led by Premier Thomas Greenway.

Mesmerized by his trust in Laurier and feeling defenceless vis-à-vis the dominance of a major party, Bourassa did an about-face, taking refuge in evasive explanations. Rather than condemn the government for contenting itself with a placebo cure that did nothing to remedy a shameful violation of fundamental rights guaranteed by the Constitution, he hailed the "wisdom" of Laurier's approach. Bourassa would later justify his refusal to support the Conservatives' remedial bill by claiming that there was no provision for tools that would "make it work."* No doubt the young MP did not enjoy having to stray from his usual rigour.

Quite adroitly, Laurier then entrusted his protégé with a delicate mission that ended up shackling him to a flawed agreement, arrived at through negotiations in which he had little say. Bourassa was named to the team of federal government negotiators dispatched

---

* Bélanger, *Henri Bourassa*, p. 38. [Freely translated.]

westward. Though it was a time-tested method, the young parliamentarian failed to grasp that he was being manipulated.

The talks resulted in the November 1896 agreement that came to be known as the "Laurier-Greenway Compromise." Historian Réal Bélanger denounced the "gulf that separated the Laurier-Greenway Agreement from the Manitoba Act of 1870, which had been so generous toward the two founding peoples," and concluded that "the very idea of a bicultural Canada so dear to the Fathers of Confederation was once again brutally called into question."* The agreement was reduced to a set of expedients: one half-hour of religious (Catholic) and language instruction per day in schools in which at least ten pupils spoke French or "any language *other* than English" [italics added]—an assimilation that clearly trivialized the status of French. In reality, it officialized the disappearance of the dual public school system in Manitoba.

Instead of attacking the agreement, Bourassa endorsed it, through linguistic oversimplification, talking of an honourable compromise and the "beginning of a settlement." Francophones in Quebec were incensed, and practically every Catholic bishop in the province rose up against Laurier as well as Bourassa. One, Msgr. Louis-François Laflèche of Trois-Rivières, said that Manitoba Catholics had been sold out and the province of Quebec betrayed, and that the so-called settlement was a mere farce. Another, Msgr. Louis-Nazaire Bégin, a moderate from the Quebec City area, described the deal as a "shameful treaty" and "an absolutely immoral act."†

To counter the opposition from the Quebec prelates, Bourassa took it upon himself to devise a strategy, which Laurier would make his own. The idea was to request Rome's intercession to call the bishops of Quebec to reason and ensure "the unity of the Church."‡

---

* Bélanger, p. 50. [Freely translated.]

† Roberto Perin, "Bégin, Louis-Nazaire," in *Dictionary of Canadian Biography*, vol. 15, University of Toronto/ Université Laval, 2003–, accessed February 29, 2016, http://www.biographi.ca/en/bio/begin_louis_nazaire_15E.html.

‡ Bourassa, *Mémoires*, lecture of October 27, 1943. [Freely translated.]

The operation proceeded apace. Pope Leo XIII dispatched Msgr. Rafael Merry del Val to Canada, who investigated and returned to the Holy See to report. The Pope then issued the encyclical *Affari vos* in December 1897, which concluded that the Manitoba law was unjust and the Laurier-Greenway Compromise "defective," but that "partial satisfaction [should] be accepted," in the hope that, over time, the situation might improve in keeping with "the value of moderation, gentleness, and brotherly love."*

For Réal Bélanger, this amounted to papal sanction of "Laurier's method of compromise"† and was to lead to "the emergence of an increasingly unicultural, English-speaking Canada: a state of affairs endorsed by Bourassa."‡

It is impossible to relate here the episodes of the many other struggles waged by Bourassa in Ottawa on behalf of the French language. The similar ways in which they unfolded are immediately obvious. Each had a disappointing outcome. Yet they reveal a Bourassa with fewer illusions about the sincerity of Laurier's promises and his ability to keep them in the face of English Canada's political clout. From then on he would make sure to secure the support of his fellow francophone citizens—and, whenever possible, that of the Church.

Insofar as we can claim to have an accurate representation of the political and social atmosphere of the time, the grandson of Louis-Joseph Papineau clearly monopolized the interest of his contemporaries. His many speeches in multiple forums were reinforced in widely published articles. He was swiftly swept up in the gyre of a busy life in which political, professional, and personal episodes continued unabated. His career was punctuated by moments of elation, confrontations, travels, joys of family life, and discouragements. At each

* Encyclical *Affari vos*, Leo XIII, December 8, 1897.

† Bélanger, *Henri Bourassa*, p. 54. [Freely translated.]

‡ Ibid., p. 56. [Freely translated.]

stage, one glimpses the life of a man of heart who was instinctively loyal to his people. A people for whom he had yearnings and ambitions that he came regrettably to feel were inaccessible.

Though it would be unwise to attempt to encapsulate Bourassa's vision of his people and its elites in a few words spoken or written in times of disappointment, some of them do reveal that he loved that people enough not to idealize it. In 1912, he wrote, "Like . . . Laurier . . . , all opportunistic politicians have indeed judged the French-Canadian people: a race of sheep, guarded by mute dogs."* Or consider this less than flattering portrayal of the elites: "They set the wrong example for a people that is in the process of becoming riffraff," he wrote, condemning the people's "lack of patriotism."† At one of his 1943 conferences, discussing the aftermath of the hanging of Louis Riel, he expressed his disappointment at the fact that Quebec voters had still "given [Conservative prime minister John A.] Macdonald a majority of seats," adding: "It was then that I began to have doubts about the political sense of my compatriots . . . , they have no opinions . . . no, they have sentiments. When they have given rein to their sentiment of the moment, they are satisfied."‡ Laurier would later tell him that he regarded their fellow Quebeckers the same way.

If Henri Bourassa had too-lofty dreams for his people—believed in a calling for them that proved too ambitious—it was precisely because he himself tended to stride on peaks. He showed greatness and courage on many occasions, but never more so than on the evening of September 10, 1910, at the Notre-Dame Basilica in Montreal, before a prestigious assembly of the most distinguished political, intellectual, and religious figures from Canada and abroad.

---

* Letter of April 15, 1912, to Msgr. Adélard Langevin. [Freely translated.]

† Bélanger, *Henri Bourassa*, p. 503. [Freely translated.]

‡ Bourassa, *Mémoires*, lecture of October 13, 1943. [Freely translated.] This assessment of the political awareness of French Canadians is often attributed to Laurier alone, when clearly it was shared by the two antagonists.

The occasion was the first-ever international eucharistic congress in North America. Msgr. Paul Bruchési, the archbishop of Montreal, along with all of the Catholic bishops in Quebec and the rest of Canada, had undertaken the organization of the event, which was to last five days. Three cardinals, seven hundred bishops, and ten thousand adherents were expected. The papal legate, Vincenzo Cardinal Vannutelli; the archbishop of Westminster, Francis Cardinal Bourne; the premier of Quebec, Lomer Gouin; the prime minister of Canada, Wilfrid Laurier; future cardinal Pierre-Marie Gerlier, archbishop of Lyon; and others were to speak. A public meeting would take place at Notre-Dame Basilica on September 10, the eve of the final solemn procession. Henri Bourassa was among the scheduled speakers.

The blows to minority rights outside Quebec in the preceding years, and the resulting controversies, were fresh in everyone's minds. Far from subsiding, the linguistic tensions had been exacerbated when English Catholic bishops entered the fray: they took a dim view of their French-Canadian counterparts' influence on the dissemination of Catholicism in the Canadian federation. Meanwhile, Irish Catholics in Ontario, led by Bishop Michael Francis Fallon, were against the continued presence of bilingual schools. Both groups felt the English language was the natural vector for evangelical expansion in North America. Moreover, they were objectively allied with English-speaking Protestants, who tended to be doubly hostile to anyone both francophone and Catholic.

Until the September 10 public meeting, Archbishop Bruchési and his colleagues on the organizing committee managed to keep a lid on the powderkeg. In their addresses, Premier Gouin, Prime Minister Laurier, and other speakers trod warily. All indications were that the event would come to a calm conclusion, albeit a muffled one, with things left unsaid.

When he reached his seat in the choir of the church, amid the most distinguished guests, Bourassa could see the crowd spilling out onto the forecourt and the neighbouring Place d'Armes. Archbishop

Bourne strode to the podium and spoke in English. Directly addressing the role of the English language and culture in Canada, he adamantly declared, "The future of the Church in this country and its consequent re-action upon the older countries in Europe, will depend to an enormous degree upon the extent to which the power, influence and prestige of the English language and literature can be definitively placed upon the side of the Catholic Church."* He went on: "It is only by bringing the English tongue to render service to the cause of truth that Canada can be made in the full sense a Catholic nation. . . . Until the English language, English habits of thought, English literature—in a word the entire English mentality is brought into the service of the Catholic Church, the saving work of the Church is impeded and hampered."†

In attendance was a young priest, the future Canon Lionel Groulx, who observed, in the choir, "the stir caused by the Archbishop's words: people whispering in each other's ears, gesticulating, agitation in the corner around Bourassa."‡ The ten thousand or so French-Canadian Catholics gathered in the church and in Place d'Armes had just heard that the language of Catholicism in Canada was not French, but English. Their mother tongue, it was claimed, had no place in Canadian Catholicism.

It caused a full-blown commotion in the crowd. Around Bourassa, dismayed French Catholic bishops shared disapproving remarks in hushed tones. Msgr. Langevin, known for his defence of minority-francophone rights in western Canada, whispered in Bourassa's ear: "Do not leave it at that. There must be a response."§

---

* *The Tablet. Supplement: Eucharistic Congress at Montreal.* London, September 24, 1910, p. 514. http://archive.thetablet.co.uk/article/24th-september-1910/37/east-and-from-the-west-from-the-north-and-from.

† Ibid., p. 515.

‡ Lionel Groulx, *Mes Mémoires*, Vol. II, Montreal: Fides, p. 198. [Freely translated.]

§ Bourassa, *Mémoires*, lecture of December 8, 1943.

Bourassa decided he would do just that. But he would have to wait his turn—which gave him some time to structure his thoughts. He hadn't counted on having to deliver a rebuke. And he was indisposed: he felt his gallstones acting up.

None of the other speakers had anything to say about Archbishop Bourne's inflammatory remarks. Then Archbishop Bruchési, the master of ceremonies, announced: "You will now hear a great orator." Abbé Groulx writes that the crowd exploded: "In one smooth motion, the assistants rise. The people want to see, to hear. The police barrier is broken; there is general pushing in the nave, in the galleries."*

The slim, upright man who strode to the ambo encircled by a metal banister was unquestionably the greatest Canadian orator of his time. In the fifteen or so years since he had entered politics, he had spoken of and debated the lot of his people on innumerable occasions, in every forum and to every type of audience. The thousands of his fellow French-speaking citizens massed around him had just heard another provocation, seen another threat to their language. Moreover, the attack had come from the must unpredictable of sources: a high Catholic authority. Bourassa, who would later write in *Hier, aujourd'hui et demain* that "language . . . comes to us from God," was distraught.† Were they claiming that God was English?

At that moment, the fiery man of faith felt the expectations flowing toward him—and realized they were hopes that he must not disappoint. He also had to consider how what he was about to say would be interpreted in various quarters. Then he embarked on an extempore address that would go down as one of the most moving and most powerful speeches in Canadian history. This was not mere oratory, but a *cri du cœur*. That of a Christian, and a citizen, who had been deeply wounded.

He began by using the outline of the speech he had planned to

---

* Cited in Michel Bock, *A Nation Beyond Borders: Lionel Groulx on French-Canadian Minorities*, tr. Ferdinanda Van Gennip, Ottawa: University of Ottawa Press.

† Cited in *Hommage à Henri Bourassa*, Montreal: Imprimerie Populaire, 1952, p. 212.

give. Then he carried on, without notes, in a riposte to Msgr. Bourne's unexpected attack: "His Eminence," he began, "has spoken on the issue of language; . . . in the name of the Catholic interests, he has asked us to make [English] the customary language in which the Gospel would be announced and preached to people."* He immediately urged the prelate to "grant . . . to the Catholics of all nations who land on this hospitable soil of Canada, the right to pray to God in the language of their race, their country, the blessed language of their father and mother. Do not tear from anyone, oh you priests of Christ, that which is the dearest to man after the God he adores."† And he concluded, "Allow me . . . to claim the same right for my compatriots, for those who speak my language . . . under the maternal wing of the Catholic Church—the Church of that Christ who died for all men and who imposed on no one the obligation of denying his race that he might remain faithful to Him."‡

At that moment, stenographer Louis Achille Cusson noted the "frenzied" reaction of those in attendance.

Even at a century's remove, at a time when religious fervour in Quebec has cooled considerably, it is impossible to read these impassioned lines without feeling the same emotions that overwhelmed those French Canadians in 1910, humiliated because of their language and loath to be forced into an agonizing choice between it and their Catholic allegiance.

Picture the orator, standing tall before the overflowing nave of the magnificent church in Old Montreal. He comes to life, striding from one side of the ambo to the other, launching one heartbreaking appeal after another: "Yes, when Christ was attacked by the Iroquois, when Christ was denied by the English, when Christ was attacked by the whole world, we have confessed and we have confessed in our

---

* Cited in Joseph Levitt, *Henri Bourassa on Imperialism and Bi-culturalism, 1900–1918*, Toronto: Copp Clark, 1970, pp. 128–129.

† Ibid.

‡ Ibid.

language. *Le sort de trois millions de catholiques, j'en suis certain, ne peut être indifférent au cœur de Pie X pas plus qu'à celui de l'éminent cardinal qui le représente ici."**

To read the speech in its entirety is to understand the immense influence of Henri Bourassa on his contemporaries, as well as their boundless admiration for his humanism and oratory skills.

Three elements came together to forge Bourassa's exploit that day at Notre-Dame: a great orator, an exceptional circumstance, and a fundamental issue. Bourassa had practised eloquence for too long to be unaware of his skills. After all, had he not once quoted Henri-Dominique Lacordaire, the famed preacher, for whom "orator and audience are one personage who are born and die together"?†

His listeners were moved to tears: here at last was someone who could express their indignation and their pride, a man with whom they were in perfect harmony, who could stir their most profound sentiments. The emotion brought on by the speech spread like wildfire, that very evening and in the ensuing days in Montreal and across Quebec.

What followed was to throw the ambiguous nature of the Church's support for Bourassa's nationalism into sharp relief. If the low clergy, the bishops and the French-Canadian diaspora generally supported and even applauded him, such was not always the case in the upper reaches of the episcopal hierarchy. It was they who had to deal with the Vatican, whose policy with regard to the linguistic rights of the French Canadians was one of fence-straddling. Bourassa himself on certain occasions had criticized concessions made by senior church dignitaries: they had decided to accept compromises that he deemed unfavourable to their flock.

The shock waves from the Notre-Dame speech reached as far as Rome, where church officials were alerted, among others, by cabinet minister Rodolphe Lemieux, who was dispatched by Laurier. The

* Ibid.

† Bourassa, *Mémoires*, lecture of December 8, 1943. [Freely translated.]

delegate met the cardinal secretary of state, Msgr. Merry del Val, who told him he found Bourassa's words "scandalous."

Bourassa decided to go to Rome himself to justify his views to Pope Pius X, who granted him an audience. Kneeling before the Holy Father, the politician explained the problematic situation of the French language in Canada. Pius X listened but, rather than replying, rose and abruptly ended the audience, saying simply, "Very well, justice will be done." His visitor was disappointed at the cool reception. "I had been given my dismissal," he said later, and found it difficult to let go of what he perceived as a "small humiliation."*

He was to pen even more bitter confidences in letters to a correspondent. In one, he wrote, "Fundamentally, men are the same everywhere and, aside from customs, decorum and manners, great men are hardly stronger or more shrewd in Rome than in London or in Ottawa." And in another, "Officials, whether of the Church or the State, are generally short of sight, narrow of mind and hard of heart. One should not expect them to direct the public consciousness or display a sense of duty."†

The year was 1910. Henri Bourassa was forty-two years old. He may have been a hero to his people, but he was disappointed as a politician and appalled as a Catholic. Had his life ended then and there, historians would surely have had an easier job of encapsulating his position vis-à-vis the Church, his faith, and the French language. He had always been a devout Catholic, but now began a period in which he lived his faith even more intensely—one might say absolutely. He began increasingly to question the importance of the link between language and religion, to the point that he mitigated and even disavowed his earlier commitment.

It would be futile to try to pinpoint where, exactly, the changes in the later life of this complex man began. There is one clear signpost,

* Bélanger, *Henri Bourassa*, p. 341. [Freely translated.]

† The letters were written to Abbé Henri Jeannotte in February and March 1911; they are cited in Bélanger, *Henri Bourassa*, p. 342. [Freely translated.]

though: a turning point as obvious as it was irreversible. He had a second papal audience, this time with Pius XI in 1926. The tenor of that meeting is evidence of the reversal that caused Bourassa to doubt the priority he had always ascribed to language over the Church's authority.

If Bourassa had shown himself to be moody in the days following his meeting with Pius X in 1910, the audience with Pius XI traumatized him. He described it as "the hardest lesson . . . of his life." For an hour, the Pope reminded him of his "first duty," which was to "defend the causes of God and of the Church . . . , other causes, even legitimate ones, are secondary and must be subordinate: a Catholic must never put them first." Bourassa then heard the Pontiff bemoan "the substitution of nationalism for Catholicism."*

Nationalism was a dirty word to Europeans, who viewed it as the root cause of the catastrophe of 1914–1918.† But Bourassa realized that it was his own brand of nationalism, his vision of the rights and the future of his people, that were the subject of the papal warning.

This time, he did not rebel. His reaction was simply one of prostration. Robert Rumilly writes that he sailed aboard the first available liner, returning home "almost without exiting his stateroom during the crossing . . . kneeling at the foot of the bunk . . . ready for every sacrifice."‡ He related to a clergyman friend his heartbreak at having to submit to the head of the Church: "I know of course that my patriotic action does not do disservice to the Church; indeed it does it

* Rumilly, *Henri Bourassa*, p. 342. [Freely translated.] Note that André Laurendeau, on page 40 of his essay "Le nationalisme de Bourassa" (in François-Albert Angers and Patrick Allen (eds.), *La pensée de Henri Bourassa*, Montreal: L'Action nationale, 1954) refers to comments by Bourassa in 1935 that attenuate the forcefulness of his initial reaction to Pope Pius XI's admonition.

† In his encyclical *Ubi arcano Dei consilio*, published a few years before his meeting with Bourassa, Pius XI had denounced "extreme nationalism" (as noted by Mario Cardinal in *Pourquoi j'ai fondé Le Devoir: Henri Bourassa et son temps*, Montreal: Libre Expression, p. 340).

‡ Rumilly, p. 693. [Freely translated.]

service . . . and yet the Pope is moved by the Holy Spirit, and the Holy Spirit is infallible."*

From then on, his major cause was to make the primacy of the rights of the Church central to his discourse. His faith in the Gospel message was accompanied by complete obedience toward the authority of the Roman Catholic Church. In 1930 he admitted that, after his first political disappointments, he had taken "the resolution . . . in all matters . . . to obey the Pope."† In 1935, he disavowed everything in his career that "had not clearly respected the primacy of the rights of the Church over race, over language and over any human interest."‡ He went even further in 1943: "[From] this decisive hour of my life, I resolved, to the very end, to do everything to combat the evil signalled by the Pope."§ The evil, of course, was the nationalism the Pope had denounced as "extreme."

It is easy to imagine the dismay that those loyal to the nationalist leader would have felt upon reading in *Le Devoir*, in January 1929, this repudiation: "It is not permitted for Catholics, on the pretext of defending the French language, to jeopardize the unity and authority of the Church."¶

One can also imagine the reaction from voters who sought Bourassa's counsel in the federal election of 1921, only to be told simply, "May God enlighten your conscience and those of your compatriots."** And what of the advice given to Armand Lavergne, his longtime disciple and lieutenant, who asked for Bourassa's support when he sought the Liberal nomination in Wilfrid Laurier's former

---

* Rumilly, *Henri Bourassa*, p. 698. [Freely translated.]

† Henri Bourassa, *Le Devoir, ses origines, sa naissance, son esprit*, brochure published in 1930, cited in Bélanger, *Henri Bourassa*, pp. 56 and 57. [Freely translated.]

‡ Rumilly, *Henri Bourassa*, p. 741. [Freely translated.]

§ Spring 1935 lecture, cited in Ibid. [Freely translated.]

¶ Ibid., p. 711. [Freely translated.]

** Ibid., p. 633. [Freely translated.]

riding of Quebec East? Lavergne's mentor suggested that he rely on "Christian resignation and hope in God."*

One cannot help but think that some drama played a part in the uncompromising soul-searching he conducted as he retreated into the silence of his later years.

Henri Bourassa was certainly not the first to realize that religion and politics do not always mix well. He had to cope (and did so poorly, by all accounts) with the impediments imposed by his religious allegiances on his political thought and engagement. It would appear that he lived with that subjugation serenely, in total surrender to his faith. At any rate, that is the state of mind one imagines he was in when, shortly before his eighty-fourth birthday and surrounded by his family, he breathed his last, having received last rites from François, the elder of his two Jesuit sons.

FIGHTING FOR INDEPENDENCE

Whether constraint or consolation, religion gave Bourassa free rein in the other great struggle of his life: the cause of Canada's autonomy.

When the young MP for Labelle arrived in the House of Commons, Canada was a dominion of the British Empire, then at the pinnacle of its power and influence over fully one-quarter of the globe. In Canada, the Empire was a source of pride and much respected, especially among the English-speaking population. In the province of Quebec, the majority of the elites, including the Catholic bishops, readily accepted British supremacy.

Henri Bourassa did not. He had a fundamental objective from which he never wavered: to break the imperial chain. He felt this was a condition for the survival of Confederation.

He described his nationalism as "a Canadian nationalism, founded on the duality of races . . . ; The homeland for us is the whole of

---

* Ibid., p. 613. [Freely translated.]

Canada. . . . The nation we wish to see develop is the Canadian nation composed of French and English Canadians . . . united in a sentiment of fraternity and devotion to a common homeland."* His speeches and texts championed "the only ideal worthy of the national ambition of Canadians . . . to show to the entire world the example . . . of a nation acceding to independence by measured degrees."† Throughout his career, he emphasized "the need to create everywhere in Canada an authentic Canadian sentiment."‡

The modern reader will find nothing revolutionary about these words; they are spoken daily by Québécois proponents of Canadian federalism. At the time, though, Bourassa's crusade was a brusque affront to public perception, especially in English Canada. Bourassa was brutally awakened to this in 1899 when London requested that Ottawa send troops to South Africa in support of the British Army's South African War campaign.

At the time, Bourassa had been a member of Parliament for three years. He admired and adored his leader, and had no reason to think that Laurier might commit Canadians to a faraway conflict. But tensions began rising across the country, especially once the war had been declared in South Africa, where British reinforcements had been sent to help English settlers in the Transvaal and the Orange Free State, both of which were controlled by the Boers. In Ontario, there was strong pressure on the government to send Canadian troops into the fray. The Empire needed its dominions, and Canada had to say yes.

In Quebec, meanwhile, there was virulent opposition. Bourassa made up his mind: he refused to consider any possibility of committing troops to assist the British. Laurier consulted aides, hesitated, and, in the end, announced that Canadian soldiers would be sent to South Africa. Appalled, Bourassa told the prime minister he would

* *Le Nationaliste*, April 3, 1904, cited in Martin O'Connell, *Henri Bourassa and Canadian Nationalism*, Ph.D. thesis (History), University of Toronto, 1954, p. 4.

† Bélanger, *Henri Bourassa*, p. 425. [Freely translated.]

‡ Ibid., p. 453. [Freely translated.]

not follow him, and would contest his decision. The eventual force, however, consisted of volunteers only, transported and outfitted by the federal government. In his biography of Laurier, André Pratte writes that 7,300 Canadians fought in the Transvaal under orders from British officers.*

Forced to choose between siding with Laurier and leaving the party, Bourassa announced he was resigning his seat in the House of Commons on October 18, 1899. Two days later, he explained his actions to his Labelle constituents and announced that, to justify his decision, he would seek their support for a renewed mandate. They responded on January 18, 1900, electing him by acclamation as an independent MP. Quebec nationalists applauded his determination in standing against Laurier and his government. On the other side, in addition to blaming him for lacking loyalty toward the Liberal Party, many were saddened to see the promising young MP isolate himself and turn his back on a career that might have taken him very far indeed.

But Henri Bourassa had made his bed and would now lie in it. He continued to urge his compatriots to maintain a safe distance from England, to avoid all risk of being drawn into imperial wars. Along with his nationalist disciples, he believed the colonies of the British Empire should develop on the bases of nationalism and autonomy. The concept of autonomy was the basis for their definition of the status of Canada as well as that of the provinces: "For Canada, in its relations with Great Britain, the largest measure of political, commercial and military autonomy compatible with the maintenance of the colonial tie. . . . For Canadian provinces, in their relation with the federal power, the largest measure of autonomy compatible with the maintenance of the federal tie."†

---

* André Pratte, *Extraordinary Canadians: Wilfrid Laurier*, Toronto: Penguin, 2011.

† From the platform of the Ligue Nationaliste Canadienne, founded in 1903 by Bourassa and journalist Olivier Asselin. Cited in Joseph Levitt, *Henri Bourassa and the Golden Calf: The Social Program of the Nationalists of Quebec, 1900–1914*, Ottawa: University of Ottawa Press, 1972.

Another controversy would furnish Bourassa with an opportunity to clearly illustrate his determination to shield Canada from imperial interference: the political upheaval surrounding the proposed creation of a Canadian navy.

The navies of Great Britain and Germany were engaged in an unbridled arms race, both countries pouring astronomical sums into the construction of new battleships known as dreadnoughts—steel-plated behemoths with displacements in the tens of thousands of tonnes and armed with massive guns. England called on the Dominion of Canada for help, requesting nothing less than for it to assume the cost of building warships for incorporation into the Royal Navy.

British leaders had reason to expect a positive response from Laurier, who had made a pledge to them at the Colonial Conference of 1897, held in conjunction with Queen Victoria's Diamond Jubilee: "If a day were ever to come when England was in danger, let the bugle sound, let the fires be lit on the hills, and . . . though we might not be able to do much, whatever we can do shall be done by the colonies to help her."* Malcontents of the time no doubt remarked that the author of this enthusiastic support for the Empire returned from that trip to London with the name Sir Wilfrid Laurier on his luggage.

By 1909, England had raised the alarm: Germany would achieve maritime supremacy in 1912. Imperialists in Canada were stirred to action: the Dominion had to come to the aid of the motherland and help it build more battleships. On January 12, 1910—coincidentally, two days after the first edition of *Le Devoir* was published—Prime Minister Laurier introduced a bill that was to equip Canada with its own naval fleet, choosing the same moment to declare to the House of Commons that "When Britain is at war, Canada is at war."†

* *The National Review*, Vol. XXIX, March to August, 1897, London: Edward Arnold, 1897, p. 784.

† *House of Commons Debates*, January 12, 1910, p. 1735. It should be noted that Laurier adopted the same ambivalence in London as in Ottawa. He blew hot and cold, with soaring pronouncements that caused his British interlocutors to hope for support that failed to materialize.

Bourassa protested in the strongest terms, demanding a plebiscite to allow the people to "manifest its will."* In English Canada, the imperialists chanted "One King, one fleet, one flag."†

Laurier's Liberals were soundly beaten in the 1911 federal election by the Conservatives under Robert Borden, who had promised to revisit Laurier's Naval Service Bill. On the strength of that pledge, Bourassa sided with the Conservative leader. His support weighed heavily in the defeat of Laurier, but it also earned him harsh disapproval from the many Quebeckers who admired the francophone prime minister. He was severely reprimanded for having formed an alliance with the Conservatives . . . and then had to suffer the shame of having been duped by Borden. For, as soon as he was elected, the Tory prime minister broke his word and announced the Naval Aid Bill, under which Canada would provide thirty-five million dollars to Great Britain for the construction of three dreadnought-class vessels for the benefit of the British Royal Navy.‡

Bourassa would once more step into the breach, this time during the Conscription Crisis of 1917, which he attacked in many speeches and editorials. But he did so with moderation, and this was remarked upon. Even as he campaigned against conscription, he was quick to express his wish that public turmoil be avoided. The day after giving a speech at the Monument-National in Montreal in June 1917, fearing the possible consequences of his fiery rhetoric, he published an article in *Le Devoir* that urged people to oppose conscription "with sangfroid."§ He was deeply concerned about rumours of possible rioting

---

* Bélanger, *Henri Bourassa*, p. 304. [Freely translated]

† Ibid., p. 305.

‡ Right from the start of their relationship, Laurier had noted Bourassa's lack of practicality. In reality, Bourassa consistently displayed a political naïveté that left him vulnerable to traps. That in particular explains the alliance with Borden to defeat Laurier in the 1911 election, which historian and biographer Réal Bélanger (*Henri Bourassa*, p. 367) described as "indecent."

§ Rumilly, *Henri Bourassa*, p. 581. [Freely translated.]

and violence. As biographer Robert Rumilly noted, "Bourassa feared, as his grandfather had, that it would all end in riots and bloody reprisals."* After that, he was relatively silent on the issue.

While he may not have dedicated himself so zealously to his repudiation of conscription, Bourassa remains the politician who most steadfastly advocated for the autonomy and even the independence of Canada.

HIS INFLUENCE

Though discreet and barely visible, the influence of Henri Bourassa continues to be felt in Canadian politics today. One needs only to revisit the writings he left us and trace his tumultuous career to see the extent to which he helped lay down the parameters of contemporary political players' thought and action.

No one analyzed the concept of nationalism in greater depth. He said that his brand of nationalism was Canadian, in the sense that he believed in a "Canadian nation, composed of French Canadians and English Canadians."† Time and again he affirmed, "for us, the fatherland is all Canada" and that he was a "Canadian above all." In his view, that fatherland was entirely compatible with recognition of the "French-Canadian nation" and "French-Canadian patriotism."‡

* Rumilly, *Henri Bourassa*, p. 583. [Freely translated.]

† Cited in H. Mason Wade, "Political Trends," in *Essais sur le Québec contemporain / Essays on Contemporary Quebec*, Jean-Charles Falardeau, ed., Sainte-Foy, Quebec: Les Presses de l'Université Laval, 1953, pp. 150–151. Bourassa was writing in the April 3, 1904, issue of *Le Nationaliste*, a weekly founded by Olivier Asselin (see Note 44) and others.

‡ The terms "French-Canadian nation" and "French-Canadian patriotism" had been employed by Jules-Paul Tardivel, "the ultramontane, anglophobe, and separatist editor of *La Vérité*" (Wade, "Political Trends," p. 150). Bourassa was replying to Tardivel's definition of nationalism in the April 2, 1904, issue of *La Vérité*. See also O'Connell, Ph.D. thesis, p. 4.

Quebec federalists certainly identify with this view, which emphasizes an attachment to all of Canada as well as an allegiance to the French-Canadian nation. It explains why they cannot abide aspersions from certain sovereigntists who attribute their federalist leanings to a lack of Québécois patriotism. In reality, many of them are like Bourassa in that their loyalty to Canada includes a love for Quebec and a sense of belonging that, to them, are just as strong as those felt by sovereigntists. And, like him, they view French Canadians as full-fledged Canadians. The motivation and arguments of federalists today, in their confrontations with sovereigntists, are therefore directly descended from Bourassa's thinking.

Bourassa consistently stood apart from the separatist leanings that he could see among some of his followers. In his day everyone, including proponents of independence for Quebec, used the term *séparatiste* (separatist) and not *souverainiste* (sovereigntist). He harshly attacked the goal of separation, even ridiculing it in texts and speeches lampooning Abbé Groulx, despite the fact that the latter was among his followers. In so doing, the austere leader revealed a sardonic side of himself that we may find hard to imagine. Speaking to visitors, Bourassa once described the future Canon Groulx amid his supporters in the "basement of a presbytery in Mile-End." Hearing one colleague attack the English, another the Americans, a third the capitalists, and seeing a fourth "unsheath Napoleon's sabre . . . , the little Abbé Groulx, who could not fight because of his priestly position, blessed the combatants."*

Bourassa went so far as to warn young people against "those who appeal to their pride in their race."† He also took pleasure in invoking a categorical argument that separatism was incompatible with Catholicism: "Is this dream [Quebec separation] attainable? I do not think so. Is it desirable? I do not believe so, either from the French point of view or, even less, from the Catholic point of view, which in

* Rumilly, *Henri Bourassa*, pp. 750–751. [Freely translated.]

† Ibid., p. 741. [Freely translated.]

my opinion takes precedence over the interest of French."* He pulled no punches in describing the "dangers" of separatism: "It would unleash civil war, sow divisions in our ranks, be harmful to other French groups in America, pit us against forces that would crush us."†

His persistence in ruling out sovereignty for Quebec as a solution to disillusionment with federalism is explained by his abhorrence of "outrageous"‡ or "savage"§ nationalism. It is thus easy to understand the discomfort of André Laurendeau and Lionel Groulx, who did not advocate that scorned form of nationalism and had to suffer unjust accusations from a man whom they otherwise admired and respected.

Laurendeau put his finger on one aspect that goes some way toward explaining their hero's anger and attacks. He felt that Bourassa would "fiercely turn against his disciples . . . when, drawing conclusions from his repeated failures, they will lean toward isolation or separatism."¶

Bourassa himself, of course, was not immune to those disillusionments. At times, he spoke of the "bankruptcy" of Confederation.** He repeatedly denounced violations of the constitutional rights of francophones, which strayed from the principle of Canadian duality. In the House of Commons in 1905, he could not help but speak his mind in what was seemingly a disavowal of the federal regime: "Every time I return to my province, I am saddened to see developing there a feeling that Canada is not a Canada for all Canadians. . . . We are

* Réal Bélanger, "Bourassa, Henri," in *Dictionary of Canadian Biography*, vol. 18, University of Toronto/Université Laval, 2003–, accessed February 29, 2016, http://www.biographi.ca/en/bio/bourassa_henri_18E.html.

† Cited in Cardinal, *Pourquoi j'ai fondé Le Devoir: Henri Bourassa et son temps*, p. 339. [Freely translated.]

‡ Ibid., p. 650. [Freely translated.]

§ Laurendeau, "Le nationalisme de Bourassa," p. 47. [Freely translated.]

¶ In Angers & Allen (eds.), *La pensée de Henri Bourassa*, p. 36. [Freely translated.]

** Ibid., p. 43. [Freely translated.]

forced to reach the conclusion that Quebec is our only country because we have no freedom elsewhere."*

For all that, he remained hopeful and, as André Laurendeau has written, "however strong his affirmation of French-Canadian identity, he chose to be Canadian. . . . He always demanded an autonomous country, a truly bilingual country with complete religious freedom; he constantly had the door slammed in his face, but continued to stubbornly express his dual wish. . . . No one was ever Canadian with as much conscience and obstinacy."† More prosaically, and using modern terminology, some would describe Bourassa's view as "tired federalism." But that would be failing to grasp that any disillusionment he felt was always tempered by hope. This tenacious individual brooked no deviations from the vision of the constitution espoused by those who orchestrated it in 1867.

If he were alive today, would he be a proponent of renewed federalism? We can no more answer that question than we can this one: How long would he have waited for a renewal of the federal regime before abandoning hope?

The central issue of his political action was the fate of the French language. His impassioned campaigns for the protection of his mother tongue even brought him ridicule. Laurier enjoyed mocking his "chivalric" impulses‡; others compared him to Don Quixote. In spite of the many insults and attacks directed at him—he was variously called a "leader of the forces of evil," a "fallen angel," a "divider of races," a "destroyer of Canadian unity," and "dictator"—he never gave up on the issue of the survival of the French language.

He was not the instigator of that great debate, in which his famous grandfather was one noted protagonist, but the passion and tenacity with which he approached it stirred in future generations

* Bélanger, *Henri Bourassa*, pp. 149–150.

† Laurendeau, *Pourquoi j'ai fondé Le Devoir: Henri Bourassa et son temps*, p. 36. [Freely translated.]

‡ Bélanger, *Henri Bourassa*, p. 76. [Freely translated.]

of Québécois an inescapable obligation to continue the struggle. In that sense, all Quebec nationalists are Bourassa's heirs.

It is largely thanks to him that promoting and defending French remain part of the everyday reality of that language, especially in Quebec. Of course, those struggles are no longer waged under the same conditions as in Bourassa's day, when the French language was "the custodian of [the Catholic] faith."* Nobody today would see a need to reconcile that fight with the demands of their faith; even less to seek a bishop's *nihil obstat*. Free of such constraints, as we are today, we cannot easily appreciate the courage and determination displayed by Bourassa, forced to overcome conscientious objections and submit to the influence of Rome, at the moment that his battle for equal rights for francophones demanded his full energy and the greatest possible room to manoeuvre.

Respect for both languages was integral to his vision of Canadian duality, a founding principle of Confederation, in the minds and in the arguments of his defenders in Quebec. This was the perspective in which Bourassa conceived of bilingualism. He himself made sure to practise bilingualism, for mastery of English was an invaluable tool for him in advocating for the rights of his compatriots in English Canada.

Precisely because he loved Canada and had great expectations for this country, he sought the greatest possible degree of independence for it. Often considered by his opponents, especially English Canadians, to be disloyal to the Empire and to Canada, Henri Bourassa was an unflinching advocate of Canadian independence. His constant calls to sever all links of subordination with England and forge a fully sovereign country surely helped nurture, in everybody's mind, the sense that national independence was a necessity.

He did win that battle, albeit posthumously. Were he alive today, he could rightly claim victory.

* "*La gardienne de la foi*," in the words of Msgr. Paul-Eugène Roy, speech to the *Congrès de la langue française*, April 10, 1911, cited in Bélanger, *Henri Bourassa*, p. 404.

Henri Bourassa's most tangible legacy today is surely the newspaper *Le Devoir*. He would doubtless remark that its editors continue to draw inspiration from values that he held dear: professional integrity, vigilance in monitoring injustices and condemning wrongdoings, allegiance to the nation of Quebec, and commitment to the French language and French-Canadian culture. While congratulating them for their resilience and appreciating the fact that readers are reminded every day of his founding role, the disciple of Louis Veuillot would surely hold his successors to account regarding their abandonment of the Church and Catholicism in favour of "ecological" proselytizing—and would probably demand a definition of the word *ecological*. He would be surprised to find so few Latin expressions in "his" newspaper, and would wonder whatever happened to the French–Latin dictionary by Quicherat that he had placed in the newsroom. And today's editorialists and columnists would be wise to have some ready explanations for why the term *Canadien français* has been replaced by *Québécois*, and to be prepared to suffer the founder's wrath upon learning that *Le Devoir* was now "separatist," a defender of gender equality, and left-leaning.

In the end, though, Bourassa would not fail to value his newspaper's vast influence in intellectual and political milieux, especially in government ministers' offices, where political attachés rise at dawn to scrutinize every word before briefing their bosses once they are awake.

Le Devoir's editors, meanwhile, would be most ill at ease if the august revenant told them he planned to take up the pen anew. For they would recall that in his day, he had opposed granting women the right to vote[*] and advised them to "do more housework,"[†] worried about the urbanization of Quebec, and, despite unequivocally condemning anti-Semitism,[‡] admired Marshal Pétain.[§] But this is vain

* Bélanger, *Henri Bourassa*, p. 444.

† Ibid., p. 462. [Freely translated.]

‡ Rumilly, *Henri Bourassa*, p. 719, p. 741.

§ Ibid., pp. 769–770.

conjecture, of course: one cannot draw incriminating conclusions from those opinions, because it would be impossible to judge a time traveller from a bygone era according to the standards and criteria of a society so foreign to him in so many respects.

There is, however, one group to whom Bourassa's influence might be very beneficial indeed: young Quebeckers, who are in need of a mentor. They would have a great deal to gain from his broad erudition and his admirable mastery of French. In getting to know him, they would also rectify some failings in the teaching of our history. Too often, the emerging generation lacks even minimal knowledge of the men and women who built the Quebec of today. In studying Bourassa, they would draw from the wellsprings of our history and discover a model of rigour, integrity, and selfless dedication. As François-Albert Angers has written, "A nation that no longer worships its great men has begun to die as a nation. . . . The reward for being faithful to that memory would be a rejuvenation that we sorely need, and the oeuvre of Bourassa could well provide us with the principle for that rejuvenation."*

Henri Bourassa's entire career also provides a lesson that all Quebec nationalists elected to the House of Commons would do well to reflect on. It would teach them that their efforts to promote the interests of Quebec within a federalist party, especially if they are given a cabinet portfolio, are likely to encounter obstacles that often cannot be overcome. Those obstacles are not fixed, because they depend on the nature of the issue at stake and the importance that the person involved ascribes to it. In a debate pitting the interests of Quebec against those of English Canada, members of Parliament from Quebec have a choice: side with the majority, or hew to a position that their constituents expect of them. They are on a necessarily subjective playing field, even more so when a question of principle arises. In such situations, Québécois MPs must expect to be reminded, as Bourassa was by Laurier, of the importance of relying on their common

* Article by François-Albert Angers in Angers & Allen (eds.), *La pensée de Henri Bourassa*, p. 186. [Freely translated.]

sense rather than idealist reflexes. Bourassa's experience, especially at the federal level, often led to such dilemmas.

One cannot doubt that the normal functioning of democratic institutions requires that decision makers, ministers, and parliamentarians show themselves capable of resolving conflicts of interest and dealing with a diversity of views. Laurier was a master at this and, in that regard among others, was arguably the greatest politician in Canadian history. But in the name of national unity, which was among his primary duties as prime minister, he had to make extensive concessions that drastically altered the equilibrium between the two founding peoples, despite its being a cornerstone of the Confederation agreement. Moreover, those actions earned him the right to be called a "traitor" and a "coward" by the scrappy MP for Labelle.

In other words, with Quebec's influence having waned in Ottawa, MPs from the province must prepare for the possibility—rare, it must be hoped—that they will have to make concessions, through gritted teeth, or else resign, which is not the goal of any political career and can only be justified by a requirement of conscience.

AN UNFINISHED WORK

Resignation does not appear to have been Bourassa's preferred remedy. True, he was exempt from the dilemmas of power since he was never entrusted with any ministerial duties. When he walked away from the Liberal Party in 1899, he was a backbencher, and he was immediately re-elected to the House as an independent. His struggle was instead one of ideas and causes. The Bourassa that his followers remember, during the most noteworthy period of his career, never admitted defeat in his defence of the French language, and maintained a fundamentally Canadian commitment.

In essence, he had a dual allegiance, melded into the representation of an ideal country that he was fiercely committed to building amid a rebellious reality—having resolved, once and for all, to endure the vicissitudes of a broken dream.

None of this can be construed to mean that the nationalist debate in Quebec and the rest of Canada has been extinguished. Nor can one infer any direct influence of Bourassa's thinking and actions on the outcome of that continuing debate. The sovereigntist camp cannot conscript, even conceptually, the ardent nationalist that was Bourassa (nor, to my knowledge, has anyone in it attempted to do so). Not any more than federalists could enrol him in their campaigns against the open nationalism of Quebec sovereigntists.

Nevertheless, one cannot ignore the reactions among succeeding generations to the torment of this disillusioned federalist. His contemporary disciples witnessed first-hand the tragedy of a man who, after pinning all his hopes on a pact structured around the equal rights of Canada's two founding peoples, had to watch powerless from the sidelines as French Canadians suffered language-based discrimination.

This great man bequeathed to Quebec nationalists an unfinished work—a failed enterprise, yes, but also an invitation to carry on. For some, the goal was renewed federalism, inspired by the ideal of Canada, while others, not trusting in any hope of renewal, sought to achieve their own ideal, a country called Quebec.

Henri Bourassa's most positive influence will be wielded above the fray, through the example of his principled view of democracy, his intellectual rigour, and his respect for others—values to which all parties ought to turn for guidance in continuing the debates that will shape our future. For the search for a solution to the nationalist question, in one sense or the other, is an ineluctable element in the unfolding of Canadian history.

One feels a futile sense of regret: that the great Canadian, and great Quebecker, who was Henri Bourassa cannot take part in those debates in person.

ROMÉO DALLAIRE AND SERGE BERNIER

THOMAS-LOUIS TREMBLAY

MILITARY MAN

LIKE TENS OF THOUSANDS of other young Canadians, Thomas-Louis Tremblay lived through the First World War at lightning speed and then returned to civilian life. Like many others who experienced the trauma of that conflict, he is somewhat forgotten today. Yet the year and a half that he spent at the front had a marked impact, still felt today, on the place of francophone Canadians in Canada's armed forces and, in a broader sense, on the country itself.

Born on May 16, 1886, in Chicoutimi, Quebec, Tremblay enlisted at age fifteen in the 6th Field Artillery Regiment* in Lévis, a unit of the Non-Permanent Militia. He was admitted in 1904 to the Royal Military College (RMC) in Kingston, which trained specialist officers, especially gunners and engineers (the latter could go on to practise their profession outside the service). He completed his education on time, leaving an excellent impression thanks to both his military and his athletic abilities. He was named the top athlete in his graduating class: on one of the honours lists in Yeo Hall at RMC Kingston, the name "Sergeant TL Tremblay" appears along with the title "Best Man at All Arms" for 1907.

* Then known as the 6th "Quebec and Lévis" Regiment, CA.

Most RMC graduates, Tremblay included, wound up in the Non-Permanent Militia, given the paucity of postings available in Canada's defence forces, which at the time were minuscule. After leaving the college, he returned to his native Saguenay region, where he was hired as a civil engineer for the National Transcontinental Railway. As there was no artillery unit in the area, Tremblay became a lieutenant with the 18th Regiment, Francs-tireurs du Saguenay. In 1911, he moved to Quebec City to open his own engineering firm, and joined the Lévis artillery, where he commanded a battery, having now attained the rank of major. He could have had no inkling that his military career would soon take on an entirely different dimension.

On June 28, 1914, while on a visit to Sarajevo, Archduke Franz Ferdinand, heir presumptive to the Austro-Hungarian crown, was assassinated by a Serbian nationalist. The incident sparked a series of diplomatic and military decisions by the major European powers, culminating in the German invasion of Belgium on August 4, 1914. The same day, Britain declared war on Germany, which automatically drew the member countries of its empire, including Canada, into the conflict. The First World War, which would ultimately result in 9.7 million dead, including 66,000 Canadians, had begun.

One week later, Thomas-Louis Tremblay and his battery were mobilized to the newly established training base at Valcartier, where volunteer soldiers were assembling for overseas postings. On August 29, he was transferred to the 1st Division Ammunition Column, and on September 22, to its officer staff. On September 26, his emergency service ended.

VOLUNTEER FIGHTER

Tremblay could easily have stayed in Canada, continued his career as an engineer, and contributed to the country's war effort in that capacity. But like many promising young men of his generation, he decided to enlist in a combat role. When he did, he was already well aware that the war was particularly demanding on soldiers, and that it would likely last far longer than originally thought. On March 11, 1915, Tremblay received confirmation that he was to become second-in-command of the only French-Canadian infantry battalion in the Canadian Army Corps, a unit that had been created the previous October and was still receiving training on this side of the Atlantic. This was the 22nd (French-Canadian) Battalion, later to become the Royal 22e Régiment and known to many as the "Van Doos."

The first commanding officer of the 22nd, Colonel Frédéric Mondelet Gaudet, was forty-eight years old in 1915. Gaudet was another RMC Kingston alumnus (class of 1887) and had joined the Permanent Militia after graduating. He had been a gunner and had completed his career in 1913 after heading the Dominion Arsenal at Quebec. Gaudet and Tremblay had very probably met: despite their age difference, they had much in common.

Why did some 15,000 French Canadians volunteer? To get a job, it is said (they were in short supply), or to earn a better wage. In reality, most of the 5,584 men who joined the 22nd Battalion between 1914 and 1918 declared that they had a trade, 5 per cent of them being farmers. The daily pay of $1.10, for a private, was lower than a civilian wage, especially in high season (summer and fall). Moreover, the danger was far greater for a volunteer soldier than for a labourer back home, who, with war-related industries burgeoning, could even expect his pay conditions to improve. And the issue of the balance of power on the Old Continent, upheld by England and challenged by Germany under Kaiser Wilhelm II, was certainly not uppermost in the minds of the vast majority of French-Canadian volunteer soldiers. Among those who left behind writings that addressed the question, a yearning for a new life of adventure was the reason most often cited. There were, of course, other motivations for enlisting, as we shall see in the case of Thomas-Louis Tremblay.

Rare among Canadian officers of the time, Tremblay kept a war diary in French, making fairly regular entries beginning on March 11, 1915: he knew he was embarking on an experience that would leave an indelible impression on his life. Unilingual French readers must thank Marcelle Cinq-Mars for her judicious annotations to the diary, large parts of which would otherwise be incomprehensible to them because so many terms are in English, the only official language of Canada's armed forces at the time.*

Tremblay's diary entry of May 21, 1914, made just after the 22nd shipped out from Halifax aboard HMT *Saxonia*, bound for England, encapsulated what would prove to be his primary motivation, and that of his men, throughout the horrendous conflict: "We are more determined than ever to prove that the French-Canadian blood flows just as purely and warmly in our veins as it did in those of our ancestors."† It was a sentiment that he would express often, in one form or another.

Since Canada had determined that its fighting force would be made up of volunteer recruits, there had been no specific requirements as to their initial mobilization. The units of the Non-Permanent Militia simply entered the names of the volunteers that came to them. Once they arrived at Valcartier, they were grouped into new numbered battalions; at first, the French Canadians had simply blended in with the crowd. But it soon became clear that their representation was completely out of proportion to their numbers in the overall population, which sparked harsh, often racist comments in the country's English-language newspapers. The 22nd Battalion owed its existence to the strong reaction to that phenomenon from a part of the French-Canadian elite, firmly supported by certain newspapers, including Montreal's *La Presse*. There is no doubt that Gaudet, along with many officers and men of the 22nd, thought the same as Tremblay: they were marching off to the battlegrounds of Europe convinced that they

---

* Thomas-Louis Tremblay, *Journal de guerre* (1915–1918); *Texte inédit, établit et annoté par Marcelle Cinq-Mars*, Montreal: Athéna, 2006, p. 332.

† Tremblay, *Journal de guerre*. Translation in Raphaël Dallaire Ferland, "Patriotism and Allegiances of the 22nd (French Canadian) Battalion, 1914–1918," accessed March 15, 2016, http://www.journal.forces.gc.ca/vol13/no1/page51-eng.asp.

embodied the military prowess and valour of the country's francophones. They were *le bras qui sait porter l'épée*, the "arm ready to wield the sword," to quote the original words of *Ô Canada*—which at the time was the national anthem of French Canadians only.

When the battalion first reached the trenches of the Belgian front, on September 22, 1915, Tremblay wrote, "All are happy and proud, and determined to honour French Canadians." On October 10, after the battalion stood firm in the face of fierce shelling, the Division Commander congratulated his men, which stoked their pride. Two weeks later, men of the 22nd fought with a group of English-Canadian gunners: "Our men prevailed, and the artillerymen had to flee. . . ."

On February 26, 1916 (the day he was confirmed as lieutenant-colonel and officially replaced Gaudet, having been interim commander since January 25 and "perhaps the youngest [battalion] commanding officer at the front"), he wrote, "My battalion represents an entire race; it is a heavy responsibility. Nonetheless, I have confidence in myself and I feel that my men respect me. My acts will be guided by our inspiring motto, 'Je me souviens.'"*

On June 23, 1916, the 1st Division under Major General Arthur Currie claimed that the 22nd had abandoned positions. Tremblay defended his battalion's actions and took his fight all the way to the corps commander, Lieutenant General Julian Byng, convincing him of the truth: that the Van Doos had in fact advanced several outposts beyond their assigned mission. The last thing Tremblay wanted was for his battalion to be scapegoated. He bemoaned the fact that the insinuations only fostered ill feeling within the Corps, and had even sparked fights between men of the two divisions. When the same allegations resurfaced on July 17 and 19, Tremblay was quite simply furious.

Two months later, Tremblay and his men had the opportunity to prove themselves fully. As they set out to take the village of Courcelette, in the Somme Valley, they knew they were going "to the slaughter." But morale was extraordinarily high, and they were "determined to prove

---

* Ibid.

that the *Canayens* are not slackers." Tremblay told his men: "We will take that village, and once we have taken it, we will hold it to the last man. This is our first big attack. It must succeed, for the honour of all the French Canadians whom we represent in France."* It was only after they were relieved, following three days of fierce fighting, that they realized the magnitude of their victory. It was, Tremblay wrote, all due to his men's ardour, perseverance, and tenacity. The other units met by the returning soldiers of the 22nd hailed them as heroes.

The capture of Courcelette was a victory shared with other battalions of the Canadian Corps, but it entered the country's military lore as the Van Doos' triumph. On September 15, 1917, by which time Tremblay was interim brigadier general, the 22nd organized a meal, simultaneously marking two years since his arrival in France and the first anniversary of the battle at Courcelette. Since then, the anniversary has been celebrated every year by the Royal 22e Régiment.

Tremblay was granted special leave to England from November 23 to December 6, 1917, at the request of the postmaster general of Canada, Pierre-Édouard Blondin. On November 27, he had a chance meeting with one Max Aitken, Lord Beaverbrook. Tremblay believed him to be responsible for the hateful campaign in the British press denigrating his French-Canadian "race": when the Canadian-born Aitken had gone to England and become a newspaper baron, he had evidently taken some of his compatriots' prejudices with him. The two men exchanged words: Tremblay told Aitken in no uncertain terms that his newspapers should cease their vilification of French Canadians, especially given Britons' admiration of their deeds at Courcelette. Beaverbrook promised he would tell his journalist to moderate his tone. Tremblay's view was that, while the British may have regretted that French Canadians were not fighting in the war in greater numbers, they did not, contrary to the assertions in Lord Beaverbrook's broadsheets, think them cowards. The press magnate did keep his word, and Tremblay later remarked that the tone of articles about his compatriots was less

* Ibid.

harsh. There was also no doubt in the lieutenant colonel's mind that "right now, the 22nd is saving Quebec's reputation."*

On July 23, 1917, the commander of the 5th Brigade, Brigadier General A.H. Macdonell, was replaced. In Tremblay's mind, he ought to have been removed long before that: Macdonell had shown no interest in what Tremblay's brigade had accomplished at Courcelette, and had even berated an officer for a meal served late while his men were being killed. Macdonell's replacement was John Munro Ross, commander of the 29th Battalion. He was less experienced than Tremblay, who found the decision difficult to accept: he regretted not having won the promotion, among other reasons because it would have favoured his second-in-command in the Van Doos.

Tremblay brought up the slight with the new brigade commander as well as 2nd Division commander Major General H.E. Burstall, who had gone to RMC Kingston and was from Quebec City. Dissatisfied with their explanations, he asked for a meeting with the new commander of the Canadian Corps, Arthur Currie. Everyone, it seemed, lauded Tremblay's work, but he did not receive a promotion. He wondered whether Freemasonry had played a role in the affair. He considered asking to be relieved of his command, but his sense of duty trumped his frustration and he thought better of it. On August 13, a major brigade exercise was held, reviewed by Burstall. The Van Doos were congratulated as the finest battalion in the division, but the compliments were hard to swallow after the injustice done to Tremblay.

A century later, such situations in Canada's military are practically non-existent, in the wake of the passage of the *Official Languages Act* in the late 1960s. That advance, which can be said to have been a necessary one, has proven effective despite causing frustrations on both sides of the linguistic divide in the ensuing years. While merit has always been the basis for all promotions, anglophones have felt they had been denied promotions because they lacked sufficient ability in French, while francophones have seen their promotions questioned by

* Ibid.

English-speaking colleagues who claimed that their advancement was due solely to their linguistic background.

ON SEPTEMBER 17, 1915, marching toward the trenches for the first time, Tremblay was beset by an attack of hemorrhoids. A year later, at Courcelette, the ailment came back to haunt him to the point that he was nearly unable to walk and take part in the battalion's and the brigade's celebrations of the landmark victory. He had to leave the front on September 22, and was transferred to England, where he underwent surgery. While convalescing, he read newspaper accounts of the Battle of Courcelette that ranked it—and the 22nd's accomplishments—among the most brilliant exploits of the Somme Offensive.

Beginning on April 15, 1918, Tremblay was again treated for the same condition, at the No. 3 Canadian Stationary Hospital in Doullens. He was there when the facility was bombed from the air on May 29—resulting in several dead, including three Canadian army nurses—despite the huge Red Cross flags flying over the building, which the German pilots must have seen. Tremblay helped save many wounded from the burning ruins. He rejoined his battalion shortly thereafter, but had to return to the Doullens hospital from June 3 to 25. Though not completely recovered, he pleaded with the physician colonel and secured the papers certifying that he was again ready for combat.

THERE WITH AND FOR HIS MEN

In the fall of 1915, with the 22nd entrenched at the Belgian front, Tremblay wrote of how, after one of the many rainstorms typical of autumn and winter weather in Flanders, the water in the trenches rose as far as the soldiers' knees and sometimes to their hips. They tried drying out the trenches, but to no avail: either more rains filled them in again or German shelling wiped out the men's work. The only consolation, he wrote, was that Canadian artillery was dishing out the same to the enemy.

Undaunted, he kept trying to improve things. In November 1915, he proposed building a sandbag wall along a road parallel to the trenches so the soldiers could climb out, yet remain out of the Germans' sight. The neighbouring battalions agreed, but the results were not exactly conclusive because of the enemy and the relentless rain. Tremblay worked often and hard, and his visits to the trenches slated to be occupied by his unit were remarked upon. Once his men were entrenched, he made frequent inspections: he did so twice on September 26, 1915, for example, only returning to his quarters at one-thirty in the morning.

It was not the only time that Tremblay would lose sleep for a similar reason. Soldiers would later recall how their commander would suddenly turn up to check the condition of the trenches or improve a firing position. This proximity to soldiers is an important aspect of command, and Tremblay's persistence brought excellent results, as well as praise for the battalion from superiors. Lieutenant General Edwin Alderson, commander of the Canadian Army Corps, made an incognito visit to the 22nd on April 14, 1916, and subsequently congratulated Tremblay on the Van Doos' trench discipline. In August, Tremblay ordered repairs made to the trenches that his men were about to vacate for the incoming 75th Battalion of the 4th Canadian Division. His superior applauded him; Tremblay replied that "the Ontario battalions wouldn't do the same for us."

Tremblay also accompanied his men on exercises, joining an October 1915 grenade-throwing practice, for example. In September 1916, as the 2nd Division was preparing for its first major attack of the Somme Offensive, he led one of the squads during a demonstration of how to capture a position in an attack, leaving to his second-in-command the task of explaining the details of the manoeuvre to the other members of the battalion.

Losses were never easy to accept. On September 20, 1915, the battalion's first day in the trenches, one man was seriously injured. Within days, others would pay the ultimate price—including, on October 6, Major Adolphe Roy, whom Tremblay described as one of the 22nd's most determined officers: he died while courageously trying to remove an enemy explosive charge that had fallen into the trench, in the process saving the lives of many brothers in arms. "For how many other officers is that fate in store?" he wondered.

From February 16 to 22, 1916, the death toll in the trenches of the 22nd was twenty-seven, a number that Tremblay considered "too high." But on March 19, after visiting the Kemmelberg area, site of their next assignment, he learned that the English battalion they would be replacing was losing an average of ten men a day. This prompted Tremblay to describe the shelling the Van Doos had endured to that point as "child's play"; he added that with his men's impending arrival in Saint-Éloi, there was "a good chance they will be seeing Heaven soon."

On April 8, 1916, having no news of one of the first two members of the 22nd to have been decorated, following a brutal German attack, Tremblay wrote: "I am anxiously hoping that this brave boy has not been killed"; he would later learn that he had. After the fierce fighting in the Battle of Mont Sorrel, in June 1916, he recommended officers, non-commissioned officers, and privates for decoration, lamenting the lack of such recognition.

Tremblay was very close to his men. On March 1, 1916, he sent two soldiers to try out a new type of explosive charge known as a Bangalore torpedo, designed for, among other things, clearing barbed wire. When they returned, he asked for a report. Private Deblois replied, "Well, colonel, you said it would blow; me, I said it would take me five minutes to go lay that charge, it took five minutes; there's no more barbed wire in that spot." Tremblay wrote that this was an example of a "clear, precise report from my men" and described the two soldiers he'd chosen as "*Canayens avec du poil aux pattes*" (literally, "Canayens with hairy paws"; figuratively, gutsy and resourceful men). Seventeen days later, Deblois was decorated for another of his many exploits. On July 17, it was Sergeant Lavoie's turn in the spotlight, when some men of the 22nd were jeered at by a bunch of English soldiers: he stopped his men, went and "laid out" the seven "blokes," and then set off again. Tremblay, who happened to witness the scene, wrote "Lavoie is a good man and a real *Canayen*," adding that what he'd done was "the only way to earn those people's respect."

Tremblay did not hesitate to share in his men's hardship, as happened on April 3, 1916. The day before, everyone had been vaccinated against paratyphoid fever, which made most of the battalion sick for two or three days. That night, they received orders to march the next day to a new position, more than fourteen kilometres distant. Tremblay protested in vain to his superior officer. The next morning, he refused to mount his horse, and led his battalion on foot. It was a shining example: only nineteen stragglers had to be picked up by the buses and ambulances that followed the battalion at Tremblay's request.

At Courcelette, Tremblay marched amid his men toward their objective. He sent the battalion's C Company forward, though they had been relegated to the rear since August for having been five minutes late for an assembly, a punishment that was supposed to last six months. More than once the lieutenant colonel wrote in his diary of how his "Canayens" showed their mettle and succeeded in reaching their objective despite multiple losses suffered while pushing through the enemy's artillery barrage. Tremblay wrote at length about the actions of several members of his battalion, a large number of whom were killed, injured, or evacuated for shell shock.

"Sublime" individual acts of courage were common, he noted on September 16. Two men, a former trapper and a scout from the battalion, went over the top to capture a German prisoner at gunpoint from a company that was busy digging a trench; the tale seemed implausible, but the prisoner confirmed it. Morale was very good, despite extreme fatigue following thirty-six straight hours of fighting. The men had taken the village and were holding it, Tremblay wrote, like "lions." They were finally relieved after three days of uninterrupted combat.

Describing the horrendous conditions of the attack on September 15—houses ablaze, bayonet charges, bodies everywhere, the continual moans of the injured—he concluded by remarking, "Man's physical and moral resistance is beyond belief," and, most famously, "If hell were as abominable as what I saw in Courcelette, then I would not wish my worst enemy to go there."*

On January 1, 1918, Lieutenant Colonel Tremblay said he hoped that the battalion would celebrate their next New Year's Day with their families. The *anciens*, who had heard him make the same promise in previous years, grinned in disbelief. These "old originals" of the battalion were the toughest; on their shoulders rested the honour of the battalion and the fact that the French-Canadian "race" no longer suffered the slurs of Beaverbrook's bunch. Would their compatriots understand this when the men returned home? Tremblay wondered. By that point, the *anciens* were few and far between: at Courcelette in September 1916, the 22nd had suffered some 300 casualties, including 207 killed; during the following engagement on October 1, the battalion lost another 300 men, including 200 dead. The year 1917 had been less bloody, but there were still dozens killed and injured.

The soldiers and officers under Tremblay's command were not the only ones to brave danger: he himself lived through his share of close shaves. On September 26, 1915, a Belgian civilian tried to shoot him; the man gave chase, but to no avail. In late October, shrapnel hit a trench he was inspecting and he wound up on his back, covered in sandbags. Two weeks later, a captain at his side was shot in the leg. On January 25, 1916, just after he was made battalion commander, his headquarters were heavily shelled by German artillery. There were forty or so men inside, but no one was injured. Noting that a pig had been killed and a cat hurt, Tremblay concluded that the enemy were choosing their targets poorly. On April 27, 1917, his shirt collar was

* Translation in Geoff Keelan, "'Il a bien merité de la Patrie': The 22nd Battalion and the Memory of Courcelette," in *Canadian Military History* 19(3), p. 12 (footnote 9).

torn by a piece of flying shrapnel, prompting him to muse that he was "not yet ready to live among the angels."

At Courcelette, Tremblay put himself in harm's way as he led his companies to the village, and then, after losing several officers and runners, directed operations himself, running from one location to another. Three times he was buried by German shelling, and on one such occasion had to be dug out by his men. At Passchendaele, speaking to wounded returning from the front lines—where the Van Doos were headed—he grasped that the conditions were horrific and that losses would be heavy. But he was not afraid; he had faith in his "lucky star," and in the prayers of his mother and his sister, a Franciscan nun. He was ready to face death again, "if it had a purpose," and concluded, "In a few hours perhaps we shall revisit hell." The 22nd lost a hundred men in the mud of Passchendaele "with no resounding glory for [the] battalion," but there was a sense that they had accomplished their duty.

Tremblay generally disapproved of small-scale offensives, for the cost was terribly high compared with the reward. He expressed this reservation often to his superiors, but always obeyed orders. When one such action was cancelled, in February 1916, he wrote that he was pleased. On August 5, 1918, preparations were underway for the Battle of Amiens, the start of what later became known as the Hundred Days Offensive. Tremblay went to see his superior, Brigadier General John Munro Ross, upset that the 22nd Battalion had been assigned a support role rather than being included in the assault wave. He suspected the real reason was that, once the initial element of surprise was absorbed, the Van Doos would then be asked to lead the attack; at that point, they would have to act without the huge preparations of the first day, with consequent greater losses. When the brigadier general refused to change his plan, Tremblay simply said he would obey orders even though his superior had broken a promise to him. The attack was launched on August 8; later that day his batman was killed beside him. On the 9th, Ross was wounded, and Tremblay became interim commander of the 5th Brigade, of which the 22nd Battalion was a part.

His promotion to brigadier general was confirmed on September 15. In the wake of the bitter fighting of that month, which saw the brigade complement reduced to that of a battalion, he would have to organize replacements.

On October 9, Tremblay, ever at the front even as brigadier general, was first to enter Cambrai, on horseback; there was no opposition, as the battalions had already pushed past the town. His brigade's contribution to the operation earned him congratulations from the higher echelons of the Canadian Expeditionary Force. The men were tired, he wrote, but feverish after their successes of the past days.

A week after the Armistice, the 5th Brigade began its march into Germany: Tremblay lamented the pointless destruction wrought by the retreating enemy forces, who in several instances blew up their munitions and left large parts of cities in ruins. On December 5, the brigade crossed the border; on the 13th, they arrived in Bonn and mustered the battalions for occupation. Tremblay was impressed by his group as they paraded past General Currie: "It is pouring rain and they are soaked to the bone," he wrote, "but my men look as proud as can be."

Thomas-Louis Tremblay was decorated several times during his time in combat. When he learned on May 29, 1917, that he was to be made an officer of France's Légion d'honneur, he said the unexpected decoration was the one that meant the most to him. At the ceremony on July 9, Tremblay was surprised by the large number of staff officers being decorated, compared with frontline officers like himself, whom he felt were those truly deserving of such distinctions.

At other times, he could not help but consider the scope of the calamity that was the First World War. In hospital in London, learning of the huge losses suffered by the 22nd just after Courcelette, he noted, "Madness reigns in Europe: it is impossible to rationalize the causes of such sacrifices. People simply do not give a damn about logic, there is no reasoning any longer." In February 1917, after his first long stay in hospital, he had to delay a few days in Le Havre. When he received his marching orders, he wrote that despite feeling well at Le Havre, he was like "the other madmen," adding, "I am eager to rejoin my unit." On September 21, 1917, he again wrote, "We are all madmen in this war." Two days later, he returned to the battlefield, as thousands of other injured or ill combatants had done once rehabilitated. Every one of them knew he was off once again to the slaughter, didn't care, and marched toward his destination as if it were his "regular occupation"—as if this enterprise were perfectly normal.

The bonds that are forged in an army unit are as strong today as they were in 1914–1918. To remain behind while one is recovering from injury or illness, as one's brothers in arms face danger, is to feel profound guilt. When confronted with an enemy determined to eliminate him, moreover, the soldier experiences a level of stimulation that he will know nowhere else. For many, the experience is akin to a drug—one they are eager to ingest again quickly, no matter the price to pay.

DISCIPLINARIAN

The young lieutenant colonel was also a harsh taskmaster, taking after Gaudet, who on June 4, 1915, following thirty instances of absence without leave, had confined the entire battalion to quarters for forty-eight hours. On New Year's Day 1916, one of the men of the 22nd left his post to meet with some Germans. Tremblay acknowledged that the soldier had returned with useful information, but, because he had not acted under orders, a reprimand was in order. In February 1917, following a disastrous raid by the 4th Division that left many casualties in No Man's Land, one of his sergeants decided to recover several of the fallen single-handed: he brought back thirteen men but suffered a bullet wound on the way back from his last incursion into the German barbed wire. Tremblay concluded that the action, corroborated by several witnesses, was "practically unbelievable" but needed to be punished. Yet he also thought it deserved the Victoria Cross, which he was unable to secure.

Unfortunately, there were other, far more serious acts of indiscipline. In November 1916, while Tremblay was convalescing in England, his replacement, Major Arthur-Édouard Dubuc, described a number of soldiers who had arrived as reinforcements following losses in the Somme Offensive as "rather degenerate," for having frequented "loose women." Venereal disease was a problem throughout the Canadian Army Corps; the battalion was then stationed at Fosse No. 10, near Lens, France, where there were many prostitutes. In January 1917, as Tremblay was preparing to return to his unit, General Turner, the then commander of the 5th Division in England, told him that there were many illegal absences among the men of the 22nd, and that he was eager for Tremblay to return and restore some semblance of discipline.

When Tremblay returned to his battalion on February 15, 1917, after four months away, he immediately realized that the exemplary esprit de corps that had existed before the Somme Offensive had vanished with the massive influx of new men and officers. He set about in earnest to restore it. The officers were severely taken to task for having let the 22nd deteriorate. On Sunday, July 15, Tremblay asked the battalion chaplain to include the issue of illegal absences in his sermon. He then spoke on the subject himself, emphasizing the gravity of the offence and the awful penalties that would ensue (two deserters from the battalion had been executed earlier that month). The honour of the battalion would not be undermined by the actions of a few, he warned, which hearkened back to his original vision of his role in the war. In all, five men of the 22nd would be executed for desertion between April 1917 and May 1918 (the death penalty was a provision in all armies of the Empire, except Australia's).

Tremblay's concern for matters of discipline continued after he was promoted to brigadier general. On December 13, 1918, shortly after the occupation of Bonn began, he saw many Germans peering out from behind the curtains of their homes but few out in the streets. That same day, he took up residence in the castle of a man named Hagan, a prominent industrialist and financier in that part of Germany. The next morning, he threw his host out into the street, saying he didn't like the face of the "dirty Boche" and adding, "I especially hate such people for the atrocities committed in France." Upon reading the instructions for the occupation, he found them severe but fair. On the 15th, he gathered the five mayors of the area under his responsibility and explained, in detail and undiplomatically, that they were to tell their citizens that their territory was occupied, that the Allies were the victors, and that their presence must not be merely tolerated. Except for murder, rape, and pillaging, he wrote, the Allies' laws of occupation resembled those of the Germans in France and Belgium, adding, "I shall enforce those laws to the letter."

AFTERMATH

Tremblay made his final war diary entry on December 20, 1918. The 2nd Canadian Division's role in the occupation was discontinued in 1919 and Tremblay, along with several members of the division, was transferred to England in April of that year. The group returned to Canada the following month, and Tremblay was demobilized on May 31. He resumed service as a major in the 57th Artillery Battery, as there was no position available for a brigadier general. On October 31, 1920, he was transferred to the Officers' Reserve. The next day, he became honorary colonel of the Voltigeurs de Québec Regiment. For several years after 1919, he served as honorary aide-de-camp to the governor general of Canada and as vice-president of Canadian Legion War Services. On April 1, 1931, he succeeded Marshal Ferdinand Foch as honorary colonel of the Royal 22e Régiment, a position he held until the end of his life. He returned to his military alma mater from 1931 to 1933 as a member of the RMC Kingston Advisory Committee.

Tremblay resumed professional life as a civil engineer and was named a commissioner of the Port of Quebec; in 1921, he became the port's general manager and chief engineer. In 1923, he was a member of the McLean Royal Commission on Great Lakes Grain Rates. In

1928, he was named president of the American Association of Port Authorities; from 1927 to 1929, he was vice-president of an association opposing water pollution. In 1939, he was appointed to the British Columbia-Yukon-Alaska Highway Commission; its report was submitted in August 1941.

In December 1939, concurrently with his role on the Alaska Highway Commission, Tremblay became inspector general of Canadian Forces in Eastern Canada, with the rank of major general. In October 1942, the Department of Defence lent his services to the Department of Labour for an assignment of nearly seven months as an assistant deputy director with the National Selection Service. He resigned his inspector general position on January 31, 1946, and retired to Lauzon (now part of Lévis, Quebec) on March 19, aged fifty-nine.

Thomas-Louis Tremblay died March 28, 1951, in Quebec City, after a brief illness. In June 1922, he had married Marie Hamel, the daughter of a Quebec City merchant; they had two sons, Jacques and Louis.

Tremblay's vision of a battalion representative of the French-Canadian "race" had proved so successful and had impressed so many that, after being removed from the Canadian Army's order of battle in 1919, the 22nd was reborn on April 1, 1920, this time as a regiment in the Permanent Active Militia.

The presence of a French-language unit in the regular land forces opened the door to enrolment by thousands of other French Canadians in the Second World War. Tremblay was well aware of this and, in a June 1944 message in *L'Auxiliaire du 22e*, a magazine published for the regiment's extended family, though he was writing as a representative of the 22nd, he could not ignore the fact that he was also the army's inspector general for Eastern Canada: "Of course, not all French Canadians are in the 22nd: there are some in most of the Canadian regiments." He then listed the other francophone regiments and hailed "the other French-language units serving overseas" (in addition to four francophone regiments there were, among others, an artillery battery, an air squadron, and field ambulances using French as their official language).

Tremblay also saw the beginning of the Korean War, in which the Royal 22e Régiment made up close to a third of Canada's infantry. But he did not live to witness the full flowering of francophone influence in the country's armed forces: a Regular Army brigade, several bases, RCAF squadrons, vessels, and, for a time, a Royal Military College. Many of these innovations were envisioned and implemented by officers and men of the 22nd. The success of the French language in Canada's armed forces was so conclusive that it influenced the discussions leading to the creation of francophone units in the federal public service beginning in the 1970s.

Thomas-Louis Tremblay probably could not have foreseen that particular outcome, but there is no doubt that, had the 22nd battalion of 1915–1918 failed in its mission, none of what we have just described would have happened—at least not the way it did.

COURAGE AND DETERMINATION

As a military man, Thomas-Louis Tremblay embodied sacrifice, courage, and determination: he appreciated his men, cared for their well-being, and showed that he was prepared to fully share their fate—all essential qualities in a great leader. He stood up to his superiors when he was convinced he was right, but once orders were given, he carried out his missions with loyalty while trying to minimize whatever negative impacts he could foresee for the men under his command.

As we have seen, he had a particular vision of his role and that of his battalion in the First World War, living according to his own culture within an English-speaking milieu that was not always receptive to it, and he hewed to that vision throughout his time at the front. Though illness, leave, or training would keep Tremblay away from the front for twelve of his thirty-one months in the war, the impact of that vision on the sociology and configuration of Canada's armed forces as well as those of the federal public service was felt over both the medium and the long term. French is far more prominent in the Canadian

Forces today than in 1915, though its use remains problematic in the major headquarters. Today's francophone minority must remain vigilant and ready, as the members of the 22nd Battalion were during the Great War, to fully assume their rightful place.

JEREMY KINSMAN

GEORGES VANIER

ON MAY 1, 1945, General Georges Vanier delivered a message "to the Canadian people" over the airwaves of the CBC, describing what he had seen in the just-liberated Nazi concentration camp of Buchenwald. A national broadcast was an ambitious undertaking for a mere diplomat. But this French-Canadian hero of the Great War, who now had become Canada's first ambassador to France, already seemed destined for much larger things.

The Canadians who heard his broadcast recognized him only as a public figure. Few knew the depth of Vanier's Christian convictions. His religious beliefs were shaken by what he'd seen in World War II, but his faith in the power of redemption through mercy was never truly extinguished. Today, Vanier has been dead for almost a full half-century. But as the scourge of modern terrorism unleashes fresh waves of violence and hatred, his message could not be more relevant.

When Vanier spoke to Canadians on the radio that day in 1945, he focused on the obligation we owed to Europe's legions of new refugees. Just weeks before, some of the first images of Nazi Germany's systemic atrocities were published in the Western press, following the liberation of Bergen-Belsen by the British and Canadian armies. When

U.S. troops took Buchenwald, Vanier pulled military rank to get aboard a military plane transporting a small delegation of congressmen dispatched to the site by President Harry Truman. (His specific task was to determine the fate of three brave Canadian officers who'd been captured during an intelligence-gathering mission—and he eventually confirmed they had been executed months before.)

Vanier was shocked. "We visited the death chambers and saw the quadruple electric lifts on which bodies were raised to the ovens of the crematorium above," he later wrote. "In the ovens, blackened forms of bodies still lay. We saw also the noise-making machine that drowned the screams of the unfortunate victims. We were told that the death quota for the camp was 80 a day. Facilities existed for the easy, continuous cremation of that many. This quota was often exceeded, however, which accounted apparently for the naked bodies, piled like so much cord wood, and on which lime was thrown."

What Vanier saw at Buchenwald challenged his faith in divine purpose, and he ruefully laid blame for the incalculable cruelty at the door of a German nation that "calls itself Christian." Yet in the same breath, Vanier also cited the atrocity as justification for "why they [Canadian soldiers] are fighting, why some of their comrades have been killed and why others bear wounds."

As early as 1942, Vanier had tried to persuade Ottawa to help save thousands of Jewish children orphaned in France after the Germans made their first round-up of Jewish adults. Later, he recalled "how deaf we were then to cruelty and the cries of pain which came to our ears, grim forerunners of the mass torture and murder which were to follow."

Vanier's humanitarian hopes were initially thwarted by institutionalized prejudice in the Canadian halls of power—as authoritatively documented by Irving Abella and Harold Troper in their landmark 1983 book *None Is Too Many: Canada and the Jews of Europe* 1933–1948. But eventually, Vanier's persistence helped move Ottawa's careerist establishment into action.

Because Vanier would go on to become governor general, we now forget that he spent much of his career being perceived as an outsider—a French Canadian walking the halls of power in what was still a largely anglophone-dominated country. During the interwar years and the dark days of Nazi occupation, he represented Canada to the people of Western Europe. He endured the electrifying experience of France's collapse in 1940, and then championed Charles de Gaulle in his agonizing effort to represent and redeem France's honour. At critical moments, when history hung in the balance, Vanier was especially insistent on two issues: that, despite reticence in Washington, Canada should recognize the legitimacy of de Gaulle's Free French government-in-exile; and that Ottawa should offer a haven for refugees displaced by war and persecution.

Events take strange turns. Though Vanier always spoke truth to anglophone power, Quebec nationalists attempted to smear him as a symbol of Anglo domination after he became governor general in 1959. Ironically, these nationalists—or separatists, as they later became—drew strength from the odd late-life choice of de Gaulle to encourage Canada's breakup. Not so many years before, Canada had featured among the first rank of France's friends during its darkest days, due largely to Vanier's efforts.

Yet it was Vanier who got the last laugh—or, at least, so it appears by today's lights. When Quebec turned away from a nativist Catholic Church that had become narrow and untrusting, Vanier offered Quebec a non-doctrinal form of inclusive humanism. And in today's largely secular French-Canadian society, it is his vision that prevails. (The separatists, meanwhile, seem very much in retreat.)

More broadly, Vanier anticipated Canada's modern spirit of liberal internationalism and the pluralistic spirit of tolerance we now take for granted—as embodied in our current government's enlightened approach to admitting those fleeing from war in the Middle East.

⚜ ⚜ ⚜ ⚜

GEORGES VANIER WAS BORN in Montreal in 1888, the son of a reasonably well-off businessman father, Phileas, whose Québécois ancestors could be traced to the seventeenth century, and an Irish mother, Margaret. She was awkward in French, and Phileas went along with English as the family language—in part because it kept him up to speed for business purposes.

After being educated by the Jesuits at Loyola College, Georges made the important decision, while still in his teens, to live an immersed life as a French Canadian. For two years, he retooled himself in language and philosophy under French tutors who instilled in him, among other things, a love of France. That nation, in time, would become his second homeland.

After earning a law degree from Laval University, Vanier got caught up in the patriotic exuberance of September 1914. He signed on with the Canadian army for a military campaign expected to be over by Christmas. It wasn't an obvious decision for a young French-Canadian professional. But there were enough enthusiasts in Quebec to form Canada's first francophone battalion—the 22nd, which, in time, would famously become known as the "Van Doos." The friendships that Vanier developed in this unit would become the most cherished of his lifetime.

Sent to France as a machine-gun officer, Vanier was badly wounded twice: in 1915, by an exploding shell, and then by gunfire in 1918, leading to the amputation of his right leg. During his long recuperation in England, Vanier drew comfort from his faith and made the decision to remain enlisted. Sir Arthur Currie, inspector-general of the Canadian Army, scoffed that it would be "impossible" for Vanier to continue fighting with only one leg. Vanier retorted: "Do you want people with brains?"

After returning to Montreal, Vanier did not let his disability prevent him from cutting the image of a tall, striking military officer. At the Ritz-Carlton hotel, on one occasion, he ran into another military veteran taking tea with a radiant young woman. The mutual attraction was instant. Pauline Archer was another child of French–English duality—her father a prominent Superior Court justice and her mother related to old French nobility. Pauline broke off a prior engagement and married Georges in Notre-Dame Basilica.

Called to Ottawa as aide-de-camp to a new governor general—Lord Byng, who had commanded Canada's troops in France—Vanier took up residence with his wife in "The Cottage," on the grounds of Rideau Hall (which, as of this writing, now serves as the temporary home of Prime Minister Justin Trudeau and his young family). Byng steered Vanier to the British staff college at Camberley, where the Canadian recipient of the British Military Cross and the French Croix de Guerre was a star, at one point receiving an invitation to lunch with King George VI.

After a spell as second-in-command of the 22nd—now upgraded from battalion to regiment—Vanier was seconded in 1927 to the Canadian delegation to the League of Nations. In hindsight, we know the League to have been a hopelessly idealistic aspiration, given the lack of U.S. participation and the growing militarism within Germany. But at the time, the organization was seen as a bulwark against a repeat of the Great War's horrors.

In grand halls set back from Lake Geneva, and on lawns where peacocks strolled, diplomats talked and talked. Vanier engaged seriously in the negotiations to limit navies and arms production, and to define rules for the conduct of war (especially regarding the treatment of prisoners, many provisions of which remain in force to this day). Still, he resisted the idea of giving up his soldier's identity for that of career diplomat. Turning down an offer to join the Canadian legation in Washington under Vincent Massey, Vanier explained to Mackenzie King's private secretary that he "didn't want to accept a position the duties of which would be entirely foreign to army work."

By 1931, however, Vanier agreed to accept an appointment as secretary to the Canadian high commission in London, the city that official Canada still looked upon as the real centre of the known universe. Ottawa's fledgling foreign policy establishment took its cues and lines from Whitehall, which paid little heed to Canadian interests. Prominent Canadians in London generally kept a low profile, aspiring to become more or less successful imitations of conservative English gentlemen.

But the stylish Vaniers were not the provincials whom the British had expected. And Londoners were struck by the tight bond between husband and wife. "We always thought of them as one," an acquaintance remarked. Pauline's vivacity complemented Georges's credentials as war hero, made vivid by his prosthetic leg, though the stress of reconciling the demands of a young family and a full official calendar resulted in a few bouts of self-doubt and depression.

The Vaniers grew close again to Byng, by now head of Scotland Yard. In what Vanier described as a "miracle of friendship," Byng insisted on paying some of Pauline's hospital bills after a serious operation. (By this time, Georges's family income had been slashed by the effects of the Depression. At one point, his mother had even been forced to sell her jewels.)

Vanier and Byng discussed the prospect of Massey becoming the next Canadian high commissioner. Byng believed the well-bred Torontonian was "too Balliol" for the job. And Georges agreed the snooty anglophile "was the least typical of Canadians." But after winning election in 1935, Prime Minister Mackenzie King felt obliged to appoint Massey (who had served him as cabinet minister in the 1920s)—though he would later say he never trusted the man.

Vanier's relations with Massey were cordial. But what Vanier biographer Robert Speaight described vaguely as an "incompatibility between two mystiques" kept them from being close. Massey's highborn persona alienated Vanier, just as Vanier's attachment to his beloved regiment mystified Massey.

More consequently, Vanier related differently to London, and to the Empire. The Vaniers loved England in many ways, but Georges bristled at the assumption that Canadians were inconsequential subordinates whom British officers would command in war and counsel in peace. He also pushed back on Canada's absence from the British Committee of Imperial Defence, arguing that when Canadian questions were being considered, Canadian participation should be mandatory.

Massey, on the other hand, took a more conciliatory approach. And his hunger for British approval would pit him against Vanier on a variety of issues. During World War II, the high commissioner pressed Ottawa not to break relations with the Vichy regime in defeated France, while Vanier argued that Canada should support de Gaulle's exiled force. Later, they would again be on opposite sides of the debate over accepting Jewish refugees, a topic on which Massey's old Toronto prejudices corrupted his judgment.

Byng died in the spring of 1935, amid an employment crisis in Britain and a rising fascist tide in Germany. When Vanier, who had spent weeks with Byng after an earlier heart attack, fell into a depression, Pauline pressed him to seek solace from R.H.J. Steuart, an ex-war chaplain and a Jesuit priest at Mayfair's Farm Street Church. Steuart's spiritual writing addressed the despair of the times in the language of a soldier: "War is a ghastly thing, but it breeds a very intimate brotherhood among wonderfully dissimilar brothers and when it is over leaves a gap that all the arts and blandishments of peace can never fill." Vanier took solace in Steuart's teachings—especially his belief that the emotional gap he spoke of could be filled by extending mercy to the less fortunate.

At the end of 1938, Vanier's career took a defining turn when Mackenzie King appointed him minister and head of the Canadian legation in Paris. (At the time, Canada still had no formally designated ambassadors or embassies of its own.) At a farewell dinner in his honour at the Savoy Hotel, attended by hundreds including members of the British cabinet, Vanier gave what King later described as "one of the best speeches ever delivered in London."

In Paris, Vanier found a country in crisis. The flappers of the Jazz Age, painters in Montmartre, and the café society of the Coupole hadn't obscured the enduring national melancholy over the appalling toll of the Great War—during which six of every ten men between the ages of eighteen and twenty-nine had either died or suffered serious wounds. The shadow over the country cast by missing husbands, brothers, and fathers had only darkened with the onset of economic depression.

France's Popular Front government, led by Jewish socialist Leon Blum, gave way in 1938 to a new coalition containing militant right-wing politicians, some of them openly anti-Semitic. The left railed against the new regime's increasing appeasement of Hitler's aggressions, while refugees from Nazi Germany streamed into France.

Optimism that the 1938 Munich agreement could bring "peace in our time" evaporated as Hitler stirred up a revanchist frenzy among Germans. As troops were being called up, Vanier predicted, "It looks like war"—though the Christian soldier still found reason for hope. "War is such a horrible thing that there are, there must be powerful moral forces—the greatest of which is prayer. . . . And so, perhaps the miracle [of peace] may happen."

It didn't, of course. Having secured the Soviet Union's partnership in carving up Eastern Europe, Germany invaded Poland in September 1939, and Canada followed Britain and France in declaring war. Vanier described the French as stoical, and predicted they would put up a fierce fight. In reporting a French cabinet shuffle on September 14, he noted the creation of the new position of under-secretary of war, but didn't name the appointee, a just-promoted general named Charles de Gaulle.

After an eight-month interregnum, the Germans smashed into France on May 9, 1940, striking to the north of the massive (and ultimately useless) Maginot Line fortifications. When news reached Paris, the Vaniers were at a dinner hosted by the U.S. ambassador. Officers got up from tables, gathered in groups, and dispersed, reminding Vanier of Thackeray's description of the Duchess of Richmond's ball in Brussels, the night before the Battle of Waterloo.

No one expected the French army to collapse as quickly as it did. Winston Churchill, freshly sworn in as British prime minister, told the House of Commons it was a "colossal military disaster," the German advance having cut off "the whole root and core and brain" of the British Expeditionary Force. But a silver lining emerged when 338,226 Allied soldiers were evacuated to Britain from the beaches of Dunkirk. Many of these troops would form the nucleus of the new armies that confronted the Nazis in the years that followed.

Vanier took the weakening pulse of French leaders repeatedly, and had a front-row seat for their rapid collapse. On June 9, 1940, Supreme

Commander Maxime Weygand, a favourite of the right who had been tasked with staunching the German offensive, told Vanier the situation was "not hopeful." This proved to be an understatement. The next day, the Ministry of War announced it was relocating to Tours. Much of the French government followed, accompanied by fleeing Parisians.

Late on June 10, with key papers having been burned, the legation's Canadian personnel also left town. From his seat in the last of five cars, Vanier captured an image of the capital in its agony: "I know Paris well and have seen it in many moods: never has it affected me as it did that night." A strong wind blew "papers in the streets in a crazy fashion—nature responding to man's folly." From out of this wind, Vanier picked out "the smell of cordite—it was the smell of the battlefield again, after 26 years."

What ordinarily would have been a three-hour car trip took more than five times as long. Vanier and his colleagues had become part of a sixty-five-kilometre line of cars and pedestrians, many pulling carts—an exodus described by Irène Némirovsky (who would die at Auschwitz) in *Suite Française* as a "confused multitude dragging feet through the dust," a "migration that obeyed its own natural laws." Creeping past dazed drivers whose cars had empty fuel tanks, Vanier imagined they were "hoping that a kind providence would send them petrol in the morning."

From Tours, Vanier cabled Mackenzie King that the deeply depressed secretary-general of the French foreign ministry, François Charles-Roux, confessed that France's "only hope lies in an immediate declaration of war by the United States. He asks me to cable their opinion to you at once, in the event presumably of your being able to influence the President of the United States in view of the well-known friendship which exists between you." (History shows that the United States, still gripped by isolationism, would not make good on this hope until after the bombing of Pearl Harbor.)

On June 14, as encircling German forces drew closer, the French government redeployed again, this time to Bordeaux. The Canadians found accommodation in a nearby village. "That night," wrote Vanier, "we received the sad but expected news that the Germans had entered Paris." Bordeaux, whose population had swollen from 260,000 to 1 million, was bombed.

Desperate diplomatic consultations intensified. Vanier often joined British ambassador Ronald Campbell in meetings at all hours with French premier Paul Reynaud and his new foreign minister, Paul Baudouin, and with the hapless Charles-Roux—at one point running after them from house to house in the middle of the night. Refusing to contemplate the idea of his government fleeing France entirely, Reynaud sought permission from his British ally to negotiate a separate peace. But Britain feared the Germans would get control of the French naval fleet, the world's second largest. Churchill countered with an offer to formally unite the two countries in one entity, which would remain at war with Germany.

The French clung to the faint hope that the United States would come to their aid; but Franklin D. Roosevelt knew that Congress would not support a war against Germany—even to save France. Far from offering aid, FDR sent a warning to the French, declaring that if their fleet was not kept out of German hands, the "French Government will permanently lose the friendship and good will of the US." As a military imperative, FDR's communication was defensible. But given the desperate plight of the French people, Vanier found its tone to be "in bad taste."

Reynaud quit as PM on June 16, after cabinet colleagues "showed no interest" in Churchill's proposal for a French–Anglo union. The development showed the strength of the pro-German right-wing faction led by Philippe Pétain, who took over as premier and went on to lead France's collaborationist Vichy regime. (After the war, Pétain would be convicted of treason.) The French fleet sailed for the open sea on June 18, disappointing British hopes it would deliver its ships to U.K. ports. At around the same time, twenty-nine Canadian dependents, including Pauline, were evacuated by a British destroyer and transferred to a cargo ship, where they joined three hundred others, including the president of Poland. Two days later, the staff followed.

Staying behind, Vanier camped out with his British colleague at the PM's office, where the cabinet was studying armistice terms. He was there when the shameful moment came, and France formally fell. The armistice divided the country into two zones: the North and the Atlantic seacoast (including Bordeaux), to be occupied by the Germans; and a nominally autonomous French-administered "national" regime under Pétain, ruled from the spa town of Vichy (where there were ample hotels to serve the new masters).

Charles-Roux tried to persuade Vanier to follow the regime to Vichy. But Vanier knew that after the armistice was formalized on June 21 at Compiègne (in the same railway car in which the Germans had acceded to their own 1918 capitulation), he would have to escape the continent altogether.

Following a midnight farewell from General Weygand, Vanier and Ambassador Campbell left for a seaside shanty. The next morning, Vanier reported, "we were hustled on to a small, smelly sardine boat. The boat was small and the waves were high. We were slewed to the top of a wave and catapulted into its trough. . . . I can say that I had never felt so brave in my life." Three hours later, following a successful rendezvous with British naval vessels, the pair were delivered to Britain, where Vanier was met by a relieved Pauline.

In the days following, diplomatic relations between Britain and the Vichy regime were shattered—the decisive moment coming when the Royal Air Force bombed the French fleet at Mers-el-Kébir in Algeria. (Almost 1,300 French servicemen died in the raid, and the episode remained a subject of French grievance for decades.) Lacking representation in France, the British hoped Vanier might relocate to Vichy so as to monitor the regime's intentions. By his account, he gave the proposition some consideration: "France is going through a period of great suffering, moral as well as material, and anything we can do to soften the pain is worthwhile."

But developments in Vichy counselled otherwise. During an August 21 meeting with British foreign minister Lord Halifax, Vanier said that the extreme tone of the Vichy regime made it impossible for

Canada to maintain a diplomatic presence. Halifax conceded the point, telling Vanier that his analysis left him "shaken."

By then, Vanier's friend René Pleven—an early joiner with the then obscure Free French forces—had brokered a fateful first meeting for Vanier with Charles de Gaulle. According to Élisabeth de Miribel, de Gaulle's secretary, the two men "liked and trusted each other immediately."

A French armoured division leader who had been named undersecretary for war, de Gaulle had resisted the armistice with Germany and formed a French government-in-exile in London. On June 18, his famous BBC broadcast to the French people marked the birth of the Free French military movement. The Vichy regime, he told fellow Frenchmen, was a betrayal of the true France, whose legacy de Gaulle sought to personify.

As it happens, few in France heard de Gaulle's speech. It was aimed primarily at the thirty thousand or so French soldiers who had been evacuated from Dunkirk. Even among that group, the exhortations were generally ineffective: most of these men chose to rejoin their families in occupied France.

As Robert Paxton put it in his 1972 book *Vichy France*, "The first Gaullists were marginal. Their number was small and their status mostly obscure. Prominent pre-war figures were mostly absent." King's diary recorded that Vanier "thought de Gaulle a gallant fellow but [with] poor political judgment . . . and [who was] surrounded by a group of men who did not amount to much." Even for Frenchmen who were sympathetic to the cause, leaving France to join the Free French was a difficult decision. And many of those who did respond to de Gaulle's outreach efforts were imagined to be desperate outcasts with questionable motives.

Vincent Massey—who was on record as deriding Pauline's "morbidly pro-French sensibilities"—was very much among de Gaulle's doubters. As he saw it, it was Vichy's Nazi quislings, not de Gaulle, who were the true embodiment of the French national will. True to his character, Vanier held a deeper view. And on June 27, he told CBC listeners that France would rise again.

Though, as Canadian historian Jacques Monet records, Vanier found de Gaulle's hauteur and intransigence to be off-putting personally, he recognized him as a natural leader—one whose Free French legions "incorporated the glorious traditions of freedom that belong to the national heritage of France." On June 28, Britain recognized de Gaulle as "leader of all the Free French, wherever they may be, who join him for the defense of the Allied cause."

Because Canadian ties to France were in flux, Vanier was left in a London limbo. But he found a new project when King appointed him commander of the Quebec military district (giving him the rank of major general), a role that Vanier took on energetically. Georges and Pauline spoke indefatigably throughout Quebec in support of the war effort. At a time when the Canadian Army was still dominated by Anglo culture, he made sure that his military colleagues became accustomed to the routine use of French.

Still the titular envoy to France, Vanier asked Prime Minister King (who, at the time, was also Canada's foreign minister) to eliminate this diplomatic title on principle, believing "the present [Vichy] government traitors in dealing with Hitler." (King wrote of Vanier at the time, "His whole view is that France has come to be very corrupt.") In a foreshadowing of Vanier's later focus on the humanitarian cost of war, he also described to King his anguish over how France was suffering from the absence of a million men being imprisoned in German prisons and forced labour camps.

King's diary records notions of appointing Vanier to the Senate and making him a member of the war cabinet, possibly as undersecretary of external affairs—or even having him run for Parliament in the Montreal riding of Outremont. Though Under-Secretary Norman Robertson "did not seem keen" on King's idea that Vanier should accompany them on a prime ministerial liaison trip to Britain in the late summer of 1942, King wrote, "I thought with the situation in France so difficult, it would be well to have Vanier along."

Eventually, King decided to send Vanier back to London with the personal rank of ambassador, accredited to multiple governments in exile—including Poles, Czechs, Belgians, and Norwegians, but especially to the Free French under de Gaulle. Vanier's mandate was to liaise with the French National Committee (FNC) "on all matters relating to the conduct of the war." An FNC press release quoted de Gaulle to the effect that "no choice could be more agreeable" than Vanier, and expressed hope that Vanier would "consult on the general interests of France in the war."

In typical fashion, King continued to vacillate on whether to extend formal support to de Gaulle. His overwhelming preoccupation was avoiding a breach in national unity back home in Canada—primarily because of pro-Vichy sentiment in Quebec, where, according to a poll that had been commissioned by External Affairs, 75 per cent believed Pétain had the backing of the French population. Only 33 per cent of Quebec respondents said they favoured supporting the Free French.

Vichy slogans of "Faith/Labour/Family" resonated with the Catholic Church in Quebec, which welcomed the end of the anti-clerical Third Republic. The province's *Le Devoir* newspaper termed Vichy "the best government France ever had," applauding Vichy's "reforms," including anti-Jewish measures. The St. Jean Baptiste Society urged Quebec premier Adélard Godbout to lobby Ottawa for a diminished war effort.

King's Quebec lieutenant, Minister of Justice Ernest Lapointe, argued that supporting de Gaulle would boost the fortunes of populist Maurice Duplessis—who had served as premier of Quebec between 1936 and 1939, and would later go on to a second, much longer tenure in the late 1940s and 1950s—and complicate the upcoming April 1942 vote on conscription. (That referendum indeed confirmed a cleavage in national opinion, with 72 per cent of Quebec voters opposing conscription while an even greater majority in the rest of Canada voted in favour.) And so the status of Canada's relationship with France was shelved.

Mackenzie King had another reason for his indecision regarding France: the Roosevelt administration's allergy to Charles de Gaulle, who was regarded by many Americans as an egomaniac. Before joining the fight against Hitler, the United States sent an ambassador to Vichy (though, in fairness, this was primarily in keeping with Washington's effort to keep Vichy from moving more decisively into the German camp). Accordingly, the Americans had little temptation to side openly with de Gaulle and his Free French movement. After the United States entered the war and an explicitly pro-Nazi Vichy government was formed under Pierre Laval, the Americans recalled their ambassador but didn't change their underlying view of de Gaulle.

Germany responded to the Allied invasion of North Africa in November 1942 by occupying the whole of France, thereby consigning the Vichy regime to puppet status. Yet even then, the United States didn't embrace de Gaulle—on the basis that the French people themselves seemed ambivalent about his mission. But as Vanier intuited, many French ignored de Gaulle not because they disagreed with his message but because they were hungry, beaten down, and depressed.

Author James MacGregor Burns reports that even though the 1942 Allied invasion of North Africa played out on French territory, FDR sought to ensure that de Gaulle "be kept out of the picture and given no information whatsoever, regardless of how irritated and irritating he may become." FDR didn't trust de Gaulle's HQ to keep secrets, and he resented the Frenchman's independence. Burns wrote that FDR also refused to make commitments to de Gaulle "that might jeopardize the freedom of the French people to decide their own political fate after the Liberation." White House antipathy toward the Free French leader seemed to be rooted in "sheer personal dislike."

In his own memoirs, de Gaulle recalls that "the Anglo-American powers never consented to deal with us as genuine allies. . . . They sought to make use of French forces for goals they themselves had chosen, as if these forces belonged to them." Vanier sympathized. From his posts in London and Paris, he had repeatedly made a similar point to Ottawa about the way the Canadian Army was subsumed in British command structures.

De Gaulle's forces suffered early reversals in their attempts to displace Vichy defenders in French colonies in Africa and Syria. When they moved against the softer North American target of St. Pierre and Miquelon, off the southern coast of Newfoundland, the U.S. secretary of state Cordell Hull worried that the operation violated the venerable Monroe Doctrine—which required Washington to oppose any European effort to conduct military operations in North or South America. Though Hull hoped for Canadian support in reversing the "arbitrary" action of the "so-called Free French," Ottawa tacitly supported de Gaulle's men—who ousted Vichy personnel and then won 98 per cent of the vote in a local plebiscite.

The Americans concluded—as they so often do—that they needed to install someone they could control. Through spy Allan Dulles in Geneva, the United States first recruited former French naval commander François Darlan in the role of "High Commissioner of the French Empire." After Darlan was assassinated in Algiers by a Free French officer, Washington went with General Henri Giraud, an escapee from German POW camps on whom they imposed the title of French Commander-in-Chief.

Once the pro-Vichy administration in Algiers was pushed out by the Allies, de Gaulle used the city as the new headquarters for his French National Committee. He invited Giraud to co-lead the committee, conceding him prime military responsibility. But a power struggle ensued, aggravated by Giraud's *amour-propre*. (On a visit to Ottawa in 1943, after the High Commission in London had bombarded External Affairs with messaging that promoted Giraud's credentials, Giraud failed even to mention de Gaulle or the French National Committee.) Eventually, he gave up and resigned. Vanier reported that FDR sent Churchill a secret message: "Can't anyone get rid of de Gaulle?"

"I feel very deeply that my place is in North Africa and later in France, where, with Pauline, I may be able to help in a humble way in its rehabilitation," Vanier wrote to Under-Secretary Norman Robertson. In Algeria, the Vaniers landed in what was a hotbed of intrigue and double-dealing. They rented a villa a bit removed from seamy Algiers, in the seaside town of Cheragas. The place soon became known as the "villa de la resistance," a gathering point for Gaullists, among whom Vanier's influence grew rapidly.

A frequent guest was a man known cryptically as "General Leclerc" (born Philippe Leclerc de Hauteclocque). This was Pauline's cousin, who had become a devoted friend of Georges. Having led French forces in reclaiming African colonies, Leclerc now was itching to participate in the liberation of mainland France. But he faced U.S. opposition to a military role for the Free French in the planning for any large-scale operation. It was Vanier who persuaded Ottawa to step in and outfit a French brigade for the June 1944 Normandy landings.

Meanwhile, Vanier continued to push for undiluted recognition of the French National Committee as the provisional government of France, with de Gaulle at its head, arguing, "There is no use closing one's eyes to the prestige and authority de Gaulle enjoys." Vanier warned, "If we do not wish to develop in the French people generally a feeling of deep resentment against us, which may be lasting and may eventually throw France into the arms of the Soviet Union, it is essential that recognition be no longer delayed."

Vanier optimistically reported to Ottawa "a much more favourable . . . attitude of the Americans on the spot (including General Eisenhower) towards the French Committee, even towards de Gaulle. They recognize that de Gaulle is the most important political figure on the French scene and must play a big part during the actual period of liberation. Their fears of a personal dictatorship seem to have greatly diminished." The British ambassador to France, Duff Cooper, called this "a diplomatic victory [that] the Canadian Ambassador had done more than anyone to achieve. No other allied diplomat, however warm his sympathies, had a parallel insight into the epic of the French Resistance."

But as D-Day approached, Lester B. Pearson forwarded to Ottawa a bootlegged copy of a cable from FDR to the British secretary of war, setting out draft instructions to Eisenhower for the administration of liberated France. It authorized "a military occupation" by U.S.

commanders, subordinating the role of the French Committee, and even suggesting that Eisenhower was to conduct the first general post-war elections in France. Though the plan was greeted in London by "stunned silence," Churchill summoned de Gaulle to London on June 4 and laid it out, alongside other U.S. intentions, including the creation of a temporary French currency showing the American and British flags but no hint of the République Française.

Informed further that, on D-Day, Eisenhower would address the French nation, urging the population to carry out his orders—with no mention of de Gaulle—the enraged Free French leader pressed Churchill to confront Roosevelt. The British PM responded, "If I have to choose between Roosevelt and you, I shall choose Roosevelt. If Britain has to choose between Europe and the sea, we shall always choose the sea." De Gaulle's meagre consolation was that, as planned, a French unit—the 1er Bataillon de Fusiliers Marins Commandos—would take part in the initial landing at D-Day. Leclerc's armoured division followed a month later. De Gaulle himself set foot at last on French soil on June 14—on the Canadian landing beach at Juno, to give a speech at Bayeux.

On his return to Algiers, he met with Vanier on June 21, "cheerfully" gratified that the first soldiers he had seen in France had been Canadian. Vanier advised de Gaulle to go to Washington, where he could appeal directly to the American public and press. Roosevelt, Vanier reasoned, would have no choice but to respond positively. His counsel proved sound. When De Gaulle proceeded to Washington in early July, FDR received him cordially at last, and even extended public recognition of the man as leader of the Free French.

A symbolically crucial issue concerned Free French participation in the liberation of Paris. From Algiers, Vanier supported Leclerc's passionate wish that his motorized brigade be the first Allied force to enter the capital. Again, Washington was opposed—but an order to U.S. general Omar Bradley, demanding that U.S. forces receive this honour, somehow never got through.

On August 25, 1944, the day after Leclerc's group led Allied soldiers (and Ernest Hemingway) into a delirious Paris, de Gaulle himself returned in triumph to pealing bells from Notre-Dame, where, despite continuing small-arms fire, a Catholic mass marked the dramatic moment. De Gaulle proclaimed: "Paris liberated! By itself, liberated by its people with the help of the French armies, with the support and the help of all France, of the France that fights, of the only France, of the real France, of the eternal France."

By "itself"? It was a myth, but one de Gaulle believed could help heal France's psychological and spiritual damage after four harsh years. Briefing Canadian media off the record when de Gaulle visited Ottawa in 1945, Vanier spoke of France's "moral devastation," and described the occupation as "the nadir of her history. The French people came out of the war morally diminished and with a deep inferiority complex."

Within days of the liberation, Vanier redeployed to free Paris, where he at last resumed his duty as Canadian envoy. Despite Ottawa's warning that dependents should stay away, Pauline joined him, wearing a Canadian Red Cross uniform. "You try to stop her!" Vanier wrote to fretting bureaucrats. On October 20, Canada's war cabinet named Georges Vanier Canada's first ambassador in Paris.

In the war's waning month and its aftermath, millions of returnees and refugees were on the move, many of them ethnic minorities uprooted from ancestral lands liberated by the Allies—in some cases, expelled by vengeful locals. A quarter of a million Jews who had somehow survived the Nazi terror sought to emigrate, many turning to a nascent homeland in British-occupied Palestine.

This teeming mass of suffering humans offered Vanier a cardinal opportunity to put into practice Father Steuart's lessons on the healing power of mercy. The Vaniers threw themselves into relief work, with particular attention to returnees and the reunification of families. The start-up Canadian embassy took on the look of a refugee-processing centre. In the mornings, Pauline would be on train station platforms, greeting returnees from the east with coffee and cookies; and in the evenings she would welcome them to the Vanier residence at the Hôtel de Vendôme. For lucky French families, it was a time of joy and reunification. For others, it was a time for bad news and heartbreak.

Vanier's argument that Canada should open its doors to Europe's refugees was not welcomed in official Ottawa. In his book *Massey*, Claude Bissell recounts how, during the lengthy freeze on immigration launched during the Depression, an "unholy triumvirate" had been forged among the Immigration Branch, the cabinet, and, to a lesser degree, External Affairs, in opposition to the admission of refugees in general, and Jewish refugees in particular.

Charles Blair, the long-standing strongman who headed the immigration service, believed Jews couldn't assimilate. It wasn't an uncommon view at the time: a sign on the entrance to the watering hole for senior officials in Ottawa, the Rideau Club, pronounced "Christians Only." Polls showed that 49 per cent of Canadians wanted Jews kept out of the country. (For Japanese, the figure was 60 per cent.) As Abella and Troper wrote in *None Is Too Many*, the official strategy was one of euphemisms and excuses: "absence of shipping, no examination facilities at ports of embarkation, (the overriding priority of) rehabilitation and repatriation of soldiers."

But Vanier would have none of it, arguing, "It simply is not true that no transport is available. This is Immigration's stock reply. . . . The real bottleneck is the lack of inspection offices, not the lack of transport." He had been dealing with Ottawa's cynically expressed resistance to Jewish migrants from as early as 1938, when the refugee ship St. *Louis* was denied permission to dock in North American ports, its human cargo eventually returning to Europe. Vanier also endured dreary obfuscations over "racial balance" from Blair and his department, which purported to justify the refusal of orphaned Jewish children from France in 1942.

But by 1946, following disclosures about the true extent of Nazi evil and Europe's suffering, Vanier's advice finally began to resonate in the halls of External Affairs. Even Massey conceded the need to take on some post-war refugees (though he suggested to King that he should accept "as many as possible Aryan Germans"). On May 1, King introduced a new policy, stressing "Canada's moral obligation." By the summer of 1948, Canada would absorb 180,000 post-war immigrants, including several thousand Jews.

Meanwhile, France was in more or less constant crisis, closely observed by Vanier, who travelled throughout the country. At de Gaulle's villa in Neuilly, the Frenchman confessed to Vanier that he might not succeed in forming a government. If so, he thought, it might be in the general interest if he left France for a time. He proposed, by Vanier's account, that he "go to Canada as a private citizen . . . as on occasion Churchill had come to France."

On January 26, 1946, de Gaulle did quit, telling cabinet in a short speech that his work to restore French democracy was done. (The real reason was that the communists and the socialists supported a constitution for the Fourth Republic that revived the dominance of parliamentary party politics and accorded relatively scant status to the office of president.) De Gaulle retreated to his austere home in Colombey-les-Deux-Églises, holding himself "in reserve" until France would again call on him (which it did in 1958, when the Fourth Republic broke up amid chaos over Algerian independence and an attempted military *putsch*). Thus ended Georges Vanier's close relationship—some might say preoccupation—with Charles de Gaulle, until the French leader's gratuitous intervention in Canadian affairs twenty years later.

IN AUGUST 1946, Vanier hosted Mackenzie King on what was effectively a victory tour of northern France. The PM's diary describes his visit to Dieppe—site of a failed raid by a Canadian-dominated force in 1942—where he found "streets lined with people, in some places several deep. They cheered and cheered. There can be no question of the feelings in their hearts for Canada." Vanier himself interpreted King's speeches to the locals (vastly improving the PM's eloquence in the process).

King was feeling his age, noting in his diary, "I am not equal today to what I was in earlier years, and also have felt so keenly some of the indifference of those around me." He exempted the Vaniers, complaining that he spent too little time with them. In fact, Vanier saw King repeatedly, and warned him of darkening storm clouds in Europe, as the Berlin crisis built and uncertainty grew in France over the U.S.S.R. and unrest in France's Indo-Chinese colonies.

The Vaniers continued their work in France, even after the devastating news of Leclerc's death in a 1947 air crash. Diplomat Charles Ritchie, who eventually would become Canada's ambassador to the UN and High Commissioner in London, recalled that "no one was better informed than Vanier about the French political scene. . . . French political leaders of varying parties and persuasions . . . came to him as to no other foreign ambassador for advice. They confided in his judgment, integrity, and discretion. The Ambassadress, Pauline Vanier, a woman of distinguished beauty and warm charity of heart, carried all before her by her spontaneity."

Vanier's decade as Canadian ambassador earned his country an unusually high profile in Europe's halls of power. Oliver Hardy, British ambassador to France, declared: "I do not think any Ambassador enjoyed such respect and affection." Ritchie, however, regretted that Vanier's focus on France's needs still was not matched by his colleagues back in Ottawa. "The Canadian Government at that time had no discernible interest in France," he later recalled. "In those days, our department at home was almost entirely Anglo-Saxon in language and mentality."

Among the Canadian Anglo establishment, Vanier always paid a price for his French roots and cultural identification. King had intimated to Vanier the possibility of his going as high commissioner to London, recording that Vanier would "be delighted beyond words." But on January 18, 1948, King noted that "Vanier is not to go to London. I am sorry for this. [Minister of External Affairs Louis] St. Laurent says if there were differences with the British Government, it would be put down to the French." Earlier, in 1945, King had even mused that Vanier should be governor general. "I would appoint him in a minute excepting it would be immediately said that here again I was body and soul in alliance with the French and Catholics." The two solitudes were intact in Canada. Vanier was a francophone in an anglophone service.

Vanier retired in 1953, at the age of sixty-five. Other posts had been offered to him—but not the top ones. His pride had been pricked.

Georges and Pauline returned to Montreal, where he joined some corporate boards. Finally, he was rescued from his boredom in 1959, when Conservative prime minister John Diefenbaker appointed Vanier to succeed Vincent Massey as Canada's governor general. The anti-Catholic sentiment of the 1940s, apparently, had eased enough to make Vanier an acceptable man for the post.

In his inaugural address, Vanier struck a humble and pious tone, while emphasizing his lifelong theme of tolerance: "My first words are a prayer. May Almighty God, in His infinite wisdom and mercy bless the sacred mission which has been entrusted to me by Her Majesty the Queen and help me to fulfill it in all humility. In exchange for His strength, I offer my weakness. May He give peace to his beloved land of ours and to those who live in it the grace of mutual understanding." Vanier proved to be an extraordinary governor general, using his office to hasten the pluralist society that Canada would become.

Ironically, his message found a more sympathetic audience among the Anglo Canadians who had once marginalized him than among his own French-Canadian society. His term in office coincided with Quebec's "Quiet Revolution," a modernization and secularization movement that took on tones of ethnic nationalism. At its core was the question of French-language rights. This was a cause Vanier had championed for fifty years, yet separatist firebrands such as Marcel Chaput and Pierre Bourgault dismissed Vanier as a *vendu* (sell-out) for surrounding himself with the professional trappings of British monarchy. At the Saint-Jean-Baptiste Day parade of 1964, the Vaniers stoically endured boos from separatists brandishing placards denouncing "*Vanier fou de la Reine*" (fool of the Queen).

TWO OF THE DEFINING CHAPTERS of Vanier's life—his support of de Gaulle as icon of a free France, and his role as a domestic unifier in the position of governor general—would crash head-on in the mid-1960s, when the French president became a champion of Quebec separatism. For Vanier, it was a form of betrayal. For de Gaulle, the development typified his personal hubris and his deluded sense that France might rediscover its colonial-era leadership role in French-speaking lands around the world.

De Gaulle's view on foreign affairs was dominated by his suspicion of Britain and the United States, which at times had marginalized and humiliated him during the early war years. De Gaulle vetoed the U.K.'s joining the Common Market—twice. Despite his eloquent praise for Canada's sacrifices on France's behalf, he came to see Ottawa as a pliant part of a post-war Anglo-Saxon agenda.

Vanier and de Gaulle both saw the horror and devastation of war first-hand in France. But they took very different lessons from it. For Vanier, the fate of Europe demonstrated the need for humanity to escape narrow tribal categories and develop a universalistic approach to human rights. De Gaulle, incapable of making this moral leap, never could escape his wounded French chauvinism. At one point, after de Gaulle had made a series of provocative diplomatic gestures, including treating Quebec's premier as the Canadian head of state, Vanier proposed to travel to Paris to reason with him. De Gaulle said that he was "touched" by the overture, but could not receive a mere surrogate for the British queen. Disgusted, Prime Minister Lester Pearson called the project off.

This conflict, between Canada and the man whom Vanier had once championed as the very embodiment of France, drained Vanier. In essence, it pitted his loyalty to his true Canadian home against his loyalty to a European nation that had become his second home. His health deteriorated during this period, aggravated by an exhausting cross-Canada centennial celebration tour that he took with Pauline against his doctor's advice.

On March 5, 1967, Lieutenant Toby Price looked in on the general, who had been watching from bed a hockey game between Detroit and his beloved Montreal Canadiens, and wished him "Good night."

"Toby, good-bye," he replied. That night, Georges Phileas Vanier died, serene in his faith.

De Gaulle delivered a terse message of condolence, which left Pauline shaken. Several weeks later, the widow would lunch once more at the Élysée Palace, where de Gaulle reportedly pontificated, "The only possible future for Quebec is as a sovereign nation." Madame Vanier left that meeting in tears.

In July, 1967, de Gaulle arrived in Montreal on a state visit coinciding with Canada's centennial-year festivities. The French president had derided the occasion, sniffing that Canada's true age actually dated back more than four hundred years, to the exploits of Jacques Cartier. But he came anyway, and the trip became infamous. The climactic moment occurred on the balcony of Montreal's City Hall, from where he pronounced to a large crowd: "*Ce soir ici, et tout le long de ma route, je me trouvais dans une atmosphère du même genre que celle de la* [1945] *Libération. . . . Voilà ce que je suis venu vous dire ce soir en ajoutant que j'emporte de cette réunion inouïe de Montréal un souvenir inoubliable. La France entière sait, voit, entend, ce qui se passe ici et je puis vous dire qu'elle en vaudra mieux. Vive Montréal! Vive le Québec! Vive le Québec libre! Vive le Canada français! Et vive la France!*"

The state visit was terminated abruptly, and de Gaulle returned to France. He maintained that his words had come to him spontaneously.

But that wasn't true. When he first disembarked in Quebec from the French cruiser *Colbert*, having received the requisite twenty-one-gun salute from the Canadian escort of two destroyers, his vacated suite was inspected by *Colbert*'s captain to ensure that no compromising papers were left. Years later, when I met the captain, Vice-Admiral Paul Delahousse, he told me that he found reams of drafts of speeches in the suite, including the lines "*Vive le Québec*—LIBRE."

To his credit, de Gaulle did reveal some remorse about his betrayal of Vanier. At his first stop on Canadian soil in 1967, he insisted on visiting the Citadel, home of General Vanier's 22nd regiment, where he recently had been buried. De Gaulle laid a wreath on the tomb of the man to whom he and France owed much.

Canadians owe Vanier more. Though I have focused at some length on the man's relationship to France, and to de Gaulle in particular, his whole life epitomized the values that are now seen as lying at the core of the Canadian identity: humane internationalism, tolerance, pluralism, a rejection of anti-Semitism and other forms of bigotry, multiculturalism (as it came to be called), enlightened monarchism, and a powerful faith in a national project founded on the union between North America's French and English peoples.

On matters of foreign policy, he was similarly far-sighted: At a time when his Anglo-Canadian diplomatic peers still rendered obsequious homage to their British counterparts, Vanier already conceived of Canada as an autonomous moral voice on the world stage. And his writings show that he understood the threat from communism—from the U.S.S.R. in particular—even before the Red Army had taken Berlin.

And then, of course, there is the issue of refugees. At the 2015 G-20 Summit in Turkey, following closely upon the November 13 terrorist attacks in Paris, Justin Trudeau delivered his first speech abroad as Canada's prime minister. In regard to refugees from Syria and elsewhere, Trudeau recalled that "Canada has tremendous examples of having integrated people fleeing for their lives. . . . Canada figured out a long time ago that differences should be a source of strength, not weakness."

Trudeau did not cite Vanier for these principles. But he didn't have to: Vanier's values have been encoded in our national DNA.

It's tempting to eulogize Vanier as a paragon of virtue and gentlemanly old-world values. But in fact, the man could be stiff, prideful, and overly formal—as the tenor of the quotations that I have included in this essay attest. And yet Vanier managed to turn even these negative qualities into virtues at important times, especially when he had to deal with de Gaulle, for whom *grandeur* was an existential preoccupation.

Vanier was that rare interlocutor whose manner of personal presentation was a match for de Gaulle's inflated self-concept.

Vanier's confidence flowed not from hubris but from his conviction in the importance of his spiritual and earthly mission. He represented Canada in the besieged capitals of Europe, during a period that we now know to have been the great moral pivot of post-war Western civilization. On every important question—opposition to the Nazis, the wages of appeasement, the treatment of the poor and despised—he sensed what the right answer was, and fought hard to convince others. His instincts were just as sound when it came to governance within the Canadian family.

Look beyond the medals festooning his outfit in official photos and portraits, and you will see the beating moral heart of modern Canada.

SAMANTHA NUTT

THÉRÈSE CASGRAIN

HISTORY IS RARELY KIND to powerful women. When the dusty books have bothered with them at all, it's as if they were conjured up by a casting agency: Cue the harpy, whore, virgin, mistress, and wife—then the princess and queen—but hold the witch and woman scorned for Act II. It's a liturgy of the broken, decapitated, divine, and defeated. Am I exaggerating? Consider the roll call of leading female historical celebrities—including Catherine the Great (or not so great, if you were a Turk or Ukrainian); Joan of Arc (lionized, canonized, and burned at the stake before her twentieth birthday); and Elizabeth the "Virgin Queen" (who ticks off not one but two of my above-listed categories). Indira Gandhi, Golda Meir, and Cleopatra offer interesting counterpoints, but only one of these achieved the apotheosis of power without benefit of royal bloodline—and the other two met agonizing ends. After this, the list runs a bit thin. There are famous female artists, musicians, poets, scientists, actors, and writers, to be sure, and an abundance of acclaimed muses, but they fall into an entirely different category.

Canadian history, that compendium of beaver pelts and Anglo–Franco accords, offers no exception to the general rule. Laura Secord is more famous as a box of re-gifted chocolates than as a heroine of the

War of 1812. Alberta's Famous Five are lauded as feminist role models, but one turned out to be an insufferable bigot, and another (perish the thought) a champion of Canada's temperance movement. As for Kim Campbell, Canada's first and only female prime minister, she wasn't in the job long enough to pen a political legacy much beyond an opening line.

The easy response is to blame the patriarchy and move on. After all, a history that dwells on the exploits of dead white men, as written largely by other dead white men, is bound to offer a narrow perspective on our country. It's one of the reasons why students find Canadian history boring. This was certainly true for me when I was in school, which is why I read the Brontë sisters through many of my classes.

Like most young girls, I preferred to read works in which women's lives comprised a central part of the story (or at least received some sort of honourable mention). How many grade-school students are still forced to make dioramas of Jacques Cartier surrounded by birchbark canoes in Iroquois villages along the St. Lawrence as he claims them for France? Scant attention tends to be paid to the fact that there were men, women, and children living in these "undiscovered" lands—people who've been fighting for the return of their property ever since. Pay attention, kids! This is the history of the *vainqueurs*, not the vanquished.

Women, Canada's First Nations people, non-European immigrants—all of these traditionally were treated as props in our central historical narrative of white, male dominion over the "new" world. So by all means, let's blame the patriarchy for that. But don't let that be the end of it. Without a doubt, men have had a head start and been afforded greater recognition in every field—science, politics, literature, business, art. But that gap is slowly, if unevenly, closing. There now exists a simple, efficient, and reliable means by which women can make sure their voices are heard: raise them.

This, in a nutshell, is a lesson that the subject of this essay, Thérèse Casgrain (1896–1981), began putting into practice almost a century ago.

AS A CHAMPION OF FEMALE suffrage, and the first woman to be elected leader of a Canadian political party (the now defunct Parti social démocratique du Québec), Casgrain is a fit subject for biography. But outside Quebec, she stands as one of the least recognized and written-about protagonists in this essay collection. This is in part because she was a more prolific political organizer and activist than essayist, and so she produced little in the way of first-person grist for biographers. Nevertheless, there emerges from her historical docket a woman who was ahead of even prime ministers Lester B. Pearson and Pierre Elliott Trudeau in seeding the modern, humanist Canadian sensibility.

Casgrain was not born into mere privilege. She was born into *exceptional* privilege. The eldest child of one of Montreal's wealthiest families, Casgrain—née Forget—grew up surrounded by servants and governesses in expansive mansions that can best be described as Downton Abbey meets Hudson's Bay Company. Her father, Sir Rodolphe Forget, was a businessman and Conservative MP whose forebears arrived in Canada in the seventeenth century. Casgrain's mother, Lady Blanche MacDonald, also was a product of vintage French-Canadian stock, her lineage traceable back to the age of the seigneurs.

Lady Blanche was described by Thérèse Casgrain as a "gentle and submissive wife and an attentive mother." Like most women of a certain social standing, her existence revolved around overseeing a household and domestic staff, and attending public functions with her husband. She was also expected to lead charitable endeavours, host fundraising events for various causes in her home, and go door to door during the holidays to deliver care packages to struggling families.

In this way, Casgrain was exposed from a young age to a spirit of noblesse oblige. When a grande dame such as Lady Blanche tended to the poor, she did not do so out of a sense of class-based guilt or obligation. Just the opposite: extreme differences in welfare among the classes often were justified on the basis of moral piety and divine will. Which is to say that the rich really were believed to be better than the poor—even if they condescended to help their "inferiors" occasionally, through entirely discretionary acts of charity. The idea that poverty had root causes wasn't yet part of the conversation. Nor was the idea that government must actively address income disparities between the classes.

This situation seemed to rattle Casgrain from a young age. While she eagerly undertook all the philanthropic duties expected of a young woman from a prominent family, she often seemed baffled that so few of her contemporaries had any appetite to understand the reason such misery existed in the first instance. While reflecting on her childhood, she writes, "Women, especially those of the comfortable classes, enjoyed playing the role of lady bountiful and distributed food baskets in the homes of needy families every Christmas. They never dreamed, however, of finding out why these people were in need."

As she matured, Casgrain began framing such questions in the language of what we would now call human rights—a set of nascent ideas then gaining prominence in Europe and the United States. While still in her mid-teens, Casgrain visited France with her family (very nearly sailing home on a new White Line luxury cruise ship christened *Titanic*). Her autobiography is silent on the specifics, but Casgrain likely would have been exposed to the spirit of humanitarianism that rose up within Western Europe in the early days of the twentieth century—a reaction, in part, to the news of Belgian King Leopold's genocidal exploits in the Congo. The miseries imposed by colonialism would become a dominant theme throughout Casgrain's life.

Women were becoming more vocal during this period, as first-wave feminism hit its stride. And Casgrain, who received her advanced education in a convent boarding school, was an unusually confident and learned specimen. She was also not one to be overly impressed by title or rank, since the Forget household had hosted dignitaries of all ranks during her childhood years. This is an important detail, because Casgrain's effectiveness as an advocate and activist emerged directly from her willingness to challenge authority—be it ecclesiastic or political.

Casgrain's sense of activist mission bloomed during her early twenties, shortly after Prime Minister Robert Borden introduced conscription during World War I. This policy was deeply unpopular among francophone Quebeckers, many of whom saw no reason to defend the British Empire to their deaths. Casgrain's father, the MP for the riding of Charlevoix, retired from the Conservative Party in protest; and her new husband, Pierre-François Casgrain, won Charlevoix as a Liberal (with Wilfrid Laurier's support). During that campaign, Thérèse would accompany her husband to areas of the riding where civic life was controlled almost entirely by the Catholic Church, and where poverty was high and education largely non-existent (she recounts that even the local mayor could barely sign his name). It was an eye-opening experience.

One might think that working the campaign trail with one's aspiring-politician husband might lead even the most intrepid and supportive of power-wives to drink. Not so for Casgrain, who felt emboldened. By Pierre-François' second campaign—the first federal election in which women were able to vote—she was delivering political stump speeches on his behalf. It was a bold move for the period, and one that caught the attention of prominent Quebec feminists, who hoped the province would follow the federal government's lead on women's suffrage. (Quebec eventually did so—but it took an astonishing twenty-one years, by which time Quebec was the only provincial holdout within Confederation.)

If Casgrain's success could be ascribed to a single character trait, it would be her tenacity—not a quality one normally associates with high-born socialites. Her commitment to women's rights would lead to a lifelong struggle; a constant campaign of persuasion, coaxing, confrontation—and sometimes, appeasement. It helped, too, that she was both a practising Catholic and a mother of four, which spared her the usual anti-feminist accusation that women's rights was a dangerous creed advanced by man-hating, childless harridans.

As the first president of La Ligue des droigts de la femme—an organization she helped found—Casgrain presided over fourteen attempts in as many years to introduce a bill in support of women's suffrage at the Quebec legislature. With both the province's premier and its Opposition leader openly opposed to giving women the vote—a position vigorously reinforced by the Vatican and the Québécois clerisy—the Ligue's political actions were widely dismissed as futile.

Fourteen attempts! I like to think that an interwar version of myself would have been up in the gallery shouting imprecations down at Quebec's sexist legislators. But then that's the kind of feminism I was born into: one that demanded, and expected, true equality. The reality was different for Casgrain.

Casgrain and her contemporaries did more than launch a series of unsuccessful petitions. The veterans of La Ligue des droigts de la femme turned their attention to other inequalities—gradually repositioning their movement in broad, humanist terms. This move proved to be strategic, as the pool of potential sympathizers expanded from a relatively small group of elite, educated suffragettes to anyone who felt mistreated or excluded. It was a long list, and one that included trade labourers, teachers, farmers, immigrants, and First Nations communities. For women and men alike, the need for a living wage often felt at least as urgent as the right to mark an X on a ballot.

Taken collectively, these projects effectively comprised the dawning of Canada's human rights movement. At the same stroke, these women were also redefining the very idea of civil society in Canada, by focusing on the protection of vulnerable groups as a public good unto itself—rather than as a religious duty sloughed onto missionaries and godly volunteers who preached acquiescence over societal change.

One very practical objective pursued by Montreal's emerging feminist organizations was the reform of Quebec's Civil Code. In particular, they sought more control for women over household financial resources, and an amendment to the adultery provisions in family law. This was a time when the state was firmly ensconced in the bedrooms of the nation.

Hard to believe, but less than a century ago, Quebec women were essentially treated as children—legal dependants of their husbands—and they held no claim to homes, bank accounts, or other assets accrued during marriage, except upon the death of their spouse. Husbands were free to leverage, gamble, or drink away every last dollar; and the women, lacking recourse, could then find themselves destitute, along with their children. It was irrelevant who had earned the money: women effectively were chattel, and the spoils of their labour belonged to the "head" of the household.

Eventually, Quebec premier Louis-Alexandre Taschereau appointed the Dorion Commission to review the Civil Code—with the result that women henceforth would be entitled to any income they earned. Nevertheless, even post-Dorion, women couldn't be granted a separation—even from an adulterous spouse, unless the cad actually brought his "concubine" (the favoured term of the era) into the family home. Needless to say, the same rule did not apply to a man, who was always free to separate from his wife if *she* was the one who strayed.

Casgrain and her determined colleagues were incredulous at this double standard, and demanded that the Commission clarify its position. In a written response, the eminent male jurists reasoned that women forgive more easily than do men, and so the blow to their psyche caused by adultery wasn't as severe. For good measure, they added that a man faces the greater burden of not knowing whose baby his wife may be carrying, whereas the spawn of cheating husbands are someone else's problems. It is satisfying to know that these men would, in very short order, find themselves on the wrong side of history.

Elsewhere in the country, the feminist movement was making more progress. On August 27, 1927, backed by the government of Alberta, the quintet of women now known as the Famous Five petitioned the Supreme Court of Canada to have women declared "persons" under the British North America Act. Here again, the intransigence of Quebec's officials, who argued the "no" side, helped assure the plaintiffs' defeat. But the Five appealed the decision to the Privy Council and, two years after filing their petition in Canada, a judicial committee in London overturned the ruling. It is not difficult to imagine how Quebec's legislators reacted to a British verdict that women, though still not eligible to vote in Quebec's own elections, now could sit in the Canadian Senate.

By this time, it must have been clear to many first-wave feminists that the path to political equality cut through Quebec—with a few stopovers in Rome. Success would depend on a strong Québécois flank, and Casgrain would come to epitomize this struggle. It was a delicate balance for Casgrain and her francophone contemporaries: they were championing progressive ideas, yet they also needed to grow their base in the strongly Catholic, rural areas that held sway over the more conservative elements of Quebec's legislature.

Casgrain received financial support for a public relations campaign on women's suffrage from high-profile activists in the United States, including the legendary Carrie Chapman Catt. Meanwhile, in an ironic turn, the onset of the Great Depression gave the women's movement in Quebec an unexpected boost. As conditions across the province deteriorated, and poverty and unemployment reached new heights, questions of protection for workers and the role of the state in advancing social welfare gained prominence. And since the labour movement was, by this time, politically and ideologically interwoven with the women's movement, Casgrain and her allies stood to benefit. (It didn't hurt that these emerging labour unions had their own antagonistic relationship with the Catholic Church.)

In 1934, members of Quebec's Liberal Party, many of whom were part of Casgrain's social circle, adapted to this rapidly changing social and political landscape by forming a new political party called Action libérale—a younger, leftist movement aligned with Quebec nationalism. It is hard to know what influence, if any, Casgrain had on party members' inner deliberations. (She claims to have remained mostly silent, though that is hard to imagine.) But in any event, what emerged was the first provincial party convention to include women, who numbered forty out of about eight hundred attendees.

Unfortunately, this moment of idealism in Quebec politics turned out to be short-lived. But for the time it lasted, Action libérale defined, for Casgrain, what politics ought to be. "It must aim at the ideal of the common good," she wrote. "At some point one must choose between one's personal interests and the cause one is fighting for and, if need be, abandon the traditional parties."

We now take for granted the link between feminism and progressive politics. But in Casgrain's era, things were more complicated. Many of the women who fought for the right to vote also embraced social conservative causes such as temperance. Casgrain championed the other wing of the suffrage movement—the ideological leftists who saw the rights of women as part of a broader struggle for equality.

On April 25, 1940, Quebec women finally won the right to vote in provincial elections. For many Québécois feminist pioneers, this marked the end of a journey. But Casgrain doubled down—pursuing the broader social justice reforms that the Ligue, labour unions, and Action libérale party members had identified as priorities. That list included universal health care, protection for children and other vulnerable members of society, better working conditions, pay equity for women in public sector jobs, and a robust social safety net. The fact that these issues are all preoccupations of the present-day Trudeau era shows that Casgrain was, in her policy instincts, very much a Canadian woman ahead of her time.

On September 10, 1939, when Canada declared war on Germany and its allies, Casgrain was in the House of Commons (her husband still being a sitting Liberal MP) to hear a speech by J.S. Woodsworth, the passionately anti-war leader of the Co-operative Commonwealth Federation. Casgrain (who herself opposed Canadian involvement in World War II) described Woodsworth as a man of deep progressive conviction who was not afraid to express views that diverged from popularly held beliefs. But his party hadn't made any headway in Quebec, where Catholics viewed his socialist leanings as a gateway to full-blown communism.

Given Casgrain's strong ties to the Liberal Party, and her husband's former high-profile position as secretary of state in William Lyon Mackenzie King's cabinet, her decision to join the CCF in 1946 must have angered many Liberals. When she then ran as a CCF candidate in 1949, against a sitting Liberal no less, it must have made them positively apoplectic. (Can anyone imagine, say, Laureen Harper, Sophie Grégoire-Trudeau, or Aline Chrétien actively campaigning for a newly formed party while their husbands helped run the country? Neither can I, but it would be fun to watch.)

Casgrain recounts an anecdote about that 1949 election campaign—which ultimately ended in a victory for Louis St. Laurent's Liberals. The CCF, St. Laurent quipped, were nothing more than "Liberals in a hurry." Casgrain claims to have shot back: "That's better than Liberals lagging behind." I am left to wonder why her response has been left out of the oft-retold historical lore (assuming the story is true—and I have found no reason to believe it was not). Is it because her party lost, and only victors get to tell their tales? Or was it simply because she was a woman, and so her sharp rebuttal was not worth remembering?

Thérèse Casgrain was not, in the end, much of an authentic socialist, democratic or otherwise. She was never without her pearls, she indulged in regular shopping trips to Paris, and she had the luxury of lifelong financial security. Casgrain tried to steer the CCF away from socialist dogma, fearing that it limited their chances of electoral success. (History suggests she was right.) Nor, in the final analysis, was she any kind of doctrinaire feminist. In fact, Casgrain went to considerable lengths to distance herself from the feminist label, opting for the neutral-sounding "humanist," despite her profound and lifelong commitment to the rights of women and girls.

Perhaps it is more accurate to describe her as a kind of self-abnegating feminist—one who always had one eye on reassuring the world that she had not given up her domesticity and femininity. Even the title of Casgrain's 1972 autobiography, *A Woman in a Man's World*, signals a sort of sexual defeatism. Frank R. Scott, a founding member of Canada's CCF, penned the foreword to the book, containing this faint praise: "She showed it is possible for a woman to play an active role in public life without losing any of her personal charm or giving up any of her duties as a wife and a mother."

Well, thank goodness for that! How unattractive it is when a woman's ambition undermines her capacity for charm. Then again, such attitudes were the natural order of things in Casgrain's day. And she learned to navigate them in much the same way as many women before and since—by checking all the boxes.

Casgrain longed for a day when there might be a woman prime minister or president, but doubted that it would ever happen, often blaming women themselves for not stepping up: "Of course it is normal for domestic tasks to absorb a large part of [women's] energies, but is that any reason to refuse to work in the public sector? Generally speaking, women are less accepted in positions of command. It would be hard to imagine a woman head of government in Canada or the United States, for instance . . . there is very little co-operation between the sexes and I admit that it is often the women themselves who set up the obstacles in their own way."

Casgrain was already into her eighth decade of life when the idea that male power structures could be challenged and potentially dismantled—even if many weren't—began to take shape in wider society. This was the 1960s. But by this time, she was locked in a generational culture war over the way women should present themselves politically and aesthetically. When asked about younger feminists in a 1975 Radio-Canada documentary, Casgrain quipped: "*Je trouve aujourd'hui que certaines Women's Lib exagèrent*" ("I find today that certain Women's Lib [advocates] exaggerate"). In a similar vein, she declared, "Our case is not strengthened because thousands of [women] throw, if not all sense of propriety to the wind, at least their bras into their fire." For a woman born into corsets, and who fled the family pool when a boy was in sight lest her personal dignity be compromised, the prospect of letting it all hang out in the name of equality seemed crass.

To understand Casgrain, and the full extent of her contribution to Canada and to feminism more broadly, is to wrestle with these contradictions. And perhaps that's what she wanted: to avoid labels that might reduce her to a cliché and thereby compromise her ability to get things done. She was a woman of action, who unabashedly challenged religious leaders, politicians, the private sector, and even foreign heads of state. Shortly after the Cuban Missile Crisis, while serving as national president for the Voice of Women, she led delegations that opposed Canada's entry into the nuclear arms race, urging John Diefenbaker's government to adopt a ban on nuclear testing and weapons. In January 1963, when Lester B. Pearson announced support for nuclear arms during a speech to the Liberal Association in York–Scarborough—just before the minority Diefenbaker government fell—Casgrain enticed a young Pierre Elliott Trudeau to give a speech on her behalf opposing the Liberal leader. (Trudeau went so far as to write an op ed accusing the Liberals of betraying their values.)

This was not an isolated instance: Casgrain had a direct line to various powerful politicians, whom she sometimes leveraged against one another. And at the provincial level, she devoted much of her energy to urging Quebec politicians to adopt policies that already had been put in place by her allies in other parts of Canada. But her infectious idealism knew no provincial borders. Her vision was of a country that respected and protected language and culture, sought to end war rather than wage it, offered free health care to all, cared for the sick and the vulnerable, provided a living wage to the poor, believed in public education, and looked after the elderly. As a member of the 1 per cent, Casgrain never quite escaped her cocoon of wealth and privilege. But as an intellectual, Casgrain did look beyond her circle of mostly white, educated, elite women, and saw others whose needs were worth fighting for.

As a Catholic, Casgrain did not abandon the Catholic Church. But she publicly defied its policies on many fronts, particularly when it came to women. It is therefore not difficult to recognize in Casgrain's activism and criticisms early whispers of Quebec's Révolution tranquille.

She was, in short, one of the most important leftists Canada has ever produced, critically contributing to many of the public policy ideas, rights, and freedoms Canadians have cherished since her time.

Which leads us back to the question of why so few outside Quebec have heard of her.

Casgrain always maintained an enviable ability to confound politicians of all stripes, but male conservatives in particular, just by her sheer refusal to go away quietly. Many tried to sideline her, though none succeeded. She always found a platform for her opinions and ideas, whether as a political wife, a candidate, an NGO or party leader, a senator, or a CBC radio host. To close the front door on her demands was to watch her climb (elegantly) through the back window, placard raised, finger pointed: *J'accuse*.

A year after her death in 1981, Prime Minister Pierre Trudeau announced the annual Thérèse Casgrain Volunteer Award, which celebrated those Canadians making a significant contribution as a volunteer. Then the next prime minister, Brian Mulroney, cancelled it. Then Prime Minister Jean Chrétien reinstituted it. Then, in 2010, Prime Minister Stephen Harper subtly slipped in a name change, renaming it the Prime Minister's Volunteer Award, and stripping away Casgrain. In April 2016, Justin Trudeau's government dutifully reversed the policy yet again, by instituting the Thérèse Casgrain Lifelong Achievement Award.

More than thirty years after Casgrain's death, there is clearly still something about this woman's legacy that some conservative men find threatening. Casgrain herself would no doubt be pleased to know that she remains a symbol of social progressivism in this country—even if she might be surprised that so much work still needs to be done.

VANIA JIMENEZ

PAUL DAVID

THE MUSIC OF THE BEATING HEART

MAY 2015. THE EMERGENCY DOCTOR remembers. It's been sixteen years since he took up his practice at the Montreal Heart Institute. Quebec's health care system is in the midst of profound change. In the intervening years, many doctors and nurses have retired, replaced by younger professionals. He remembers . . .

APRIL 1999, AS A YOUNG DOCTOR, he began his career at the Institute, founded by Dr. Paul David in 1954. He was among the first to practise emergency medicine in this sanctuary for the treatment of cardiac illnesses. To get acquainted with the premises—a six-storey building in an E-shaped layout in east-end Montreal—and with the staff in the different departments, he set out to tour its various wings and rooms.

Something wasn't right. Wherever he went, he saw eyes reddened by tears. Why, he wondered? Everyone he spoke to welcomed him merely with polite curiosity. He knew that Dr. David, whose specialty was cardiology, had been against the construction of a multi-purpose emergency room in "his" facility. This new ward was a sort of transgression, so the young doctor could have expected some degree of reticence. But tears?

He soon learned the reason. Paul David was dying. The father of one of the world's top five cardiology institutes had reached his final days.

The young emergency physician was a music lover. The night before, he had been to a concert at Montreal's Place des Arts. Bach, the master of counterpoint.* Back in his days as a medical student, when he pressed the bell of his stethoscope to a patient's chest, the sound of the beating heart was a call, urging him to consider cardiology as his specialty. As it turned out, his university training led him to specialize in emergency care; still attracted by the music of the beating heart, he compromised and chose to practise at the Heart Institute.

Was it that same music of the heart that had prompted Paul David to become a cardiologist? The young doctor, curious, already knew that a love of music ran in the David family—crystallized in the founding of the Orchestre symphonique de Montréal by Paul's parents.

But what muse had inspired the young Paul? Clearly, he had realized a dream, and been guided by a melody, on top of which there were certainly counterpoints: he may initially have been loath to betray a lineage of lawyers and politicians, but he felt a desire for autonomy in his career choice, and this drove him to step outside the family tradition. A counterpoint, already.

Systole, diastole. Beep-BEEP, beep-BEEP. Image and sound. The young emergency doctor set out on a search for Paul David, in the music of the beating heart, and beyond the stunning achievement that the Institute represented. Intrigued, as soon as he had some free time he went through the archives. Who was this man whose imminent demise had stirred such sorrow?

Another question fascinated him: what music was playing in Paul David's head when he spoke those history-making words in 1968?

* Music that is written with two or more melodic lines in superimposition.

Mozart? Brahms? The founder's voice echoed in his ears: "The heart transplant has been achieved and the procedure is complete."

That first day at the MHI, the young doctor met an older nurse. When he asked her about Dr. David, she first apologized for the tears welling in her eyes. Then she smiled, quoted Walt Whitman's "O Captain! My Captain!"* and reminisced about the fundamental goodness of the ailing cardiologist: "The most respectful man I have ever known," she said. Then she added, deferentially: "But he could be so intense . . ."

The young doctor wondered: is that "intensity" a hallmark of great men? Are they instruments of destiny led to accomplish great work, or are they the artisans of their own vision? Unless those are merely two ways of saying the same thing . . .

"Intense." "Obstinate." "Kind." "Respectful." All of these words were used to describe Dr. David. Still more adjectives would later light the young man's way (perhaps explaining the internal dynamics of David's determination in remaining distinct from Université de Montréal), especially the paradoxical designation "nationalist federalist."

Throughout his life, this slender man with the receding hairline and tortoise-shell eyeglasses seemed to have embodied a tension that somehow guaranteed he would accomplish his mission. His was a strange and wonderful destiny: he disappointed his father, Athanase, by choosing medicine over law, and then specialized in cardiology. At once invested with and dependent on that weighty, refined heritage, but following his own impulses, he stood apart—at least in terms of his chosen profession—from his male forebears, who were lawyers.

His great-grandfather Stanislas David, son of the sculptor Louis-Basile David, was born in 1794 in Sault-au-Récollet (today part of the Montreal borough of Ahuntsic-Cartierville) and took part in assemblies of Patriotes, as a militia captain. Stanislas's son Laurent-Olivier (grandfather of Paul and father of Athanase) was a lawyer, journalist, and politician, and a friend of Sir Wilfrid Laurier. As a member of the

* "O Captain! My Captain!" was written by the American poet and humanist in honour of President Abraham Lincoln.

Saint-Jean-Baptiste Society, he helped create the Monument-National theatre in Montreal. An ardent Quebec nationalist, he wrote *Les Patriotes de 1837–1838*, and in the introduction to that essay collection left no doubt as to his political leanings: "The sole objective of this book is to show that they (the Patriotes) deserve our recognition, and that we must accept the offering of their sacrifices and their blood for the honour of our nationality and the triumph of liberty."*

Laurent-Olivier David had ten children, including a single son, Athanase, born in 1882, who was a very important politician in Quebec during the first half of the twentieth century. After becoming a lawyer, Athanase married Antonia Nantel, herself descended from a dynasty of politicians and teachers. He was a great lover of music, and his wife was a musician, having studied piano in Montreal as well as opera at the Conservatoire de Paris. She had planned on a career as an opera singer until she met the politician who would become her husband. The heartbeat of Antonia, both a music lover and a musician, of course accompanied Paul David before his birth, which came on New Year's Day 1919. He had a twin sister, Suzanne.

Antonia Nantel was exceptionally sensitive to music, thought the young emergency doctor. He felt he was close to an answer to his question: what was the connection between music and Paul David? He thought of how in dance classes, it was common for the teacher to ask her students to tap out the rhythm of their own heart: each dancer then discovered how every pulse is different, and how, by following that rhythm, their movements become more fluid.

Music was omnipresent in the David family: Antonia played a key role in the 1930 founding of the Montreal Orchestra, Quebec's first professional symphony orchestra. She was a member of its executive committee, but quit in 1934, protesting that the orchestra's soloist recruitment policies discriminated against francophones. Determined that the city should have a francophile orchestra, she founded

* Laurent-Olivier David, *Les Patriotes de 1837–1838*, Montreal: Eusèbe Senécal & fils, 1884. [Freely translated.]

the Société des concerts symphoniques de Montréal that same year. Paul David and his twin sister, Suzanne, were by then aged fifteen. In 1935, Athanase hired Wilfrid Pelletier as the orchestra's first artistic director. The next year, along with Pelletier, Antonia established the Festivals de Montréal, an annual celebration of classical music that would endure until 1965.

The same year as the Montreal Orchestra was founded, Paul David began his secondary-school studies at Collège Stanislas in Paris. He continued his studies there from 1934 to 1939, eventually obtaining his baccalaureate degree. Thus music, and its advent in his life, accompanied his first steps toward a career in medicine.

After returning from Paris, Paul entered medical school at Université de Montréal. Around the same time, in 1940, angiocardiography—the radiographic examination of the heart's chambers and blood vessels—was coming into widespread use. And by then, the future cardiologist probably already knew that his musician mother suffered from heart problems.

THE SOCIAL CONTEXT

The context of post-war health care in Quebec—the setting in which Paul David became a medical doctor and accomplished his projects—is worth describing here. Put simply, the major societal shifts in the province included the transition from a system in which health care was primarily the responsibility of religious orders to one of secular administration.

Quebec was slowly emerging from the years of the so-called Grande Noirceur under Premier Maurice Duplessis. The medical profession in francophone society, which until then had humbly toiled in the shadows of the renowned—and English-speaking—McGill University, was gradually flourishing.

It is often thought that modern Quebec only began after the death in 1959 of Duplessis and the election of Jean Lesage in 1960. It is true that prior to those years, French Canadians wielded little economic power and their potential for advancement in the working world was limited. Social and cultural conservatism had arrested intellectual, educational, and material development, primarily among the middle and working classes, though the French-Canadian elite and bourgeoisie (to which the David family belonged) were much advantaged by comparison. The movement toward modernization begun in the 1930s broadened and intensified in the post-war years, propelled by challenges to traditional ideologies as well as openness to new currents of Western thought.*

Prior to this shift, the francophone health system was almost entirely in the hands of the religious orders, supported by philanthropic initiatives. Doctors were hired by hospital administrators, not the state. The modernization of Quebec's health care system was one product of the so-called Quiet Revolution. With that sea change approaching, those religious orders that could afford it took very seriously the training of administrators for their institutions; for example, Sister Rachel Tourigny, the first head of the Montreal Heart Institute, was a member of the American College of Hospital Administrators.

Medicine in Quebec, on both the English- and French-speaking sides, benefited from the work of clinicians, surgeons, and physiologists from Europe and the United States, which led to a broadening of diagnostic and therapeutic knowledge and techniques. Knowledge transfer was facilitated by study trips and fellowships.

Specialization grew, and in that context many young physicians helped change the face of medical practice in Quebec's hospitals. Although cardiology was not yet a specialty, the first cardiology clinic in the province was established at McGill in 1926.

Post-1960, the health care sector was one theatre for the transformation of class dynamics in Quebec: where once there was a clerical elite,

---

* Paul-André Linteau, René Durocher, François Ricard, and Jean-Claude Robert, *Histoire du Québec contemporain, Volume 2: Le Québec depuis 1930*, Montreal: Boréal, 1989.

there was now a new stratum of lay administrators who came from intellectual circles. Before 1960, the state had subsidized health care only for the poor. Private insurance existed, but only 43 per cent of the population had coverage. Quebec signed on to the federal hospital insurance program in 1961, and in 1970 passed the Health Insurance Act, giving birth to the health care regime in its present form.

In 1960, 58 per cent of hospitals were owned by religious orders, with one-tenth still managed by them. The Hospitals Act of 1962 withdrew their ownership and administration rights. Members of religious orders were thenceforth a minority voice on hospital boards of directors, and could no longer chair them (nuns who remained in such positions also began to earn salaries). Consequently, secular men replaced religious women as the heads of Quebec's health care institutions.

The Montreal Heart Institute was founded against this backdrop of the shift from private to public health care.

THE CALL OF MEDICINE

Heading back to the emergency room on that day in early April 1999, the young doctor recalled a passage from a book that he found particularly moving:

> A voice speaks to him, calls him, keeps him spellbound. It overwhelms the interior silence of the human being, simultaneously revealing to him that it permeates the universe. . . . This inaudible utterance seems to come from afar, yet clearly it is there, present, immanent. To manifest, it takes the form of vocation and belongs to the various modes of perception to which human temperaments are subject. . . .*

* Alfred Tomatis, *Écouter l'univers. Du Big Bang à Mozart : à la découverte de l'univers où tout est son*, Paris: Robert Laffont, 1996, p. 277. [Freely translated.]

The young doctor pondered this "calling of medicine," this appeal from the heart that he himself had heard. Paul David had surely heard it too: the proof was in that series of counterpoints to his lineage, the marching forward in spite of—and thanks to—his predecessors.

And what did Dr. David himself believe, privately, about his profession? A likely echo comes to us in a novel written by Nellie Maillard, his first wife and the mother of his six children:

> And yet we love this métier! We love it fiercely and religiously all at once. There is so much to do, so many struggles to wage! Fighting every step of the way against death, suffering, and every physical decline. The physician is the champion of life, and in that capacity has no right to mediocrity. He who is not a good physician can only be a poor one. *Noblesse oblige!* . . . Yes, we love this métier, an inexhaustible source of charity, that commits every one of a man's strengths: his conscience, his soul, his intelligence, and also his family, inspiring in all a militant spirit, keeping everyone spellbound, alert at the brink, staring into the misery of the world. . . .*
>
> But you see, even after but a few years' practice, I have been near my share of sick people, of all classes, all ages, all conditions. I have seen some die; I have, alas, seen the slow agony of cardiac patients, whom medicine can only assuage and prolong their lives. It is in those last few months of existence that one is able, perhaps, to judge a man, to discover his deepest resources. I assure you, Monsieur, sometimes culture, science, human knowledge and all the refinement of our civilization are utterly powerless to allay his anxiety and his anguish. This man, confronted by suffering and close to the end, is stripped little by little of that which constituted his life; everything crumbles around him—career, friendships, artistic and intellectual joys!

* Anne-Marie (pen name of Nellie Maillard-David), *L'aube de la joie*, Montreal: Le Cercle du livre de France, 1959, p. 9. [Freely translated.]

> And then, religion comes to his rescue; religion alone brings him peace, resignation, the answers to the terrible questions that haunt him.*

Bringing relief to bodies to liberate minds. As a deeply religious, practising Catholic who respected others' beliefs, this is no doubt how Paul David would have spoken of his métier.

EARLY APRIL 1999. The days went by and Dr. David's condition did not improve. The Heart Institute, where he was hospitalized, had no neurology department, so neurologists in other institutions were consulted. Perplexed, the young emergency physician wondered whether it was opportune for a specialized institute to be located so far from a general hospital. Would creating this type of autonomous facility, independent from a general hospital, even be conceivable today? Did Wilder Penfield roll over in his grave when the Royal Victoria Hospital moved so far away from the Montreal Neurological Institute, which he had founded?

Intensely curious, he kept at his research: After earning his physician's degree in 1944, David had begun specializing in cardiology at Notre-Dame Hospital. Heart disease was then the leading cause of death in Quebec. In 1946, he trained at the Massachusetts General Hospital in Boston with Dr. Paul Dudley White and, a year later, returned to Paris to study at Hôpital Lariboisière with Pierre Soulié and Jean Lenègre. All were eminent cardiologists. Even at this early stage, David was eager to learn from the two great traditions, American and European. The scientific advances then occurring in the United States were fascinating.

When David returned from Paris in 1948, the Sœurs Grises (Grey Nuns), administrators of Notre-Dame Hospital, held discussions with

* Ibid., p. 21. [Freely translated.]

him. In 1950, he took a position as a cardiologist there. A visionary, he foresaw a method of correcting congenital valvular disorders, which at the time were impossible to treat.* Under his direction, Édouard Gagnon became the first physician in Canada to perform surgery to correct mitral stenonis.†

That same year, 1950, David attended an international cardiology congress in Paris, which likely provided the impetus for him to advance the discipline—and perhaps the idea of an institute wholly dedicated to the development of cardiology was already germinating. Upon his return, he insisted that the cardiology department occupy an entire floor of Notre-Dame Hospital, but under separate administration.

The existence of the Montreal Neurological Institute was probably another spark fuelling David's determination to create a cardiology institute. An institute, uniting clinical, teaching, and research disciplines under one roof, allowed close correlation between medical and surgical practice on the one hand, and experimental and clinical research on the other. As the second half of the twentieth century dawned, there was assuredly fertile ground for such seeds to grow under the stewardship of great research minds like Armand Frappier, Hans Selye, Jacques Genest, and Antonio Cantero.

In 1951, the Sœurs Grises asked David to set up and head the cardiology department of the future Maisonneuve Hospital; it would eventually be built in 1954. Per David's wishes, the department would occupy the top two floors as an independent entity, the Montreal Heart Institute. David became its first director.

Those fragments of information gathered, the young emergency doctor returned to the compelling question of the role of music in David's life at the time. The Montreal Orchestra had folded six years after its inception, and by 1953 the francophile Société des concerts symphoniques de Montréal, founded in 1934 by Paul's parents, Athanase and Antonia, was officially known as the Orchestre

* Defects, existing at birth, in the valves controlling blood flow through the heart.

† A narrowing of the mitral valve, located on the left side of the heart.

symphonique de Montréal, under the baton of illustrious maestros, the first of whom was Wilfrid Pelletier.

Athanase David died that year, followed two years later, in 1955, by his wife, Antonia. Between those two dates, in 1954, the Montreal Heart Institute was founded.

BUILDING AND CRYSTALLIZING THE DREAM

As the first centre in Canada dedicated to cardiology, the MHI indeed consolidated services, teaching, and research under one roof. For assistance, David enlisted Dr. Arthur Vineberg, a renowned cardiac surgeon at the Royal Victoria Hospital who had pioneered a revascularization procedure whereby the internal mammary artery was implanted into the left ventricle to treat cases of coronary artery narrowing or blockage.*

As soon as the Institute was created as a distinct entity of the Maisonneuve Hospital, David had an experimental operating theatre built there, along with a kennel under the supervision of a biologist. Another physician developed new surgical instruments, and a social worker was hired—a first step toward multidisciplinary work.

The Institute was the site of several milestones. In 1957, the first experiments in Quebec with open-heart procedures were conducted there, using cardiopulmonary bypass.† In 1961, the first pacemaker in the province was implanted at the Institute. And the first coronary angioplasty in Canada would be performed there in 1980.‡

* The mammary artery, now more commonly known as the internal thoracic artery, supplies the breasts. In bypass surgery, it can replace a coronary artery (i.e., one essential to the proper operation of the heart muscle) without inconvenience to the patient.

† Blood circulation, normally occurring inside the body, with the heart's pump action irrigating all vital organs, is temporarily transferred outside the body using a mechanical pump, called a heart-lung machine.

‡ Angioplasty is a minimally invasive procedure that enables relief of narrowed or blocked coronary arteries without need for major surgery.

Long before that, though, early successes drove expansion. The original Institute had only forty-five beds and a single operating room. With patients being referred there from all over, a new facility would be needed. The initial plan was to build on land adjacent to Maisonneuve Hospital.

Eventually, it was announced that a hundred-bed hospital would be built on Bélanger Street, at its intersection with Viau Boulevard. At the start of construction, in 1964, the Institute's president, Claude Robillard, wrote in a newsletter, "This newsletter will keep you abreast of the progress of construction and the work that has been conducted for ten years now by Dr. Paul David and his team of doctors, surgeons, researchers, nurses, technicians, etc." The Institute moved to its new (and current) location in 1966. The building was enlarged in 1973 to 172 beds.

Between 1960 and 1970, research at the MHI focused on cardiac catheterization techniques,* treatment of bacterial endocarditis,† and open-heart surgery to repair congenital defects. Late in that same decade, thousands of kilometres away in Cape Town, South Africa, a heart surgeon named Christiaan Barnard, who had previously performed kidney transplants and successfully transplanted hearts in dogs, was preparing to perform the world's first human heart transplant. The milestone operation, using a team of thirty doctors and nurses, took place on December 3, 1967.

In the great "symphony hall" of the Montreal Heart Institute, preparations were underway to perform the first heart transplant in Canada, the eighteenth such procedure worldwide. Paul David, by then the general manager of the Institute, wrote in its annual report, "Last April, in Lima, as President of the Interamerican Society of Cardiology I was able to meet on several occasions with Dr. Christiaan Barnard, the most in-demand guest at the VIII Interamerican Congress.

* In catheterization, a probe is inserted via a thin tube inserted in a natural orifice, a vein or an artery.

† A bacterial infection of the endocardium, the inner layer of the heart.

On the basis of his presentations at the congress, reports in the press and a lengthy conversation, I returned absolutely convinced of the merits of this surgery. All that remained was to trust in the abilities and skills of the surgeon and of the large team who would attempt to perform the procedure successfully."

After months of preparation, the go-ahead was finally given. At 11:30 p.m. on May 30, 1968, Canada's first heart transplant began in the operating theatres of the Montreal Heart Institute.

Dr. Pierre Grondin operated on the recipient, fifty-six-year-old Albert Murphy of Laval, removing his diseased heart while his other vital organs were supplied with blood and oxygen for ninety-five minutes using a heart-lung machine. Meanwhile, Dr. Gilles Lepage removed the heart of the donor, Mrs. Gérard Rondeau, aged thirty-eight, who had died of a cerebral hemorrhage. After the transplant, Murphy survived for forty-one hours before succumbing to an infection. Subsequent patients did not survive for very long either.

Thinking back to what happened following those initial transplants, the young emergency physician, on his first day at the MHI in April 1999, had better insight into the Institute staffers' heartache. Paul David, deeply driven by ethics, had a different relationship to celebrity than did Dr. Barnard. Confronted with the dismal reality that, worldwide, cardiac transplant patients' survival times were so brief, he was the first to recommend a moratorium on the procedure until immunosuppressive drugs could be developed that would prevent a recipient's body from rejecting the transplanted organ. A man of conviction, even in the face of opposition from his colleague, the distinguished Dr. Grondin, David unhesitatingly ordered a stop to transplants at the MHI—a decision that was far more difficult to make than the decision to perform them in the first place. And the world followed suit, beginning in 1969.

Heart transplants eventually became routine in the late 1970s and early 1980s, once anti-rejection drugs were perfected. In 1983, a twenty-one-year-old woman became the first recipient of a new heart as part of the second phase of the Institute's cardiac transplant program.

The Montreal Heart Institute Research Centre was founded in 1976, focusing initially on clinical (applied) research and eventually expanding into fundamental (pure) research, the most important outcome of which was the finding that cyclosporin, a immunosuppressant drug already in use for treatment of autoimmune disorders,* could prevent rejection of transplanted organs. This paved the way for the tremendous growth in transplants of all kinds after 1980.

"NUCLEAR WAR"

Paul David's career path was not free of obstacles, however. One aspect that proved laborious was university and hospital alliances.

Some days later, the young emergency doctor came across another of the counterpoints that had marked the esteemed cardiologist's work, and was able to measure the scope of the controversy around the university–hospital alliance—something that had personal repercussions for David himself during his dying days. The decision to build the MHI away from the Université de Montréal campus had led to, in the words of the elderly nurse, a "nuclear war." Noting the young doctor's surprise, she smiled and qualified her choice of words: it wasn't so much a war as a "forced marriage"—a particular aspect of the relationship between hospitals and medical faculties in francophone Quebec.

During the first half of the twentieth century, the teaching of medicine in Quebec followed the pragmatic and operational criteria of the French clinical tradition, and professors were enthusiastically francophile. Everyone had to heed the supremacy—the "aristocracy," even—of the clinic. The 1940s, however, brought growing interest in biomedical science, especially the spectacular advances seen in the United States. McGill University, a distinguished and prosperous institution that had enjoyed an international reputation since the turn

* Diseases in which the body's immune system attacks its own healthy tissues.

of the century (and was supported by the Rockefeller Foundation), already exemplified this trend. Members of the Université de Montréal and Université Laval medical faculties, too, had shown interest in scientific research, though it was rare. Too often, willingness to reconcile fundamental and clinical science was thwarted by the dearth of financial resources at the French-language universities, the absence of stable scientific policies, the needs of hospitals, and an unfavourable economic context.

The connections between care delivery, teaching, and research, which to the casual eye should flow naturally, consistently proved difficult to make. Conflicting interests or a thorny issue always seemed to rear its head; hence the "forced marriage." Without having to be a union of love, it might at least have been one of reasons . . .

As far back as the 1920s, the Université de Montréal Faculty of Medicine had wanted to establish a university hospital adjacent to the central building of its new campus on the northwest slope of Mount Royal. The idea of combining hospital services, the teaching of advanced surgical techniques, and research was laudable, and it seemed that it would come to fruition.

At the time, Université de Montréal had already been upstaged by McGill. Under the aegis of Dr. William Osler, who had always favoured the amalgamation of clinical and fundamental science in hospital settings, the Royal Victoria Hospital's university clinic had been inaugurated in 1924, in what was then the most modern facility in Quebec.

By the early 1930s, with Université de Montréal reeling from the impact of the Crash of 1929, the project was halted. Even the Rockefeller Foundation, in view of the economic downturn, withdrew its support for construction of the wings that were to house the new hospital.

At the same time, a new hospital (Maisonneuve) was being planned for east-end Montreal, with the support of the provincial government. The project to build a teaching hospital adjacent to the Université de Montréal medical school progressed in fits and starts, but was abandoned when the Duplessis government considerably reduced funding for universities. Hope was rekindled in 1959, but controversy arose regarding the proposed site on Mount Royal. The newly elected Liberal government did an about-face, and the death knell rang for the project.

Unlike university hospitals, with their arduous birth pangs, the emergence of specialized institutes was relatively uncomplicated, thanks to a smoother fit: the hospital remained a hospital, and the institute remained a specialized entity. The Montreal Heart Institute specialized in care delivery as well as teaching and research, conducting work on electrical defibrillation* and cardiac electrostimulation, and even experimenting with open-heart surgical techniques on animal subjects.

The approach was so successful that, in 1959, an affiliation between the Université de Montréal Faculty of Medicine and the MHI was considered, and won the favour of Premier Paul Sauvé and the university's rector. An agreement was approved in 1961, whereby the Institute would retain its autonomy but its academic personnel would thenceforth be attached to university departments. All went well until the idea of building a teaching hospital on the campus of Université de Montréal was revived. This time, it was the status of the Institute within the future hospital that was problematic: it was feared that an independent MHI right next door would leave the hospital with a grossly inadequate cardiology department. In reality, this meant even greater specialization of some physicians, to the detriment of general practice.

In the end, neither project saw fruition. No teaching hospital was built up on the mountain, and the MHI was not integrated into the university. Land was purchased on Bélanger Street in 1964 for construction of a new location for the MHI. It left the Maisonneuve Hospital site in 1966, and as a result was further separated from the university. Nevertheless, the work being done at the Institute was perfectly in line with one of the university's missions: to conduct leading-edge research.

---

* The treatment of abnormal contractions of the heart muscle by electrical discharges, and stimulation of an element of the nervous or muscular system by electric current.

As for teaching at the Montreal Heart Institute, it was wide-ranging, and was provided to physicians from the Montreal area and elsewhere, who benefited from state-of-the-art expertise, as is evident from the list of interns at the time—physicians with names like Abi-Saleh, Alvarez, Borromeo, Eibar, Zakrzewski, Perez, and others.

Coinciding with the fortieth anniversary of the Institute, construction of a six-storey building was completed in 1994.

SCIENTIFIC REPUTATION

The same year, to ensure maximum antibacterial protection for patients, six rooms were converted into two sterile units. Specialists from several countries visited them, including Dr. Christiaan Barnard himself.

The considerable success of research conducted at the MHI, and the legacy of Dr. Paul David, is evident in the number and quality of scientific publications by researchers there. Between 1954 and 1979, seven hundred papers were published, 43 per cent of these in U.S. journals, 18 per cent in European journals, and 39 per cent in Canadian journals.

The Institute's researchers published dozens of papers in the most prestigious journals, and took part in numerous medical congresses. In 1968 alone, MHI-affiliated physicians and scientists presented an imposing number of clinical and scientific papers at such gatherings as the Interamerican Congress of Cardiology in Lima, the first Conference on Heart Transplants in Cape Town, the Annual Meeting of the American Heart Association in Miami, and meetings of the American College of Cardiology in Vancouver and the Ontario Hospital Association in Toronto. A documentary short film about heart transplantation commissioned by the National Film Board of Canada, directed by Claude Fournier, was distributed by Columbia Pictures around the world.

But one final paradox about that difficult birth remained for the young emergency doctor to elucidate: that of Paul David himself. He was very sensitive to the multiple dimensions of patient care, so why was he so fixated on asserting the Heart Institute's identity and independence? An example of what motivated him in this regard was the glaring lack of radiology and neurology facilities at the MHI. David was intent on a protected budget, and had insisted on an autonomous cardiology facility to ensure it could develop unfettered by competition from other departments.

It was obvious that, at the time the Institute was founded, medicine was far less advanced than it is today, and one specialty could do without the others. The young doctor knew deep down that in 1999, as opposed to the 1950s, to ignore interdisciplinarity would be unthinkable.

Would the Institute have forged such a strong reputation had it been confined to the bounds of the university? To shine, a diamond must be plucked from its natural surroundings. While it was true that the Institute had done extremely well in uniting considerable means—laboratories, libraries, animal houses, specialized personnel affiliated with research programs—there was a price to be paid elsewhere, notably the difficulty faced by Maisonneuve-Rosemont Hospital in obtaining a cardiac surgery department. But who could say whether the decision not to integrate the MHI into the planned-but-never-built campus on Mount Royal had been a hindrance or a blessing?

Roger Dufresne, the assistant dean of the Université de Montréal Faculty of Medicine and a friend of David's, had pushed for the outright assimilation of the Heart Institute into the future teaching hospital. David replied: "To integration, we prefer collaboration; to annexation, we prefer a more thoughtful formula of agreements based on respect and sincerity." He remained committed to maintaining the distinct character of his Institute.

Imagining that tension between friends, the young emergency doctor was reminded of the fraught relationship between Quebec and the rest of Canada. The province was de facto part of Canadian Confederation, but not integrated, not assimilated.

Indeed, the elderly nurse he was speaking to mentioned that when Dr. David was taken ill, he had had to be referred to Maisonneuve-

Rosemont Hospital for expert neurological care. Thus a price was being paid in 1999 for the leading-edge advances and expertise obtained decades earlier by emulating the American method and its remarkable discoveries.

FRANCOPHONE PRIDE

In Paul David's vision of the Institute, it collaborated with the university while remaining distinct from it. That vision was perfectly coherent and a mirror image of his political position: he was a "nationalist federalist." As president of the Association des médecins de langue française du Canada and editor of its *L'Union médicale du Canada*, a scientific journal renowned for its great rigour, he helped ensure the reputation of francophone medical expertise in Quebec, the rest of Canada, and internationally.

In June 1970, David wrote, "At the dawn of this very important step in the evolution of our society,* we see in the Association des médecins de langue française du Canada the organization most representative of French-language medical thought in Canada." In his acceptance speech after winning the 1977 Montreal Hospital Council Award, he said, "As a Québécois, my individual nationalism was to prove that it was possible for a francophone to create a body of work with a reputation that grew progressively in Canada, the United States, in Europe, and around the world. It is now up to the younger generation to sustain that prestige and excellence. During the often difficult hours of this achievement, I put up with indifference from those who did not speak my language, but I never understood the frequent apathy on the part of those who share my cultural objectives."

Two years later, on the occasion of the Heart Institute's twenty-fifth anniversary, to an audience that included the mayor of Montreal, Jean Drapeau, and the Quebec minister of social affairs, Denis Lazure,

* The advent of the Quebec public health insurance regime.

he said, "Allow me to express my satisfaction in having demonstrated to Quebec the excellence of a Montreal-based undertaking, to Canada the success of a Quebec endeavour, and to the world the leadership of a French-speaking Canadian team."

As the saying goes, though, the apple never falls far from the tree. Paul David may not have followed in his forebears' professional footsteps, but his values remained close to theirs. After all, his mother, Antonia, had walked out on the Montreal Orchestra over the issue of discrimination against francophones.

At the end of his first day on the job, the emergency doctor was still pondering what music played on an endless loop in Paul David's head. Haydn, speaking of Mozart, once said, "I have just discovered that which I have been searching forever: harmony."

In music theory, the term *harmony* is synonymous with counterpoint.

OTHER INNOVATIONS

There was one more striking paradox: in spite of his insistence that the Institute remain a distinct entity, Paul David had foreseen a new type of global, or holistic, medicine—one emphasizing prevention and a humanist approach. Persuaded of the obvious link between body and mind, he stated repeatedly that cardiovascular conditions are often caused or aggravated by stress and family problems. As we have seen, he had been quick to hire a social worker at the Institute.

"A happy and motivated staff depends, among other things, on having a pleasant place in which to eat well," he said.* The young emergency physician could not help but notice the MHI's magnificent cafeteria.

"One of my father's colleagues from the earliest days of the Institute told me that when he went on his rounds, the first thing he

* Françoise David, personal communication, March 9, 2015. [Freely translated.]

would do was to sit with the patient and engage in a warm conversation," David's daughter Hélène relates.*

Without forsaking science, David had predicted a return to "the art of medicine," with its emphasis on the physician–patient relationship. The young emergency doctor couldn't help but think of the spiritual kinship that he felt with Norbert Bensaïd, a French general practitioner he admired who was the author of a 1974 essay, *La consultation*. Dr. David, he thought, would surely have approved of these words by Bensaïd:

> We can see patients much faster; we can, on the surface, reduce our entire action to the elementary gestures of consultation: interrogation-examination-prescription. Nothing will ever keep the person inside the physician, with his ideas, sentiments, education, and milieu, and the person inside the patient, with his background, and all of society, from being part and parcel of that action.†

Was David a health care reformer before his time? Years later, responding to intense criticism of the "dehumanization" of health care, many faculties of medicine were to implement sweeping changes, restructuring their curricula. The associate dean of undergraduate studies at the Université de Montréal explained the shift in 1990: "Medicine in the coming century will require an integrated form of fundamental physician education reliant on both the natural sciences and the humanities."‡

The idea of global medicine, with emphasis on prevention, had attracted attention as early as the 1960s. In 1968, David, decidedly

* Hélène David, personal communication. [Freely translated.]

† Norbert Bensaïd, *La consultation: le dialogue médecin/malade*, Paris: Bibliothèque Méditations, 1974, p. 301. [Freely translated.]

‡ Denis Goulet and Robert Gagnon, *Histoire de la médecine au Québec, 1800–2000: de l'art de soigner à la science de guérir*, Quebec City: Septentrion, 2014, p. 332. [Freely translated.]

avant-gardist, had thrown his full weight behind a pilot study, the Étude Pilote de l'Institut de Cardiologie (ÉPIC), which aimed to demonstrate the benefits of exercise on the cardiovascular system. Several MHI physicians and researchers took part. The findings were clear: the best way to prevent heart problems was to engage in physical activity. David himself didn't exercise! The ÉPIC Centre was eventually built in 1974 and integrated into the Montreal Heart Institute in 1983, as its preventive medicine and exercise centre. It is now Canada's largest centre for cardiovascular disease prevention.

HUSBAND AND FATHER

The Davids passed on Christian values to their children, and the family attended church every Sunday. Both parents (especially Nellie) imparted the social teachings of the Gospel message while insisting that their children never make disparaging or improper remarks about people of other faiths.

The university embodied the quest for knowledge, through teaching and research. For a learned man such as Paul David, dissension with that powerful symbol could only be a source of great suffering, and the torment caused by the tensions between Université de Montréal and the Heart Institute affected him deeply. Nellie supported him unconditionally through those times. A paragraph in one of her novels (premonitory, because it was written before Paul faced those difficulties in real life) takes the full measure of that distress:

> He did his utmost to appear optimistic, but I could sense he was depressed, disgusted; he went and got a sleeping pill, gulped it down, and lit another cigarette. Finally he turned out the light. Moments later, I could feel him turning this way and that, trying in vain to get to sleep, or at least to calm down; he punched his pillow repeatedly, muttering jumbled words. . . .

Concerned with issues of ethics, Dr. David was a staunch advocate for free care and services[*] and, invoking the Hippocratic Oath, was deeply upset when Quebec physicians went on strike in 1970.

He was a loving father to his children whenever he was home, delighting them with dozens of photos brought back from one trip or another.[†] One such picture, printed in the Montreal Heart Institute's annual report for 1968, shows him with Dr. Christiaan Barnard at the VIII Interamerican Congress of Cardiology, receiving a medal as Commander of the Order of Hipólito Unanue, awarded by the Peruvian Health Ministry.

Among Paul David's descendants, there were no wrong notes. If his ancestors were people of exception, so were his progeny. He and Nellie had six children: four girls and two boys.

Pierre David is a well-known film producer and president of the Independent Producers Association (IPA). With his sister Anne-Marie, he administers the Fondation du Docteur Paul David.

Françoise has been co-spokesperson of the left-wing political party Québec Solidaire since 2006 and a member of Quebec's National Assembly since 2012.

Thérèse's company has won five Félix awards as best media relations agency in the performing arts field, four Coqs d'or awards for ad campaigns for *Le Journal de Montréal*, and three Rubans d'or awards for promotional campaigns for the former TQS television network.

Anne-Marie was from 1974 until recently a professor of social work at CÉGEP du Vieux-Montréal, and is a long-time labour activist.

Hélène has been Quebec's minister of culture and communications since 2014. She was a psychology professor and researcher at Université de Montréal and the institution's associate vice-rector from 2005 to 2008, and has authored some one hundred papers as well as poster sessions for symposia and other scientific gatherings.

---

* Paul David, "À l'aube de l'assurance maladie," in *L'Hôpital d'aujourd'hui* 22(1) (January 1970).

† Françoise David, personal communication, March 9, 2015.

Charles-Philippe is a professor of political science at Université du Québec à Montréal, holder of the Raoul Dandurand Chair of Strategic and Diplomatic Studies, director of the Observatoire sur les États-Unis and twice a Fulbright Scholar; he has also written several books on U.S. politics.

Nellie Maillard died in 1969. Ten years later, Paul David was remarried to Yvette Lemire, herself a cardiologist.

THE RETIREMENT THAT WASN'T

In 1985, at age sixty-five, Paul David retired. He planned to spend his time reading and travelling. But, after the fashion of his ancestors, a connection to power and politics was perhaps inevitable, and before long he received a phone call from Prime Minister Brian Mulroney, who wanted to appoint him to the Senate. David was deeply religious and devoted to serving others, and now his calling transcended the frontiers of medicine, leading him to become a senator. It was a return to family roots, as both his father and grandfather had previously served in the Red Chamber of Canada's Parliament.

But here again, there was a glaring counterpoint.

Unlike his father and grandfather, who were Liberals, David was appointed under the Progressive Conservative banner, believing he would join a group of "sages." It is said that he was disappointed by the grossly partisan nature of the Senate, but nonetheless fulfilled his duties, serving from 1985 to 1994.

In 1992, the father of cardiovascular medicine in Quebec suffered a stroke, which left him paralyzed on the right side of his body. Despite this handicap, he remained active, working from home.

By the end of the young emergency doctor's first week at the Montreal Heart Institute, the inevitable happened: Paul David died on April 5, 1999.

MAY 2015

The emergency doctor is young no longer. He has treated his share of emergency cases. But whenever he is called to care for a patient suffering a heart attack, when he requests that a patient be transferred to hemodynamics, when a patient is declared brain-dead but their heart can be transplanted,* he thinks: no matter the tensions between Paul David and his friend Roger Dufresne, regardless of the fact that the Institute never became part of the Université de Montréal campus, there can be no doubt that the life of Paul David endures—in the lives of so many who owe their lives to his pioneering work.

More than two thousand heart transplants have taken place in Canada since the procedure came back into widespread use. The Montreal Heart Institute is a jewel in Quebec's health care crown, shining in the rest of Canada, in North America, and across the globe. Doctors at the MHI perform between twelve and fifteen heart transplants per year—a number that is limited by the scarcity of organ donors.

But questions still grate at the emergency room doctor and music lover. When someone's heart is transplanted into another person's body, who exactly is the person who wakes up in the recovery room?

Paul David was born of the marriage of politics and music. If the heart of a politician and lawyer had been transplanted into his body, would he have lived up to the ideal of his father, Athanase? Genetically, one is never purely the product of one's father, or of one's mother. Paul became a medical doctor, the embodiment of heart and compassion, a fusion of his father's legal mind with his mother's musical one. And fate did not stop at the crystallization of that alloying of elements. It had to go further: Paul's destiny was to become a cardiologist.

May 13, 2015: the emergency doctor opens that morning's *La Presse* and reads:

* Protocol today allows for transplanting of hearts that have been "dead" for up to twenty minutes, unlike in Dr. David's day, when the donor organ still had to be beating.

Yesterday, researchers at the Montreal Heart Institute looked like a gang of kids about to embark on a treasure hunt. Pharmaceutical giant AstraZeneca has just provided a bank of 80,000 DNA samples for them to scrutinize. The goal: identify the genes responsible for cardiovascular disease and diabetes, and develop new designer drugs to combat them. The staff is delighted: this is the most extensive bank of its kind, and a clear endorsement of the Institute's unique bioinformatics capabilities."*

Something tugs at the doctor's memory. He searches, and searches again. Finally he finds it: a text that he'd read during that first week at the Institute. Forty-seven years earlier, Paul David had written: "With the recent acquisition of its own computer, the Institute will be able to rely on a growing number of programs for assistance with its research projects, follow-up on illnesses, and medico-administrative statistics."† A visionary.

That day, the doctor runs into a member of the David family by chance. Recalling his first day on the job, he smiles to himself and realizes that he still has no idea what music had played in the mind of Paul David.

He asks, and is taken aback by the answer.

Among the family members, though he liked classical music well enough, Paul wasn't the most fervent fan of Mozart or Gregorian chant. Over and over, he listened to so-called popular music. Top of his playlist: *The Sound of Music*.

Montreal's symphony orchestra flourished under the baton of several illustrious maestros, he muses. The Heart Institute had Paul David as its first "conductor." And while a number of directors succeeded him—and succeeded in their positions—within the walls of the Institute, the baton of its first maestro still ruled.

A feeling of profound affection swells within the doctor's heart.

---

* Philippe Mercure, "Des chercheurs montréalais partent à la chasse aux gènes," *La Presse*, May 13, 2015. [Freely translated.]

† Montreal Heart Institute, *Annual Report*, 1968. [Freely translated.]

But it is tinged with bitterness. Quebec's health care system, and all of Canada's, is in the throes of crisis. Access to a family doctor is problematic; financing for the public health care system is increasingly in jeopardy. He intensely feels the absence of the simple man, respected by one and all, who was Paul David, and wonders what the founder of the Montreal Heart Institute would have to say about the storm currently lashing the medical profession in Quebec. If he had to describe it in musical terms, what composition would be best suited? Verdi's *Requiem*, perhaps—that gargantuan argument between an atheist and God.

No, he remembers. Paul David wasn't enough of a classical music fan!

On the cusp of the medicare era, in a January 1970 article published in *L'Hôpital d'aujourd'hui*, David had described problems identical to those of today. The issue of forced marriages between universities and hospitals was as acute as it is now.*

"In 1958, when I supported the adoption of hospital insurance, which was already available to patients everywhere else in Canada, I was roundly censured," David wrote. "And yet, the public in general and the medical profession in particular have reaped incredible benefits from that legislation. With the same vigour and for the same reasons, I now accept medicare."†

At the end of the article, David cited a paragraph from the book *Strength to Love*, by Martin Luther King Jr.: "The means by which we live have outdistanced the ends for which we live. Our scientific power has

* "The report's authors also note 'a clash of two visions' at the CHUM [Université de Montréal Hospital Centre]: one academic, the other having to do with hospital management. . . . In the surgery department, this conflict even resembles 'outright war' between university and hospital leaders." (From an article on the report on medical management at the CHUM by inspectors Michel Baron and Claude Desjardins.) Cited in Ariane Lacoursière, "Les médecins doivent collaborer davantage," *La Presse*, April 24, 2015. [Freely translated.]

† Paul David, "À l'aube de l'assurance maladie," in *L'Hôpital d'aujourd'hui*, 22(1) (January 1970), p. 22.

outrun our spiritual power. We have guided missiles and misguided men. Like the rich man of old [the rich man in the Biblical parable], we have foolishly minimized the internal of our lives and maximized the external. We have absorbed life in livelihood."

Paul David's heart had beaten to the rhythm of his intelligence and his ability.

And, the aging emergency doctor thinks to himself, today's health care system is deeply in need of a harmonious counterpoint, guided by the music of the beating heart.

MARGARET ATWOOD

GABRIELLE ROY

IN NINE PARTS

1. PREAMBLE

I read my first work by Gabrielle Roy when I was sixteen. It was 1956. I was in my last year at a suburban Toronto high school.

The Second World War had ended barely a decade earlier, yet to us it felt like ancient history. Many things about that war, including the Holocaust, had been deliberately buried. The Cold War was underway; West Germany was an important ally, and needed to be treated with tact. The U.S.S.R.—such an essential partner in the war—was now the enemy, and Smiling Uncle Joe Stalin had become Evil Big Brother. A whole sheaf of wartime attitudes and memes had been tossed out along with the rationing books. The post-war cornucopia of consumer goods was in high spew.

At the beginning of the 1950s, propaganda images of domestic bliss had been promoted to hustle women out of the work force, making way for the men returning from the war. The baby boom was in full swing, and four kids, an automatic washer, and a split-level bungalow was the ideal pushed by advertisers and politicians alike. Although Simone de Beauvoir's *Le Deuxième Sexe* was published in 1949 and translated in 1953, second-wave feminism was nowhere to be seen, or not by us high school students. (The book did not gain traction with our generation until Betty Friedan's *The Feminine Mystique* appeared in 1963. Moreover, we felt that these books described our mothers and grandmothers, not us.)

Nor were the boys of our age bedevilled by the woes of the men in grey flannel suits, veterans used to a lot more adrenaline than a nine-to-five job could provide. These men were already being lured away from their bungalows and wives into Playboy Bunnyland by their fellow vet Hugh Heffner.

By comparison, we teenagers of the 1950s were floating in what might be called the Early Betty and Veronica Age. Archie Comics still described a reality we could identify as ours: old-maid schoolteachers, balding and comical principals, and girls who made pans of brownies in Home Economics so the boys taking Shop could make yum-yum noises and rub their stomachs. Sex was Archie with a heart drawn above his head. That was as far as things went, because love and marriage went together like a horse and carriage. Nobody had got around, yet, to asking the horse about its opinion.

Meanwhile, in the wider world, annihilation by atomic bomb hovered as a fearful possibility, and McCarthyism had made any talk of social welfare or workers' rights sound almost treasonably Communist. Since the Hungarian Revolution had just been quashed by Soviet tanks, we all knew what a bad thing Communism was. Catchwords that had been all the rage in the 1930s and the 1940s were now out. You couldn't say "working class" or even "world peace" any more without attracting suspicious glances. In the world of B movies, invasions of Martians who would take over your brain and turn you against your fellow citizens were much in vogue: outer space was full of Communists, evidently, but so was inner space. They were everywhere.

Thus, Gabrielle Roy's masterpiece of 1945, *Bonheur d'Occasion*, must have seemed like dangerous fare to the nervous educators of the 1950s. Not only did it blurt out "the working class" right on its 1947 American-edition flyleaf, but it focused on economic and social inequalities, and its most idealistic character looked forward to a "just society." After Roy, we'd have to wait for Pierre Trudeau's leadership speech in 1968 to hear this phrase given such pride of place again. (It's odd to remember this now, when the themes of the "1 per cent" income equalization, and job creation have taken centre stage once more, but that's how it was in the timorous 1950s.)

2. GABRIELLE ROY IN THE HANDS OF MME WIACEK

The Cold War politics of the day may explain why it was Gabrielle Roy's *La Petite Poule d'Eau* that was on my high school curriculum, rather than *Bonheur d'Occasion*.

Roy's novel was a set text for the French Literature final examination, and those finals determined whether a student would go to university. We *élèves* pored over every word under the guidance of our meticulous teacher, Madame Wiacek. As her name might suggest, Madame Wiacek was neither French nor Québécois; she was Polish—French being, at that time, the second language of choice for educated Poles.

Thus it was that a roomful of Canadian anglophones with terrible accents were studying French through a book written by a francophone from Manitoba, under the often amused tutelage of a woman who'd escaped both the Nazis and the Russians, immigrated to Canada, and somehow fetched up in a middle-class and very mundane post-war suburb of Toronto.

The most alarming event on the horizon was not likely to be an invasion of storm troopers or commissars, but the Friday night hop, at which a bunch of adolescents rocked and rolled around the gymnasium under the supervision of the German teacher, who was Bulgarian, and the Latin teacher, who was of Indian descent by way of Trinidad. This ethnic mix of students and teachers was not untypical: our high school fancied itself as Scottish, though some students were Chinese and a number of them were Armenian. This incongruous mixture was very Canadian, and would have been fully appreciated by Gabrielle

Roy herself—for among the many areas of Canadian life that she explored, long before this exploration became fashionable, was its ethnic multiplicity.

The approach we took to Gabrielle Roy's book was intensely French. We practised the classic *explication de texte*—a close reading of the work itself. We unravelled the sentence structures of the text, but discovered little about its author. In English studies, too, New Criticism was the favoured method, so biography was barely glanced at: we learned everything about *The Mayor of Casterbridge* but nothing about Thomas Hardy's life (possibly just as well, considering its gloom).

This absence of biography was normal for me at the time, but it seems very curious now—especially since the story of Gabrielle Roy is just as interesting as the story of Luzina Tousignant, the heroine of *La Petite Poule d'Eau*. Who was Gabrielle Roy? How did she become a writer? And why was her work chosen for a high school curriculum otherwise dominated by European authors, in both French and English? Dead male European authors, I might add. There were a couple of women among the English ones, but they, too, were dead.

Yet here was a living female Canadian author, still alive, right on our curriculum. This astonishing fact passed without comment. The dreaded *dictée* hogged all our attention in our French class, and matters such as gender and nationality and class and colonialism and the bizarre circumstances of individual artists' lives were hidden in the wings, preparing to make their appearance onstage over the next decade.

But the unknown wise and good who selected Gabrielle Roy must have had their reasons. How did Gabrielle Roy pass their scrutiny?

3. GABRIELLE ROY WAS VERY FAMOUS

The short answer is that Gabrielle Roy was very famous. We weren't told about this fame of hers, but her fame was well known to the generation of teachers who'd chosen her.

The book that had made her so famous was *Bonheur d'Occasion*, her first novel. The French original was published in Montreal in 1945, just as the Second World War was drawing to a close. The translation, entitled *The Tin Flute*, appeared in English in 1947, and was adopted as the monthly selection by the Literary Guild of America—at that time a major force in publishing. The bestselling first print run was seven hundred thousand, a number that would be almost unheard of today, especially for a literary novel. There followed a triumph in France, where this book was the first Canadian novel to win the prestigious Prix Femina. It also won the Canadian Governor General's Award.

A film contract was signed, translation rights were sold in twelve languages, and Gabrielle Roy became a literary celebrity—so much so that she returned to Manitoba to escape from the demands being made upon her by the press and her admirers. The scale of her success was unprecedented for a Canadian writer, surpassing even that of Gwethalyn Graham, whose 1944 novel, *Earth and High Heaven*, was the first Canadian book to top the *New York Times* bestseller chart.

4. A CINDERELLA STORY, MORE OR LESS

Part of Roy's appeal was her rags-to-riches Cinderella story. But Gabrielle Roy had no fairy godmother: she'd come up the hard way, and most Canadians could empathize with that, having come up the hard way themselves. Moreover, the hard way was in literary vogue: the roaring twenties gave us tales of the rich and profligate such as *The Great Gatsby*, but the dirty thirties had been characterized by such iconic poor people books as John Steinbeck's *The Grapes of Wrath*. Plutocrats were out, except in romance novels; "the masses" were in. Not only Gabrielle Roy's novel, but her life, was in tune with the times.

Roy was born in Saint Boniface, a largely francophone district of Winnipeg. Her parents were both immigrants to Manitoba, attracted by the boom times following Confederation. Her father was originally from the Acadian community of New Brunswick; her mother was from Quebec. Politically Léon Roy was a Liberal, and when Wilfrid Laurier's Liberals gained power in 1896, he was employed by the federal government as an immigration agent, helping foreign incomers settle in the province. (But live by the government, die by the government: when the Conservatives won the election of 1915, M. Roy was fired, six months short of a pension.)

Although Roy's family wasn't wealthy, it was never dirt poor. Before he lost his job, M. Roy was able to build a large house on Rue Deschambault, in a newly developed section of Saint Boniface. It was this house that became the focus of Roy's semi-autobiographical series of stories, the 1955 *Rue Deschambault*. (Translated as *Street of Riches*.)

Gabrielle was the youngest of eleven children, of whom eight were living. Her year of birth was 1909, the same as my own mother's. Thus, by the time of Roy's extraordinary fame, she was just over forty. She was five when the First World War broke out, nine when it ended, and ten when the 1919 Spanish flu epidemic swept the planet, killing twenty million worldwide, including fifty thousand Canadians—which, in a population of eight and a third million people, was substantial.

During Roy's childhood, smallpox was still a killer, as were tuberculosis, diphtheria, whooping cough, red measles, tetanus, and polio. Infant mortality rates were high, as were maternal death rates. Both having a baby and being a baby were riskier than they are now, and this is worth noting since babies feature largely in Roy's work.

Also in 1919 the Winnipeg General Strike took place—perhaps the single most important event in the history of Canadian labour. Roy's political leanings—Liberal, egalitarian, sympathetic toward the exploited—were formed early in her life, not only by the events around her, but by her family's attitude towards them.

Roy's family was francophone, but due to a legislative quirk she received a bilingual education. When Manitoba was established as a province in 1870 it was bilingual. However, over the decades the status of French as an official language had declined, and in 1916, when Gabrielle Roy was seven, Manitoba passed a law making English the only language of instruction in public schools. (This move was deeply resented by francophones, who saw it as a gross betrayal of the province's founding principles.) But Roy attended the nun-run Académie Saint-Joseph for twelve years, where she was educated in both English and French. Thus not only was she fluently bilingual, she had access to the great literatures of both languages. For a future novelist, this was a tremendous advantage.

The direction Roy took after receiving her grade twelve diploma was a common one for young women of her era. She went to Normal School—a crash course for young teachers—and became a public school teacher in rural schools. The job choices for young women were not numerous, especially during the Depression years, which began in 1929 when Roy was twenty. Roy then obtained an English-language school in Winnipeg, so she could teach and live in her parents' home at the same time.

Roy saved up her teaching money, but unlike many young women, she did not then get married. Instead she went to Europe with the intention of becoming a professional actress.

During her school-teaching years Roy had been acting, in both French and English. The companies were of the kind that abounded in the Canada of those days—semi-amateur "little theatres"—and Roy acted with both the Cercle Molière and the Winnipeg Little Theatre. She was passionate about acting, and due to some favourable critical reception, thought she might make a career of it. Looking at photos of her as a young woman it's easy to see why: she had the high cheekbones and chiselled features of the screen beauties of the 1930s. At the same time she was writing, and had managed to get some pieces published in periodicals both local and national.

In 1937 she was ready to make her move. It was a move that Canadians and indeed Americans bent on an artistic career of any kind—painting, acting, music, writing—had been making for decades. You needed to expand your horizons; you needed to travel to Europe, where art was taken seriously, or so went the myth. (As this was still the pattern in the early 1960s when I myself was a young artist, I understand it well.)

Despite hostility from her family—as an unmarried daughter, wasn't it her duty to stay at home and take care of her aged, widowed mother?—off to Europe Roy duly went. Her first stop was Paris, where she stayed only a couple of weeks—I speculate that she had some problems with her "provincial" accent and the resulting snobbery, which North American francophones have been known to experience. Then she went to England. In those days the British Empire still existed, and it was fairly easy for Canadians to get into Britain. In London, Roy mingled with other young expatriates, including friends from Manitoba. She also enrolled in the Guildhall School of Music and Drama, which had added "Drama" to its name only two years previously.

Guildhall was not the top drama school in England, but even so it must have been demanding for Roy. It's hard to imagine what the experience must have been like for someone of Roy's intense and ambitious character. Amateur theatre in Canada was one thing, but it would have been much more difficult in England, land of actors, for Roy to maintain her acting dream. In each of the cultural capitals of her world—Paris, London—Roy would have been swiftly identified as being from the margins; indeed, the margins of the margins. *Manitoba*—where was that? In fact, *Canada*—where was *that*? Up to the 1970s, when I myself experienced it, this was the attitude of English people to colonial upstarts. (It was not the attitude in Scotland, Ireland, or Wales, but that's not where Roy travelled.)

So, while doing the usual young-tourist things—the visits to the museums, to the theatres, to the countryside—Roy fell back on her second string, writing. A talent for mimicry can come in handy in fiction just as it does on the stage. She already had some previous publication experience, and she managed to place three pieces in an important Paris magazine. It was in England, paradoxically, that she became convinced of her vocation as a writer, and of her chances of success.

It was now 1939. As many foresaw, a second world war was on the way. Roy made one last visit to France, this time to the countryside, then sailed back to Canada in April. Despite more family pressure—having had her fling, shouldn't she *now* be supporting her aged mother?—she did not return to Saint Boniface. Instead she settled in Montreal, where she began the long, hard, dedicated grind that would result, five years later, in the great success of *Bonheur d'Occasion*.

5. MONTREAL, SIN CITY

Montreal at that time was the only Canadian city comparable to New York. It was the financial capital of Canada—bustling, cosmopolitan, multilingual, and sophisticated, with impressive architecture both ancient and Victorian, and a lively nightclub scene frequented by A-list jazz musicians. It was also Sin City, known for its freely flowing liquor, its many prostitutes, and its civic corruption.

Toronto was small and provincial by comparison: Protestant-dominated, repressed, and stiff with "blue laws" that dictated such things as who could drink what, and when (almost nobody, almost nowhere). Ottawa, although the capital of the country, was thought to be even duller than Toronto. Vancouver then was a smallish port, as was Halifax. Winnipeg had made its bid for glory toward the end of the nineteenth century—the completion of the trans-Canadian railway made it a staging point for Western products such as wheat and cattle—but the glory had not lasted. Calgary and Edmonton were still small bumps on the railway. But Montreal was in full bloom, even though it was a festering lily rather than a spotless rose.

And there was Gabrielle Roy, inspecting it with a critical outsider's eye. She had to work hard to make a living, as she was a freelancer, not an employee of a newspaper like Mavis Gallant, who was working for the *Montreal Standard* at points during this period. In the war years of the early 1940s, Roy wrote for several periodicals, including *Le Jour* and *La Revue moderne*. She also wrote for *Le Bulletin des agriculteurs*, which, notwithstanding its title and its rural readership, was a general-interest magazine. For it she wrote several long series of what we would now call "investigative journalism." For these various magazines she was also writing "reportages"—non-fiction about current events—as well as descriptive pieces, which could contain impressions as well as observations. In addition, she was contributing essays, which would contain well-argued opinions.

These projects took Roy into the intimate life of the city, especially its seamier side. She was able to take a keen look at Montreal, especially its lowest layer, where she saw abject, dead-end misery up close. Though she herself had grown up in modest circumstances, she'd never lived in an urban slum. Her own family had experienced some belt-tightening, especially after the death of her father, but nothing compared to the hardscrabble life she was now witnessing.

Following Hugh MacLennan's 1945 novel *Two Solitudes*, it had become fashionable to think of Canada as divided into two kinds of people—francophones and anglophones—who did not communicate with each other. But Montreal contained a third solitude: the Jewish community. This last group was soon to be given in-depth literary treatment by Mordecai Richler, a teenager growing up in the Saint Urbain district while Roy was writing her first novel. And, like Richler, Roy identified yet another layer of solitude, since the extreme poverty she saw first-hand in the Saint-Henri slums just down the hill from rich and privileged Westmount was fully as isolating as ethnicity and religion. The great divide in *Bonheur d'Occasion* is not only linguistic. It's a class divide.

6. *BONHEUR D'OCCASION*, ITS APPEAL AND STRENGTHS

Bonheur d'Occasion was a novel that made radical departures from tradition while weaving in other strands familiar to readers in both French and English. It challenged received opinions, including patriotism, religious piety, the position of women, and the expectations of what was still called, unselfconsciously, "the working class."

The book was ahead of its time, but not so far ahead that it left its readers behind. It was unsparing in its observations, but not overly judgmental about its characters. It described hard times and hard people, but it allowed the occasional dollop of empathy to soften its gaze.

The title, *Bonheur d'Occasion*, has several layers of meaning in French: "*bonheur*" is "happiness," but though "*d'occasion*" can mean "used" or "second-hand," it can also mean "bargain," "chance," or "opportunity." So, a shopworn happiness that is also a happy chance. This describes the determining events in the lives of the novel's main characters, who snatch at whatever small, tawdry opportunities fate makes available to them.

The English publishers wisely concluded that they couldn't cram all of these meanings into a snappy title. They fell back on *The Tin Flute*, which points to a significant object in the novel: the tin flute is a toy passionately desired by little Daniel Lacasse, which, although cheap, is nonetheless too expensive for his impoverished mother. He finally gets his longed-for flute when he's dying in the hospital of what is described as "leukemia," but by then he's no longer interested in it. And so it goes, for quite a few of the characters in this densely populated book.

All novels come from their own time. For *Bonheur d'Occasion*, this is wartime. Money is chinking, but it's not chinking for everyone: the effects of the Great Depression are still being felt, and many lives have been warped by it.

Roy rarely names her characters without having a semi-hidden meaning in mind. You'll be told by name-tracing ancestry sites that "Lacasse"—the family name at the novel's core—comes from a Gaulish word for "oak," that sturdy and useful tree, and may also refer to a box-maker. But "*casser*" is the verb "to break." The Lacasse family contains some oaks at least sturdy enough to survive despite what they've been through, but they're nonetheless trapped in a box. They're also broken: they limp rather than sprint. Even so, they're losing ground.

The father of the twelve Lacasse children—eleven when the book opens, ten when one of them dies, but eleven again when another one is born—is named "Azarius." This isn't a common name, even in the

French Canada of that time. It's the name of a sedative herb, but it's also the name of a Biblical character. In the French version of the Bible, "Azariah" is the name given to one of the three youths put into the fiery furnace in the Book of Daniel.

In English translations, the "Prayer of Azariah" is omitted as apocryphal, but it appears in Catholic versions after Daniel 3:23. Part of it goes like this: "And thou didst deliver us into the hands of lawless enemies, most hateful forsakers of God, and to an unjust king, and the most wicked in all the world. And now we cannot open our mouths, we are become a shame and a reproach to thy servants; and to them that worship thee. Yet deliver us not up wholly."

Gabrielle Roy's character names have a tendency toward irony, so Azarius Lacasse is no Biblical hero. Instead he's an impractical dreamer who goes from one job to another, always with the idea that he's going to make it big with some new scheme. He spends a lot of time shooting the breeze with other men from Saint-Henri, coming in late, and getting fired. As his eldest daughter Florentine puts it, he never has much luck.

But if I'm right about the derivation of his name, we see the head of the Lacasse family undergoing an ordeal by fire at the hands of a wicked and unjust king. In the context of the novel, the unjust king would seem to be Montreal's wealthy and powerful—the manipulators of the social system who, in wartime, ask everything from the men of Saint-Henri including their lives, but deal out only injustice and inequality in return. One Saint-Henri man who has enlisted in the army puts the case. Finding himself in Westmount, home of the wealthy English, he muses:

> Looking up toward the high fences, the winding gravel walks, the sumptuous facades of the houses, he wondered: *Do they give all they have to give?*
>
> The rich, polished stone glittered like steel, hard, indecipherable. And suddenly he felt the enormity of his presumption and of his innocence. . . . 'Nothing on earth is to be had cheaper

than your life. We others, stone, iron, steel, silver and gold, we're the things that cost dear.'*

If these unjust kings require their arms, legs, and lives from the men of Saint-Henri, what do they require of the women? In a word: babies. Not just any babies: babies born in wedlock, since society had no great wish to support orphanages.

In Quebec, this was the age of *la revanche des berceaux*—the revenge of the cradles. The term originated in Quebec before the First World War, the theory being that if French Canada could succeed in breeding faster than the English, they could out-populate them and thus avenge the fall of New France and the subsequent anglophone domination. Thus motherhood—especially prolific motherhood—was officially promoted and idealized, whipped on by both the Church and the civic authorities in Quebec. Families of ten, twelve, fourteen or more children were praised, and their mothers were seen to be doing their duty to the francophone Catholic community.

Those who paid with their bodies, their health, and the health of their children were the women of the fertile poor—the rural poor, who got a fictional going-over somewhat later by Marie-Claire Blais in her 1965 novel *Une Saison dans la Vie d'Emmanuel*, but especially the urban poor, who lived in slum conditions even more crowded than those on barebones farms. Babies were born with minimal care and ceremony: public health care had not yet been instituted, and hospitals were dreaded—partly because of the expense, but also because of the humiliation. While hospitals might waive their fees for the poor, such patients were looked down on as charity cases. In Saint-Henri, babies were more likely to be delivered by midwives at home than in hospitals by doctors.

In this, as in much else, the family's mother, Rose-Anna Lacasse, is typical: she avoids hospitals. "Rose-Anna" is a maternal name, for "Rose" is the "rosa mystica," a term for the Virgin Mary, and "Anna" is

* Gabrielle Roy, *The Tin Flute*.

Saint Anne, mother of the Virgin. Rose-Anna's entire life is centred on her family. She wears herself out slaving to put food on the table and keep a roof over the head of her brood, though the family is always hanging by a thread. They live packed in like sardines, barely making ends meet, and are kicked from one substandard dwelling to another—dwellings sought out by Rose-Anna.

Rose-Anna doesn't get much thanks for her efforts: she's exploited by the older children, especially the mooching oldest son, Eugène, and also resented by them when she asks them to contribute to the family's expenses.

Every once in a while, Rose-Anna breaks down and delivers an outpouring of misery: The family is falling apart, there's nowhere she can turn, what can be done? She can't pay enough attention to the younger children because there are simply too many of them. When she finally takes little Daniel to the hospital because of the big purple bruises on his legs, the doctor upbraids her with a lecture about malnutrition. No wonder the pre-adolescent daughter Yvonne says, when asked if she's looking forward to growing older and getting married, that, on the contrary, she intends to be a nun. A religious vocation was almost the only alternative to a life of constant childbearing—unless of course you could afford to go to Normal School and become a schoolteacher.

The novel's other main female character is Rose-Anna's eldest child, Florentine. Again, she is not named thoughtlessly. The word's primary meaning is "blossoming," and Florentine is indeed a pretty girl of nineteen. But a "Florentine" is also a flat, brittle pastry, and these adjectives describe Florentine's shape and manner: she's very thin, and she puts up a haughty, dismissive front to disguise her fear and insecurity.

A Florentine is also an inhabitant of Florence, which suggests Savonarola's famous "Bonfire of the Vanities," and Florentine's main characteristic is her shallow vanity. She exists by reflection: her own reflection in mirrors, and the reflection of herself in the eyes of other people. She works at the lunch counter of the "five and dime," and although she gives some of her earnings to her mother, she uses the rest to buy adornments: cheap makeup, cheap perfume, cheap trinkets. Her daydreams involve leading men on and then rejecting them, but she tries this once too often, and finds herself falling in love; although it's a love that's mixed with pride and avarice, because what she really wants is to conquer and possess.

As in *Wuthering Heights*, and indeed as in the *True Romance* magazines popular in the 1940s, she has two suitors. One of them is cast in the Linton mould—a cut above Florentine socially, idealistic, and a nice guy, but not a man to whom she is drawn sexually. The other is a quasi-Byronic, cynical, passion-inspiring no-goodnik, like Heathcliff. Here the plots diverge, for in *Wuthering Heights* the no-goodnik is devoted to the heroine, while in *Bonheur d'Occasion* he has his way with her and then skips town.

Florentine finds that her first slip from virtue—which is described more like a semi-rape—has left her pregnant. The man involved is suggestively named: Jean Lévesque. In Quebec, "Jean" is always John the Baptist—a hermit and a Herodias-denouncing misogynist. "Lévesque" is "bishop." As we are told by another character, Jean doesn't like women much. So, no hope from him, even if Florentine could locate him; which, humiliatingly, she can't.

Terror is the word used by Roy to describe Florentine's state of mind when she discovers her condition. She's frantic: disgrace and ruin are staring her in the face. Should her pregnancy become known, her family's last shreds of self-respect would be destroyed. And where could she turn? There was no social support for unmarried mothers at that time. It would be almost impossible for her to get a (highly illegal) abortion; indeed, the thought doesn't even cross Florentine's mind.

Pregnant girls might be packed off to a "home for unwed mothers," usually run by a church; the neighbours would be told they'd gone to visit an aunt, but everyone knew what that meant. Their babies would be removed from them at birth, and either offered for adoption or placed in an orphanage. The consequent loss of respectability would affect a girl's ability to get a job, and she might even end up as a low-rent prostitute of the kind that some of the novel's men are in the habit of frequenting. No wonder Florentine is distraught.

Seduced and abandoned, sometimes pregnant, sometimes not, the list of such fictional girls in nineteenth-century novels is long, as is the list of consequences: poorhouses, madness, suicide, prostitution, starvation, suicide. Such women had to be punished. Even if a girl had not actually "fallen" but had been trapped in compromising circumstances, the result would be the same: Maggie Tulliver in George Eliot's *The Mill on the Floss* is just as "ruined" as Tess of the d'Urbervilles, and so is Lily Bart in Edith Wharton's *The House of Mirth*.

But tough little Florentine has a strong will to survive, and devises a solution for herself. Without telling anyone of her plight, she goes after her other suitor—nice but not sexy—and hooks him into marriage, even though she doesn't love him. Tellingly, her saviour is called Emmanuel. He's in the army and about to go overseas, so she acquires not only a father for the child, but a war-wife allowance that will enable her to live in relative comfort. Salvation comes to her through the war. Her happiness may be second-rate, but at least it's something. And she buys a new coat.

One of Roy's accomplishments in *Bonheur d'Occasion* is her rejection of received pieties. Not for her the noble, good-hearted peasant: Rose-Anna's mother, who still lives the rural life, is a cold-hearted, criticizing monster, although generous with food. Not for Roy, either, the virtuous poor: these people are too hard-pressed for virtue. (At one moment, when Rose-Anna is praying and might, in another, earlier novel, have had a vision of a saint, she has instead a vision of a huge roll of dollar bills.) Rose-Anna's dogged perseverance is amazing, but she's also a dreary pain in the neck.

The only character who might be called morally virtuous is the modestly middle-class Emmanuel. But he's deluded by his own idealism, especially when it comes to Florentine. He makes her acquaintance only because he's slumming: the poor sap is afflicted with a social conscience, which leads him to hang out with the no-hopers of Saint-Henri, and to marry down. Not surprisingly, his own family is not pleased by the match.

Roy's refusal to buy into earlier views of "the poor" while at the same time suggesting that they were owed a better deal was certainly part of the novel's success. And its moment of publication was propitious: the war was ending, and those who had survived it were ready to consider a fairer distribution of wealth.

But perhaps the biggest contribution that *Bonheur d'Occasion* made to its society was in the area of women's rights. Roy doesn't use the language of feminism; in fact, first wave get-the-vote feminism was by that time outmoded, and the language of the sexually liberated second wave had not yet been invented. So Roy must show rather than tell, and what she shows is a situation that is both cruel and unjust. How can a human being be expected to give birth to, feed, and support so many children, with almost no help at all? Quebeckers took a good look at its own policies through the eyes of Roy, as did hundreds of thousands of readers outside Quebec, and they were appalled.

Even before the second wave of feminism got underway in English North America, it was already underway, in a different form, in Quebec. The Quiet Revolution of the sixties broke the grip of the Church on women's reproduction. The daughters of the dozen-child families refused to emulate their mothers. It's no accident that the feminist movement in Quebec was earlier, stronger, and more vociferous than anywhere else in North America: there was more to react against. From having had the highest birth rate on the continent, Quebec moved within decades to having the lowest. This has caused other problems, but that's another story.

7. SECOND NOVEL SYNDROME

It's not always a blessing for a writer to have an astonishing success with a first novel: expectations for the second one can be paralyzing.

And when a novel has hit the keynotes of its own time so exactly, what to do when that time has passed? By the end of the 1940s when the excitement over *Bonheur d'Occasion* had died down, the anti-communist reaction had set in. Roy couldn't return to the subject matter that had made her fortune. The two novels Gabrielle Roy wrote after *Bonheur d'Occasion* were both "little people" novels, but the little people were not from urban slums in Montreal.

The first was *La Petite Poule d'Eau*, that text I sweated over in 1956. (The translation was titled *Where Nests the Water-Hen*, which makes the book sound flowery and Tennysonian, which it decidedly is not.) For her setting, Roy turned to the Petite Poule d'Eau region in Manitoba, where she'd taught briefly before her European excursion.

As with *Bonheur d'Occasion*, the French title is much more appropriate. "*Poule*" means "hen," and invokes the Biblical hen who gathers her chickens together. It's a motherly word, and aptly describes Luzina Tousignant, its heroine. And it's *La Petite Poule d'Eau*, not *La Grande Poule d'Eau*: this world is little, not big.

"Luzina," like "Azarius," is an uncommon name. My guess is that Roy chose it for its component "Luz," meaning light. "Our Lady of Light" is an epithet of the Virgin Mary, and Luzina is a light-bringer, for her efforts are focused on bringing education to her very remote corner of Manitoba so that her children can pursue a better life than hers. (They do, but the price she pays is that they leave her.)

La Petite Poule d'Eau is a sweet book, mild and nostalgic in comparison with *Bonheur d'Occasion*. You can see why the Ontario curriculum-setters of the 1950s would have decided—quite apart from its social-justice views—that the first book was not healthy fare for teenagers. Florentine's unwanted pregnancy would have led to outraged letters from parents, sniggering in the classroom, and embarrassment for Madame Wiacek.

Not that *La Petite Poule d'Eau* was without its pregnancies: its yearly pregnancies. This too was a terrifying prospect for the young female readers of my generation in those days before effective birth control. Would we, too, end up dropping babies like kittens? But Luzina regards her pregnancies with equanimity, for they give her a chance to travel, expand her horizons, and go shopping in a city.

Roy's next book of this period was *Alexandre Chenevert* (1954). It, too, is about a little person, but he's little in so many ways that readers have to stretch to find him interesting. Roy's attempt is heroic: place a constricted individual in a constricted situation, then bombard him with the noise of post-war modernity—advertisements everywhere, constant bad news in the papers. Alexandre doesn't enjoy anything—not his marriage, nor his one vacation to the countryside, which ends with nervous boredom. To make his life complete, he then gets cancer and dies a painful death. Only at the end of the book does he have a vision of human sympathy.

I tried hard with *Alexandre Chenevert*. Perhaps I could connect it with Tolstoy's *The Death of Ivan Ilych*, but it would suffer by comparison. Or I could tie it in with Marshall McLuhan—the global village, of which Alexandre is unwillingly a part, and the interest in advertisements, explored earlier and more humorously in McLuhan's 1951 book, *The Mechanical Bride*. But finally, after pausing to applaud the attempt, the empathy, the writing, and the closely observed detail, I must turn briskly to the next stage of Roy's career. It is a lot more compelling, for it concerns the formation and role of the artist.

8. PORTRAITS OF THE ARTIST

Over the eleven years between 1955 and 1966, Roy published three books that explore the process of becoming an artist: *Rue Deschambault* (1955), translated as *Street of Riches*; *La Montagne Secrète* (1961), translated as *The Hidden Mountain*; and *La Route d'Altamont* (1966), translated as *The Road Past Altamont*.

The second book of this trio—*La Montagne Secrète*—is about the spiritual growth of a trapper and self-taught painter, Pierre Cadorai, whose subject and milieu is the boreal forest of Canada. The model was the Swiss-born painter René Richard, who, like Roy, had spent time on the prairies and also in the north, and who became her friend when he was already an established artist and she an established writer. It's perhaps not much of a leap to suggest that the admirable and adventurous coureur de bois figure of earlier francophone Canadian literature, seeker and capturer of beavers, has morphed into the admirable and adventurous artist figure, seeker and capturer of beauty, that Roy depicts.

Again, the book is of its time: Farley Mowat, with *People of the Deer* (1952), had already kicked off a new look at the northern and natural themes that had preoccupied several earlier generations of writers and painters. But Roy was less fascinated with the North, as such, than with the aesthetic and mystical experiences that her hero experiences in these surroundings—and the process by which his experiences are transformed into art.

The two books flanking *The Hidden Mountain* belong to a noteworthy literary family that we might call "Portrait of the Artist as a Young Girl." This motif is opened in *Street of Riches* and expanded somewhat—though obliquely—in *The Road Past Altamont*, as Roy picks up the thread of journey-as-story and the transmission of narrative gifts from one person, and generation, to another.

These books are part of a larger tradition: the female writer as her own subject. Women had been writing for some time, but it was only with the popularity of the *Bildungsroman*—the novel of formation or education—that they began to write fictions about the formative years of female writers. (None of Jane Austen's heroines is a writer, for instance. Nor are any of George Eliot's.)

Frequently, but not always, these semi-autobiographical fictions are disguised as "girls' books." The grandmother of these artistic literary girls may well be Jo, of *Little Women* fame (1868). And one of her granddaughters is certainly Sybylla Melvyn of the Australian Miles Franklin's novel *My Brilliant Career* (1901). Another is L.M. Montgomery's Emily, of the *Emily of New Moon* series (1923). Emily, in turn, was an inspiration to Alice Munro, who produced her own version of the genesis of a female writer, *The Lives of Girls and Women*. Margaret Laurence's variations can be found in her story collection, *A Bird in the House* (1970), and again in *The Diviners* (1974). Mavis Gallant's account of her own formation is perhaps most compactly contained in her "Linnet Muir" stories. In francophone Canada, the female writer perhaps most occupied with the process of becoming a female writer has been Marie-Claire Blais.

Why so many in Canada? Three possible factors may have encouraged artistically inclined young Canadian women to try their hand at writing in the first half of the twentieth century. One was the narrow range of other options. School teaching, secretarial work, nursing, home economics in its various forms, or dressmaking: that was about it. (Some jobs were opening up in journalism, though not yet on the news desks.) Another factor was the closeness of much of Canada to frontier conditions, and the resulting attitudes toward artistic pursuits. Men should handle practicalities: farming, fishing, engineering, prospecting, logging, medicine, the law. Art—flower painting, amateur acting, or a dabbling in verse—was an acceptable hobby for women, as long as they weren't serious about it. And writing was something you could do at home in your spare time.

But the third factor was the presence of women writers, in the world but also in Canada, who were already both successful and visible. In England, there were Virginia Woolf and Katherine Mansfield; in the United States, Edith Wharton, Margaret Mitchell, Katherine Anne Porter, Clare Boothe Luce, and Pearl S. Buck, this last a winner of the Nobel Prize. In Canada, L.M. Montgomery and Mazo de la Roche. And in France, Colette—a national institution, and frequently the subject of her own writing. Writing might not have been encouraged for girls, but it was not seen as completely impossible for them, because other women had succeeded at it.

The writerly coming-of-age stories in *Rue Deschambault* are set in the second and third decades of the twentieth century, when Roy was a young child, then an older child, and then a teenager. On the surface of it, the stories—at least the ones in the first part of the collection—aren't about writing at all, but about various incidents that take place in and around the family house in Saint Boniface, where the semi-autobiographical "Christine" is growing up.

The street is heterogeneous: There are two African-Canadian boarders, an Italian immigrant family, a woebegone Dutch suitor. Then there are the incoming settlers Christine's father is helping: Doukhobors and Ruthenians. This is far from being a tightly enclosed francophone community. Instead it is—like the book itself—loosely structured, shifting, multilingual, and filled with stories both happy and tragic. This is multiculturalism at its most generous.

Toward the end of the book, in the story called "The Voice of the Pools," young Christine, now sixteen, climbs up to the attic room where she has done so much reading, and looks out the window. In this fictionalized version (for Roy proposed several others over the years), this is the moment at which the writerly vocation strikes.

"I saw then," she says, "not what I should later become, but that I must set forth on my way to becoming it. It seemed to me that I was at once in the attic and also far away—in the loneliness of the future; and that from yonder, committed at so great a distance, I was showing myself the road. . . . And so I had the idea of writing. What and why I knew not at all. I would write. It was like a sudden love. . . . Having as yet nothing to say. . . . I wanted to have something to say."

She announces this discovery to her long-suffering mother, who reacts the way you might expect: "Maman seemed upset."

As *mamans* are. But this Maman goes on to say quite a mouthful:

> "Writing," [Maman] told me sadly, "is hard. It must be the most exacting business in the world . . . if it is to be true, you understand! Is it not like cutting yourself in two . . . one half trying to live, the other watching, weighing?"
>
> And she went on: "First the gift is needed; if you have not that, it's heartbreak; but if you have it, it's perhaps equally terrible . . . For we say the gift; but perhaps it would be better to say the command. And here is a very strange gift . . . not wholly human. I think other people never forgive it. This gift is a little

like a stroke of ill luck which withdraws others, which cuts us off from almost everyone . . ."*

Ah, the *poète maudit*, doomed by the poisonous gift. It was indeed the age, if not of the doomed writer, then at least of the consecrated one: the priest of art, forging the uncreated conscience of his race, like Joyce's Stephen Dedalus. If you were a woman artist, so much the worse: no helpful wife for you, you'd be on your own. Maman doesn't include gender in her response, and neither does Christine; but considering the time of writing, that's what would have been hovering unsaid.

However, young Christine isn't buying Maman's warning wholesale. "I still hoped that I could have everything: both a warm and true life, like a shelter . . . and also time to capture its reverberations . . . time to withhold myself a little along the road, and then to catch up with the others, to rejoin them and cry joyously, 'Here I am, and here is what I've found for you along the way! . . . Have you waited for me? . . . Aren't you waiting for me? . . . Oh, do wait for me!'"

It's not a certainty, this pleasant dual future. Or not in the story. Though Gabrielle Roy did manage to have it all, after a fashion, in her life.

9. GABRIELLE ROY: MESSENGER OF THE FUTURE

Gabrielle Roy took the names of her characters seriously, so let me conclude with a small riff on her own name. "Roy" is a king: it sets the standard high. But "Gabrielle" comes from the Archangel Gabriel, messenger of messengers. Gabriel delivers "good" messages—to the Virgin Mary, the news that she's going to have an unexpected baby, but not just any old baby—and also "bad" messages—here comes the end of the world.

* Gabrielle Roy, *Street of Riches*.

What is the role of the writer? Every age, and indeed every writer, has something different in mind. For Roy, in *Bonheur d'Occasion*, it was the annunciation of the future to the present. It's pleasing to think of her turning up at Rose-Anna's moment of worst despair and saying, "The future is going to be better."

In her other books, there's a different mission. She opens the curtains on windows people did not suspect were there—a remote corner of Manitoba, the ordinary life of an ordinary man, the lost but teeming past of her natal province, the many journeys of an artist—and asks readers to look through. Then—whatever the smallness, harshness, or oddness of the view—to understand, and then to empathize. For the Angel Gabriel is above all the angel of communication, and communication was a skill Roy valued highly.

THE 2004 CANADIAN twenty-dollar bill has a quotation from Gabrielle Roy on the back, in both French and English: "*Nous connaîtrions-nous seulement un peu nous-mêmes sans les arts?*" "Could we ever know each other in the slightest without the arts?"

No, we could not. As we contemplate our politically splintered society, as we reach the limits of data-collecting and the divisions and specializations of science, and as we finally turn back toward a more holistic view of human being, Roy's vision has more relevance to us than ever.

CHRYSTINE BROUILLET

JEHANE BENOÎT

CANADIAN CUISINE'S GRANDE DAME

"GET ME THE JEHANE BENOÎT from the shelf, would you?" my mother said one July day in 1966. "You're old enough to help me cook now."

After all that waiting, the time had finally come: if she thought I was worthy of hefting the heaviest book in the house, it meant I wasn't a little girl any longer. I was eight years old, I could read the author's name, and I'd seen Mum crack open that book dozens of times. I'd also seen it at our neighbours', and at my aunts'—*everybody* had a copy of *L'Encyclopédie de la cuisine canadienne*.* It was the go-to culinary bible for homemakers of the time: more than a thousand pages of recipes making life easier for them, teaching them all they needed to know to prepare healthy and delicious meals for their families. Jehane Benoît knew the importance of understanding the fundamental principles of cooking and food conservation: once learned, they could be applied and multiplied into variations on many themes. She encouraged her readers to use their imagination—to add their own personal touch

* In English, *The Encyclopedia of Canadian Cuisine*, published under the auspices of *Canadian Homes Magazine*, Montreal: Southam Printing, 1964.

once they'd mastered the basics. Intuition and knowledge brought more freedom and, without denying tradition and the classic time-tested recipes, a measure of curiosity about cuisine from other cultures—a welcome touch of the exotic. Open the pages of Madame Benoît's encyclopedia and you'll find recipes for *veau printanier*, beef Wellington, the inevitable meatball stew, fricassee of lamb, fried chicken (serves ten to fifteen!), as well as desserts of all kinds, from fruit shortcake au Paris–Brest to coconut cream pie and *Gugelhupf*. The crystal-clear explanations guaranteed the success of every recipe—as well as phenomenal success of the book: the *Encyclopedia* sold more than a million copies.

The key to that success? Jehane Benoît's unique, sparkling, remarkable personality. She was a visionary. A woman lucky enough to have had a forward-thinking father who refused to see her confined to the roles of wife and mother. Who allowed her to study—in Montreal and Paris, no less. The enriching experiences of those early years, made possible by her father's broad-mindedness, prompted Jehane to follow her own path—to dare, to act on impulse, to try one adventure after another. That tremendous audacity would bring her fame right across Canada and even beyond its borders.

Jehane Benoît was a bona fide celebrity in her lifetime. So I was flabbergasted, as I set about researching this essay, to find so little documentation about her. That absence, that inexplicable lack of interest in a luminary who was so widely published, was paradoxical. I couldn't help but wonder: wouldn't a man with such reputation, reach, and influence have several biographies and a wealth of articles celebrating his fame?

Having consulted the few sources that exist, however, I can presume that Benoît would not have paid that slight much mind: she was far too busy to complain about it. Busy going forward, discovering, and learning. Tasting, studying, comparing, and admiring. Giving, changing, and travelling. Understanding and cherishing life.

And it had all started when she was a child. On both her father's side and her mother's, there was no room for laziness. Her paternal grandfather, Hilaire Patenaude, a farmer and livestock trader established in Saint-Isidore-de-Laprairie, south of Montreal, had been sufficiently well off to send his sons to school "in town." Ésioff Patenaude (later a lawyer and the seventeenth lieutenant governor of Quebec) and his brother Alfred (Jehane's father) left the countryside and settled in Montreal. Alfred started out as a City and District Savings Bank clerk, quickly moving up the ladder to an enviable career in banking. Despite the demands of that profession, he had enough spare time for a sideline. Well aware that being bilingual had helped him flourish in anglophone environments, he was keen to help others study English, and devised a method for teaching the language. By 1918, his method was in use in several French Catholic schools in Quebec. And his daughter, a front-line test subject for his novel teaching approach, grew up perfectly fluent in both French and English.

The young Jehane was clearly more interested in learning languages than sewing, a skill that her mother, Marie-Louise Cardinal, might otherwise have passed on. Marie-Louise, the daughter of bakers, was a very stylish woman with a gift for decor and fashion, but Jehane never shared those passions. Mother and daughter would remain distant, but Jehane fondly remembered her grandmother Rose-Anna and her uncle Joseph, who was the first baker in the country to produce butter croissants commercially. Within the two branches of the family, one conservative and the other liberal, there was agreement on one thing: the importance of fine food. Hilaire Patenaude was a promoter of temperance, unlike Jehane's grandfather on the Cardinal side (he read Voltaire, whose books were then on the Index, the Catholic Church's list of banned publications), but they both loved a good meal.

Jehane Patenaude was born in March 1904. From 1910, she attended a boarding school, the Pensionnat de la Congrégation des Sœurs des Saints-Noms-de-Jésus-et-de-Marie—which meant she could enjoy family meals only at Easter, at Christmas, and during the long summer vacation, even though the school was just a stone's throw from home. Later, she went to the Dames de Sacré-Cœur du Sault-au-Récollet school. At the time of the armistice ending the First World War in 1918, she was looking ahead to graduation, and hoping to attend McGill University. Her application was rejected, however: only anglophones were admitted at the time.

No problem: Jehane turned resolutely to the French side of academia. She yearned to explore Paris and secretly dreamt of taking theatre classes there, so she settled on a curriculum that was unavailable in Montreal—in the process avoiding the early marriage that her mother wished for her. Jehane left the family home in Westmount for the Ville Lumière, studying toward her baccalaureate at the Sacré-Cœur Convent, where she loved meal times so much that she kept a diary of her culinary observations. She also took classes at the Cordon Bleu cooking school, the august institution that had been founded in 1895. And she walked! She roamed the streets of Paris, strolling spiritedly all over the city—while trying not to shudder at the sight of so many young men ravaged by the horrors of the Great War. At the same time, she approved of the changes she saw in French society: more and more women were working outside the home.

And when eighteen-year-old Jehane returned to Montreal, she herself felt no desire to fall into a woman's traditional domestic role. But how would she go about avoiding the "nice young men" her mother would want to introduce to her?

The answer was obvious: return to Paris, which celebrated culture, while in Quebec the priests in their pulpits condemned Montreal's vaudeville theatres as palaces of sin . . .

Back to Paris, then. But to do what? Why, study food chemistry at the Sorbonne! And try to get into a theatre class given by the famed actor Charles Dullin. Craftily evading the vigilance of her mother, who had accompanied her to Paris, Jehane managed to meet Dullin at L'Atelier, his studio in the 18th arrondissement—only to have to endure disparaging remarks about her Québécois accent. She agreed to modify her diction, but the snickering didn't stop and it eventually forced her to give up her dream of a performing arts career. Jehane was bitterly disappointed but couldn't know that what she'd learned from

Dullin—how to articulate and project her voice—would eventually be useful in her radio and television work.

She found things much easier at the Sorbonne, marvelling at the teachings of Édouard de Pomiane, the author of twenty-seven books, chef, savant, and physician who explained the physical and chemical changes that foods underwent when cooked. He believed that gastronomy was as much science as art. That food was directly related to health—and intrinsically linked to economic conditions as well: the Great War had forced housewives to find inventive alternatives to staples like butter, sugar, and flour, which were in desperately short supply. De Pomiane, who was of Russian and Polish ancestry, also believed that every country had its own cuisine. What, then, characterized the national cuisine of his student from Montreal, born in a dominion of the British Empire but living in a French-speaking province thereof? Jehane Benoît would devote her entire life to that question, one which to this day continues to fascinate great chefs and researchers alike. While in her university classroom she plumbed the mysterious properties of foods and acquired the techniques for exploiting them, she also busied herself with "field research," working in restaurants in Paris as well as *en province*, learning all she could about the cuisine of France, the secrets of its *terroir*, the wonders of its vineyards.

She enjoyed France immensely, and was flattered by her mentor's suggestion that she settle in Paris for good to become a chef. Yet she rebuffed his offer. Was she homesick, or mindful of the fact that she would always be a stranger in that culinary capital, already home to so many talented chefs?

Not knowing what to expect, Jehane returned to Quebec, but never forgot a lecture given by Auguste Escoffier that she attended at the Carlton Hotel in London. The legendary chef spoke of the ownership of recipes and the importance of protecting copyright. After all, he was the sole inventor of peach Melba, created in honour of the eponymous soprano Nellie Melba, and *timbale Garibaldi*, named for the Italian patriot Giuseppe Garibaldi. She also committed to memory a favourite expression of Édouard de Pomiane's: "We are what we eat."

As for Jehane, she was thenceforth an artist and a scientist. By the time the steamer docked in the Port of Montreal, she knew she had found her calling: culinary art.

Only months later, she found a husband as well: Carl Otto Zimmerman, whom she married in April 1926 in a parish some distance from Westmount: Sainte-Catherine d'Alexandrie. A daughter, Monique, was born a year later, on April 17, 1927. There is scant information on this first matrimonial adventure: it is known that Zimmerman was a travelling salesman, and one supposes that the couple were still together in 1934 when Jehane opened a restaurant on St. Helen's Island, in the St. Lawrence River east of Montreal, commemorating the arrival of Jacques Cartier four hundred years earlier. Madame Benoît rarely spoke about this first marriage; had it simply been a way for her to leave the family nest and escape the grip of Marie-Louise, who was less than enthusiastic about her daughter's career ambitions?

Jehane, fortunately, believed in herself. Perfectly aware that the teaching of cooking was then the exclusive preserve of the religious orders, she opened her own school in 1935. It was not aimed at young girls but at wives looking for easier ways to prepare not only daily meals but elaborate dinners as well. Jehane's students were mostly urban women, at a time when both the clergy and the government, wary of the growth of Quebec's cities and the accompanying rural exodus, were preaching the virtues of home-economics classes as a means of equipping young women with the skills to create the ideal household and ensure their husbands remained in the countryside. Those skills were known as *la science du ménage*, or domestic science, and their acquisition exalted as something noble. Woman was the soul of the family; it was in her "nature" to devote herself to her loved ones. In other words, through women, the dominant elite sought to promote and preserve traditional values—in the process keeping women in their place, in the home. Where they had much to do: most domestic tasks before 1940 revolved around food. Meal preparation, of course, but also tending to the vegetable garden, preserves, the chicken coop, the creamery, the bakery. Before the Quiet Revolution, women baked their own bread and churned milk into butter. And a *ménagère* (housewife) was expected to *ménage*; that is, to be sparing in smartly managing expenses in times of hardship, whether brought on by the Great Depression or by Second World War–era rationing.

School inspectors appointed by the Duplessis government in 1937 were tasked with ensuring that home-economics teaching upheld moral, religious, and national values among French-Canadian families under threat from modernization: children were going to university and husbands were leaving to work in the cities, fuelling fears that the traditional family structure would disintegrate. And other dangers lurked over the horizon: Communism, American materialism, and the empowerment of women, who had won the right to vote in 1940, gone to work in wartime factories, and smelled the intoxicating scent of freedom . . .

Against that ultra-Montanist backdrop, Jehane's decision to open a lay cooking school without financial support was resolutely avant-gardist. But she was proven right: newspaper ads and word of mouth did their job. The first enrollees in the *Fumet de la Vieille France*, as the school was known, were women from the English-speaking bourgeoisie attracted by its "French touch" and the fact that its founder had studied at the Sorbonne. But they were soon joined by francophones. Some eight thousand women would eventually benefit from the courses, given in downtown Montreal, not far from the Ritz-Carlton Hotel. The popularity of the Fumet (also called the School of Culinary Art) led to a problem, however: how to feed all those students! Jehane was inspired by a new trend in the U.S., where restaurant patrons served themselves at a huge buffet. It was a fairly simple system, and it would save time: her students wouldn't have to leave on their lunch break, and she could serve them healthy food as well. She called her concept Le Salad Bar, in the process seizing an opportunity to restore the somewhat tarnished image of fruits and vegetables. Word spread quickly in the neighbourhood about the welcoming "canteen," and soon businessmen as well as the students' husbands were also enjoying its delicious fare: potato salads, cole slaw, carrot salads, and a wide selection of sandwiches, all made with quality ingredients.

One of those new Salad Bar patrons was a young twenty-two-year-old named Bernard Benoît, who was in his final year at the École des hautes études commerciales and planning a career in advertising and business. One day in August 1940, at his mentor's urging, Bernard arrived at dawn at Jehane's (at the time, she was living upstairs from her cooking school) to pitch an idea he had for radio advertising. She was waiting with a plate of warm brioches, and he never forgot their heady butter-and-ginger aroma—or the gentle smile of the woman who'd baked them just for him.

The radio project fell through, but Jehane, who'd been immediately smitten by Bernard's voice, offered to help out with another venture. He agreed, and soon saw that Jehane was so busy—cooking, teaching, writing down recipes in the evenings before going to bed—that she had little time to attend to the administrative side of her business. Bernard knew enough about accounting and running a company to relieve her of that burden. Before long, he was sharing Jehane's life, going out with her to the movies and to restaurants. From their friendship grew deeper feelings and, though Bernard was thirteen years Jehane's junior, they became lovers.

Their idyll was interrupted by the Second World War: Canada joined the Allied effort in the fall of 1940, and Bernard enlisted. He would spend several months in Brockville, Ontario, before shipping out. Jehane visited him there often, but she now had to run the school and Le Salad Bar alone, and be as efficient as ever despite the anxiety gripping her at the prospect of Bernard's imminent posting to Europe. He sailed for England on April 13, 1943.

Not long after they said their goodbyes, Jehane faced another ordeal: a fire broke out at Le Salad Bar. The lodgings where she and her daughter lived were spared, but the fire and water damage downstairs was extensive. Rebuilding would take several months and would be costly. In those days of austerity, investing that kind of money was a dicey prospect. Jehane hit upon a less financially demanding solution: she began giving private cooking classes and soon landed her first job in radio, presenting adapted recipes that helped people cope with rationing. She was now forty years old and wondered whether the Salad Bar fire was a sign. Maybe it was time to think of herself and Bernard, to go and meet him on the other side of the Atlantic. Her skills might be needed overseas; she could prove her worth by offering her services to a charity like the Red Cross.

Through friends, Jehane found a job that seemed tailor-made for her: a position as an auxiliary with an organization bringing food aid to victims of the war. The plan was for her to help refugees in England. As it turned out, however, she did not leave Montreal until August 1945, by which time Bernard was able to meet her in London. The years of war and the horrors he'd witnessed had left their mark, but his love for Jehane was undimmed, and they were married on August 23, 1945. Her status as a new bride allowed her to travel freely in recently liberated Europe: she saw her beloved Paris again, reading in people's faces the deep wounds of the Occupation, and then went to the Netherlands, where Bernard had been posted. They lived there until February 1946, then returned to Montreal—where everything had changed. Jehane had to resign herself to living at her parents' house for a few months with her new husband. With a post-war boom coming, Bernard planned to turn his gifts for business and advertising to advantage and move ahead with a number of projects showcasing his wife's many talents. Jehane resumed her radio career, gave lectures, and wrote recipe books for food manufacturers.

In June 1947, Jehane and Bernard founded their own publishing house and culinary information firm. New food products were constantly being brought to market, and their promoters, aware that adoption depended on clear, accurate, and attractive preparation instructions, called upon Jehane's educational acumen. She stopped using the name Patenaude and, as Jehane Benoît, began publishing *Mes fiches culinaires*, "a hybrid form of [recipe that] could be used either as a booklet or as tear-out cards filed in a box."* She translated them into English, as she would almost all her other publications.

In the ensuing years, with Bernard often working in the U.S. for a company based there, Jehane became a fixture on the airwaves of Radio-Canada, the French network of the CBC, contributing three times a week to the program *Fémina*, hosted by Louise Simard. She shared recipes inspired by Québécois and other cultural traditions, tips to ensure they turned out right, and tidbits from the history of cooking, showing that a touch of elegance added to daily meals could be a source of pride.

Because of her success on radio, television beckoned in the following decade. Producers at the CBC were aware of Jehane, who since 1956 had written columns in *Canadian Homes and Gardens* and *The Canadian*, and hired her as a regular guest on the programs *Living* (hosted by Elaine Grand), *Open House* (with Anna Cameron), and *Take 30* (with Adrienne Clarkson). Since all three programs were broadcast from Toronto, Jehane was constantly shuttling back and forth between Ontario and Quebec. She also did plenty of travelling within La Belle Province, as Bernard had bought a farm in Sutton, in the Eastern Townships. He would have to renovate the property, but that also meant that Jehane could spend more time with Monique, who had married and settled nearby and was raising two children.

Madame Benoît wouldn't live full-time in that picturesque rural setting for several years yet, but the frequent travel between city and country didn't slow her down: in 1959, remembering her maternal grandmother's "little book of secrets," where she'd discovered the secret to her delectable baked beans ("a topping of sugared apples that caramelized during cooking"), she published *Recettes et secrets du cahier de ma grand-mère*.† In the foreword, she wrote of her faith in the

* Elizabeth Driver, *Culinary Landmarks: A Bibliography of Canadian Cookbooks, 1825–1949*, Toronto: University of Toronto Press, 2006, p. 248.

† Revised and translated as *My Grandmother's Kitchen*, Toronto: McGraw-Hill Ryerson, 1981.

"cuisine de chez nous . . . celle où les choses ont le goût de ce qu'elles sont et non point celle qui dissimule toutes les saveurs." While honouring the ingenuity of her female forebears and cherishing their heritage, Jehane was also the exemplar of the modern woman, contributing columns to the monthly *La revue moderne* (the ancestor of the French edition of *Chatelaine*), edited by Léo Cadieux.

Alongside those activities, she busied herself with collating notes, texts, and recipes for the exhaustive encyclopedia she hoped to write. When Bernard was posted to the Paris offices of the Rheem Manufacturing Company in 1962, Jehane dropped everything to follow him. But she knew she wouldn't be bored, since it meant rediscovering the city she loved—and, though she hadn't brought along the trove of research material, which would have made things easier, she began writing the encyclopedia anyway, relying on her formidable memory. Ensconced in an apartment not far from the Eiffel Tower, she created the massive tome that would cement her reputation, sending the manuscript in successive bundles to her secretary back home. Amazingly, none was ever lost in the mail, and *L'Encyclopédie de la cuisine canadienne* rolled off the presses in September 1963, just as the Benoîts returned to Montreal. In all, a million and a half copies were sold in the decades to come, given as wedding presents and to children leaving home to go to work or school. Since the price of the 1,200-page volume—twenty dollars in 1960s currency—was potentially prohibitive, the *Encyclopédie* was also sold in weekly instalments in Steinberg's department stores, so buyers could spread out the cost.

Carl Zimmerman died in 1964, and Jehane married Bernard Benoît in a religious ceremony in Westmount, despite his having had an affair that produced a son. Jehane would eventually welcome that child into their home in Sutton, once the couple settled there permanently. At around the same time, *The Encyclopedia of Canadian Cuisine* was published in English. It did just as well as the original edition and, at the behest of *Reader's Digest*, Jehane wrote *My Secrets for Better Cooking*, published in English only and distributed in Canada, the United States, and Australia. She continued to be featured on radio and television and, though she was the perfect guest on shows like *Take 30*, *Femme d'aujourd'hui*, and *Bonjour Madame*, her celebrity was fuelled not so much by those programs as by her myriad appearances in commercials. Several companies hired Madame Benoît to extol the virtues of their products—everything from ingredients to utensils. She was the ideal spokeswoman: she wasn't a beauty queen but exuded a folksy, unassuming charm. It made her all the more reassuring and credible; this was no seductress teaching the art of cooking, but a woman of privileged upbringing who spoke with a distinguished accent, who showed a certain refinement but was not in the least pretentious.

Jehane was the picture of success, simultaneously vivacious and comforting in the increasingly fast-paced world of the 1960s. Milkmen gradually stopped leaving their bottles of milk and cream on customers' doorsteps because those housewives now preferred to stroll the aisles of the new supermarkets in search of that new kettle, brand of rice, or type of chocolate that Madame Benoît had mentioned. While there, they picked up the brochures that she wrote for Cadbury, Dow, Dainty Foods, Steinberg's, and the Canada Sheep Marketing Council, which counted on her to make lamb (at the time unjustly maligned) a mouth-watering alternative to beef and pork.

Jehane was particularly well suited to that task: in Sutton, on the slopes of Mount Echo, where the Benoîts had settled for good in 1967, some 1,200 sheep grazed on a magnificent 499-acre spread. Their dusky-coloured feet, heads, and snouts prompted Bernard to name the flock, and the estate, "Noirmouton." They were Hampshires from Scotland, a breed that Jehane's paternal grandfather, Hilaire Patenaude, had been the first to import to Canada. They inspired Jehane to concoct delectable dishes ranging from the obligatory navarin to grilled chops, barbecued lamb shoulder *en papillote*, moussaka, and Oriental breast of lamb. In the *Encyclopedia*, there are nearly as many recipes for lamb as for beef, though the latter was far more popular at the time. Many, such as Bengali-style lamb curry, Armenian lamb casserole, and shish kebabs, reflect Madame Benoît's interest in foreign cuisines. (As a teen, she had often visited a Greek grocery run by the Basil

Brothers, discovering seeds and spices that could not be found in the mainstream *épiceries*.) She asserted that taste for global foods in 1982 with *La cuisine du monde entier*, a compendium of recipes from all over the world. The dishes, with enticing aromas and names that conjured visions of faraway locales, were very much of the time: Canadians' memories of long lineups to visit the Moroccan, Thai, and Mexican pavilions at Expo 67 were still fresh, and there was an ongoing fascination for exotic, more refined cuisines. People wanted to learn to cook *tajines*, *pastilla*, imperial rolls, and tacos. Another sign of the evolution of gastronomy in Quebec was the 1968 founding of the Institut de tourisme et d'hôtellerie, which provides specialized training in the culinary arts as well as restaurant and hotel management.

The Benoîts soon became known for their warm hospitality at Noirmouton: TV personalities and crews loved the rural setting—and Jehane's cooking. She had enough space in the farmhouse for a personal library comprising some three thousand cookbooks. Reporters and photographers followed her to the vegetable garden and the sheep pen. It was clear the city girl had perfectly adjusted to country life. She provided moral support to Bernard, who upon acquiring the property had decided to open a boutique selling sheep products, both woollens and meat. Jehane's fame brought a steady stream of visitors, including her earliest fans as well as day trippers to the Townships. She hired her grandson to welcome the groups spilling off the tour buses, and could also rely on the able assistance of Sylvie Delbuguet, daughter of Micheline and René, a couple who had often hosted Jehane at their French restaurant on Montreal's Guy Street, Chez la Mère Michel, starting in the 1960s. René, also an advertising photographer, had a close working relationship with Jehane, having taken the cover pictures for many of her books.

Sylvie Delbuguet also provided a shoulder for Jehane to lean on after the untimely death of her daughter, Monique, from cancer. Despite her grief, Jehane continued to write and work. The books kept coming—one devoted exclusively to lamb recipes, another all about cider. Jehane was now over seventy, but no less active and just as popular. In 1973, in recognition of her life and career, she was made an Officer of the Order of Canada. A staunch federalist since the day when, as a young girl, she had heard a speech by the then prime minister, Sir Wilfrid Laurier, she was doubly thrilled to receive the honour. Governor General Jules Léger draped the medal over her shoulders and onto her long dress of brown silk, and later, at the reception, Madame Benoît was reacquainted with the current prime minister, Pierre Elliott Trudeau, whom she had known in her youth.

Before long, the tireless empress of the kitchen took up a new challenge: explaining the benefits of a recently marketed innovation, the microwave oven. Many people at the time were skittish about the strange new appliance, but to Jehane—who had always preferred gas to electric ovens for their faster cooking times—the tremendous time-saving advantages of the convection oven were obvious. In short order, she won over the doubters, adapting her recipes to the new technology, which was completely safe and did not spoil the taste of food. Microwaving was also handy for quickly thawing the three daily meals she prepared for her husband whenever she had to be away for a personal appearance to promote the miracle oven, or was too busy writing a new recipe book, such as *Madame Benoît's Microwave Cookbook*, published in 1975 (the French translation, *La cuisine micro-ondes*, appeared a year later). The fact that she had studied food chemistry at the Sorbonne lent her a certain "savante" status that was reassuring to consumers. Representatives of Matsushita, the makers of Panasonic ovens, wasted no time hiring Madame Benoît to promote them both in Quebec and in English Canada, and she criss-crossed the country as their microwave missionary from 1975 to 1987, helping to substantially boost sales. (The company would even market a special-edition model bearing their spokeswoman's monogram.) Jehane had always had a fascination for Japan; she admired works of art and design depicting floral arrangements, and had met the Japanese-French painter Léonard Foujita during her student days in Paris. Now her association with Matsushita allowed her to realize a long-held dream: she visited the country and its temples, learned more about Buddhist spirituality, and strolled through gardens suffused with calm and serenity. And, of course, she relished the opportunity to expand her knowledge of Japanese cuisine, having already included recipes for fondue and tempura in the *Encyclopedia*. Between 1975 and 1986, she would travel three times to Japan, where she was welcomed with great deference (which she jovially attributed to her advanced age; in fact, according to her husband, their hosts were astounded to learn that their ambassador, who was quite spry despite a recent hip operation, was eighty-two years old on her last visit to their country).

While most people would have retired twenty years earlier, Jehane Benoît agreed to take on another assignment, entrusted to her by Canada's Metric Commission: to promote the SI system of units, which she had been familiar with since her studies in Paris. On yet more coast-to-coast tours, she spoke to cookbook authors, community groups and home-economics professionals, demystifying metric measures and demonstrating their simplicity.

Late in her career she also placed her talents as a teacher in the service of the younger generation: by now a great-grandmother, she decided to write a microwave cookbook for children. She eventually slowed down her work schedule, however, acquiescing to the wishes of Bernard, who was worried about her health. He himself had had some difficulties, and thought Jehane increasingly fragile; she had lost weight. Early in November 1987, she was hospitalized with heart failure, but the prognosis was encouraging, and she returned home to rest. On November 24, she was feeling well enough to think about making supper for Bernard, with the help of her grandson's wife, when she suffered heart failure. Bernard rushed to her bedside and an ambulance was summoned, but the paramedics were unable to save her, and by the time they reached the hospital, it was too late.

Jehane Benoît was buried in the cemetery in Sutton. Twenty-five years later, the nearby Sutton Museum held an exhibition in her honour, gathering numerous testimonials to the widespread and genuine affection for the woman who had come to exemplify Québécois cuisine.

In the foreword to the *Encyclopedia of Canadian Cuisine*, the author asked, "*Avons-nous une cuisine canadienne? Oui, mais nous avons surtout une cuisine québécoise. . . . La cuisine d'un pays témoigne de sa géographie, de son histoire, de l'ingéniosité gourmande de son peuple et de ses atavismes. S'y ajoute une longue période de tâtonnements et d'expériences.*"*

More than fifty years after those words were written, it is amazing to consider the enduring relevance of Jehane Benoît's definition of Québécois gastronomy. It can be encapsulated in one word: *métissage*, or hybridization. There is the legacy of First Nations peoples, who introduced the first French colonists to corn, fruit, and herbs, as well as techniques for smoking meats. The heritage of French savoir-faire, which allowed dishes to be adapted to regional needs. That of the English colonists, who made dishes like sea pie (which begat *six-pâtes* and then *cipaille*, in French) and imported brown sugar and molasses. And, finally, cooking traditions from neighbouring provinces and states: the Maritimes, a bastion of seafood, and northern New England, with its endless variations on pumpkins and squash. As historian Michel Lambert has written, "Quebec cuisine is that unique fusion of foods and recipes originating here and elsewhere, and of a consensual taste sensitivity born of our founding cultures, laden with emotions linked to our family and collective history."† Jehane Benoît perfectly understood and cultivated that notion.

The esteemed food writer Rollande Desbois adds that Madame Benoît "provided the needed clarifications and explanations to the recipes passed on from mother to daughter, from generation to generation." She clarified traditions but also simplified and synthesized things: from the French school, Jehane retained the structure of a dish and the details that make it sing, but she democratized *cuisine française*, doing away with frilly "grace notes" and explaining in lay terms the food-chemistry concepts she'd learned at the Sorbonne. Drawing on

---

* *Encyclopédie de la cuisine canadienne*

† Michel Lambert, "Retour aux sources," in *Continuité*, No. 130 (Fall 2011), p. 25. [Freely translated.]

North American tradition, she emphasized the time-saving benefits of products increasingly available in Canadian supermarkets: soups, canned sauces, chili, or mayonnaise, for example.

She was indeed a hybrid, with one foot in Europe and another in North America. She straddled two eras as well, complementing classic methods with the convenience of modern technology. And she exemplified both the rural and the urban. Nothing eluded Jehane Benoît; her gift was that she drew inspiration from everywhere. Case in point: the first edition of her *Encyclopedia* featured an Aboriginal recipe for squirrel stew! It also included a hundred suggestions for avoiding food waste, reflecting her awareness that, at the time, a wife and mother's merits were judged according to her ingenuity in home economics. Where today's renowned chefs similarly respect the full potential of ingredients—Normand Laprise, of Toqué! fame, uses the leaves, roots, seeds, and juice of tomatoes and, at harvest time, cans them to ensure a ready supply all winter—they echo Madame Benoît, who dedicated substantial space in her books to methods for freezing, sterilizing, and conserving foods: marmalades, jams, leaf jellies, marinades, chutney, ketchup, mincemeat, as well as preserved meats, poultry, and fish.

When France-born Jean Soulard, who spent two decades as a chef at the Château Frontenac, arrived in Quebec, he was amazed to see a copy of Jehane Benoît's *Encyclopedia* in every home. As part of the process of writing his own cookbook, *Le Soulard de la cuisine*, comprising some 1,100 recipes, he consulted the grande dame of Canadian cuisine's masterwork. To this day he finds it astoundingly modern. Soulard draws many parallels between Jehane Benoît's teaching and current Quebec gastronomy, with its revisiting of the classic dishes that she originally added to the canon and its reliance on a long list of forgotten vegetables including celery root, salsify, cabbage, and Jerusalem artichoke, which she always championed. He recalls how prominent lamb dishes were in her books: by insisting on including so many recipes (and raising sheep herself) she was instrumental in ensuring the popularity of this meat, which continues to this day. Soulard also praises Jehane Benoît for including recipes that used all types of organ meats. They may still be a long way from widespread acceptance in Quebec, but they are far more visible on modern restaurant menus. The same is true of game, which had pride of place in the *Encyclopedia*. Quebeckers have permanently adopted duck, for example, and many of us with a gourmand bent have tried our hand at guinea fowl with chorizo, jugged hare, caribou tartare, or quail with cherries.

In our day there is a growing focus on responsible fishing; fifty years ago, Madame Benoît's *Encyclopedia* offered a variety of recipes for fish, including many non-threatened species. She also devoted a chapter to the importance of healthy eating, long before the boom in books touting diets that guard against cancer, heart disease, or overeating. Our definition of health food has, of course, evolved since the *Encyclopedia* was written: some of the recipes are too rich for our taste, such as the suggestion of *fondue bourguignonne* for a fancy dinner to be followed by a generous dessert (!), and the recommended portions are more suited to the physical labourer of fifty years ago than today's Web-surfing cubicle dweller. Yet Madame Benoît was clearly a trailblazer when she opened Le Salad Bar, anticipating the vegetarian and vegan movements. And while today we might log on to Google in search of a quick and easy dish, or subscribe to cooking magazines, Jehane made sure her recipes were accessible to everyone by making them available in instalments at Steinberg's.

Is there any aspect of food and dining that escaped Jehane Benoît's attention? The answer would appear to be no. With undeniable talent and peerless generosity, this impassioned visionary played a vital role in the evolution of Quebec society.

KEN DRYDEN

JACQUES PLANTE

I WAS SEVEN YEARS OLD when Jacques Plante played his first full year as goaltender of the Montreal Canadiens. It was 1954, and I was growing up in suburban Etobicoke—about to play my own first hockey season, also as a goalie, with the Humber Valley Hornets of the Toronto Hockey League.

My family had moved into a newly built house the year before. To provide my brother and me with a place to play under the watchful eye of our mother, our father paved the backyard and installed full-size goalie nets (painted red, just like the ones in the NHL). It became the neighbourhood ball-hockey rink.

In our daydreams, the backyard was Maple Leaf Gardens. Foster Hewitt's voice was in our heads, telling the world about how we'd just won the Stanley Cup, in overtime, in the seventh game, each of us scoring our own winning goal—the fans delirious, our grateful teammates carrying us off on their shoulders.

This is an essay about Jacques Plante, not about me. But a little bit of my own story will help demonstrate the state of unawareness about all things Québécois that prevailed in that age.

I knew almost nothing about Quebec, nor did my friends. I had never been there. The neighbour kid who lived behind us had moved from Montreal—his father worked for Texaco—but he was a unilingual anglophone, and so seemed no different from the rest of us. Likewise the kid on my hockey team, who wore the Coronation Park Aces hockey jacket of his former Montreal West team, called his hockey gloves "gauntlets," and goalies "goalers."

I had learned in school about Cartier and Champlain and the founding of Quebec in the 1600s. I knew about Arvida and Thetford mines because that's where aluminum and asbestos came from. I loved the rhythm of town names such as Chicoutimi and Chibougamau, which you'd sometimes hear on the national weather report. Other than that, Quebec was a place connected to me only through random snatches of words—like a Rudyard Kipling limerick my grandmother once taught me:

There was a small boy of Quebec,
Who was buried in snow to his neck;
When they said. "Are you friz?"
He replied, "Yes, I is—
But we don't call this cold in Quebec."

I knew of no writers from Quebec, no actors, no dancers or musicians. I didn't begin to learn French until high school, when everyone else did. I vaguely knew who Maurice Duplessis was, but not Wilfrid Laurier. At Ungava Bay, a large body of water in northern Quebec, some cosmic object apparently had struck the Earth eons ago. I would go see it, I promised myself. Someday.

And I knew one more thing about Quebec, which towered above all the rest: I knew that Quebec was home to the Montreal Canadiens. It's the thing everyone knew.

From the mid-1950s to the late 1970s, the Canadiens won fifteen Stanley Cups. Their stars—Plante, Rocket Richard, Jean Béliveau, Doug Harvey, Boom Boom Geoffrion, Dickie Moore, Henri Richard,

Doug Harvey, even their great coach, Toe Blake—were heroes to kids *everywhere* in Canada.

Yet we rarely *saw* the Canadiens play. The only TV game of the week was on Saturday night. And in Toronto, the CBC showed only the Leafs, who, like the Canadiens, always played at home on Saturdays. (The teams played each other mid-week—in Toronto on Wednesdays, in Montreal on Thursdays.) It was only in the playoffs that we got a chance to see the Canadiens—and even then, only if they were playing the Leafs (or if the Leafs had already been eliminated).

This was an era when, in Toronto, it was rare to hear English spoken by anyone who didn't speak it as a mother tongue. Here and there, depending on the neighbourhood, you would encounter Italian- or Polish- or Greek-accented English. On TV, we'd hear a cartoon Chinese accent in Charlie Chan movies, or Mexican-English in Westerns that had minor characters in sombreros who grinned a lot. The French accents we heard in movies—think Maurice Chevalier or Charles Boyer—sounded sophisticated and unattainable. But the French hockey players we sometimes saw on TV being interviewed in English didn't sound like Chevalier. We decided that they couldn't be very bright.

JACQUES PLANTE WAS BORN in 1929 in the small village of Notre-Dame-du-Mont-Carmel, the first child of Xavier and Palma Plante. Five brothers and five sisters would follow. Not long after, the family moved a few kilometres north to Shawinigan Falls (now known simply as Shawinigan, again made famous in more recent times by *p'tit gars* Jean Chrétien), where Xavier got a machinist job at Alcan.

Situated at a long drop in the Saint-Maurice River, Shawinigan Falls had been created in 1898 by foreign investors as a company town for the newly formed Shawinigan Water and Power Company. At the time, Montreal was hungry for new electricity sources—and thus did Shawinigan Falls become a thriving boomtown, providing the Plantes with a comfortable existence. Hockey in the winter. Baseball in the summer. Family, school, and church year round. This was Jacques Plante's childhood.

Biographies of great athletes often feature harrowing tales of overbearing parents, tyrannical coaches, and hardship. But Plante experienced none of that. He was loved and cared for by his mother and father, performed his chores dutifully at home, and earned a reputation as a conscientious student at school.

Plante's home sat across the street from a neighbourhood outdoor rink, where he lived out his hockey fantasies. The Canadiens were his favourite team. He never actually saw them play, whether at the Forum or on television: *La Soirée du hockey* was still more than a decade away. Instead, he saw the Canadiens through the radio voice of Jean-Maurice Bailly. His favourite player was goalie Bill Durnan—who, to Plante's ears, never let in a bad goal.

Indoor skating facilities now are common in Canada, but they were scarce when Plante was a child. Even large cities such as Montreal and Toronto had only a handful, and these were usually reserved for teams with the most talented older kids. In order to get more ice time, Plante joined multiple teams in different age groups, and came to play against Marcel Pronovost, who would go on to become a Hall of Fame defenceman with Detroit and Toronto; and the Wilson brothers, Johnny and Larry, who lived a block from Jean Chrétien (with whom they became close friends).

Plante didn't begin as a goalie—a position that often attracted players whom other kids considered too young or too small to play as forward or defence. It was asthma that put him in the crease: long stretches of skating left him breathless. But though he came to the position late, Plante was an almost immediate sensation.

In a town of modest size, top talent becomes public knowledge quickly. Scouts began showing up to watch Plante play. (This was before the NHL draft had been implemented; in these early days, NHL teams could sign players of almost any age.)

Plante turned down approaches from a New York Rangers junior team, among others, then finally got the offer he wanted, from the Canadiens. His timing seemed right. Durnan was nearing the end of a great career, and Gerry McNeil, preparing in the wings to take his place, wasn't the formidable presence the team needed to beat the Leafs and the Wings (and their Stanley Cup–winning goalies, Turk Broda and Terry Sawchuk respectively). Nevertheless, Plante drifted in the minor leagues for five years. He would occasionally get called up to the Canadiens when McNeil was injured, sometimes for extended stretches. But until 1954, he never broke through.

These days, Plante is remembered as a legend. But in the mid-1950s, he was known outside Quebec for one very odd and specific reason: he liked to knit. That was his hobby. It said so in the little cartoon drawing on the back of his hockey card. This was the 1950s. *Women* knit. Men didn't. And certainly not NHL hockey players.

But Plante's quirks were largely forgotten in 1956, when the Canadiens won the Stanley Cup with him in goal. Then they won again the next year. And the year after that. And the year after that. And the year after that, too. When you win five straight championships, no one cares if you fashion toques in your spare time.

If being an important part of six Canadiens championships were all Plante did, he would still deserve his place in the Hockey Hall of Fame. And yet his greatest contribution to the game had more to do with what he came to wear on his face. Since the first hockey game at McGill University in 1875, goalies had never worn masks.

In November 1959, at New York's Madison Square Garden, Plante was hit in his bare face by a shot from the Rangers' Andy Bathgate. At the time, NHL teams carried only one goalie. If Plante didn't come back on to the ice after getting stitched up, the Canadiens would need to use an assistant trainer or a practice goalie provided by the Rangers as a replacement. Plante had previously worn a mask in practice, but Toe Blake, his coach, insisted that he would never allow him to wear one in a game.

Plante refused to return to the game without his mask. Blake relented. It was a hockey-changing moment.

To modern readers, goalies' willing exposure of their heads to hockey pucks surely seems like an exercise in extreme stupidity. But we goalies had our reasons.

I didn't wear a mask until I was an eighteen-year-old freshman at Cornell University in upstate New York (and even then, only because masks had become mandatory at the university level). The few times I'd tried one previously, I'd reacted the way most goalies did during this period. "I can't wear a mask because I can't see a puck at my feet," is what we'd say. In retrospect, it's obvious that if any of us truly wanted to see a puck at our feet, we could have just tilted our heads downward by a few degrees. The truth is that we didn't want to wear a mask at the time because wearing a mask somehow felt like the "wrong" thing to do.

Hockey players in the early twentieth century did not play their sport in isolation: equipment was minimal across the athletic spectrum. Football players didn't wear helmets. Baseball players wore tiny gloves that fit snugly to the outline of their fingers (literally, *gloves*). Hockey players wore skates—and little other equipment. Sport was intended to be a test of body, mind, spirit, and the human capacity to overcome pain. Equipment was allowed only to the narrow extent that it was necessary to experience the purest essence of the sport, not intended to protect the players.

Then, little by little during the course of the twentieth century, attitudes evolved. A player would get injured. He'd put on a pad to protect his injury until it healed . . . and then he'd just keep wearing it. To prevent similar injuries, other players would mimic this.

A player gets hit in the shin with a hard wrist shot or an opponent's stick. He notices that the bruises accumulate in the same place. Does it take away from the game, or from the player's manhood, if he uses a rolled-up magazine to lessen the impact?

These changes in equipment, in turn, changed the nature of the sports themselves. A football player, having suffered many blows to the head, puts on a helmet—which not only protects his skull but also transforms the top of his head into a weapon. He tackles differently, blocks differently, runs differently.

Likewise the baseball player who wants to avoid the sting of a line drive. He extends the leather on his glove beyond the ends of his fingers, and fills the space between with webbing. Suddenly, missed fly balls and bobbled grounders become less frequent.

For hockey's first half-century, goalies wore almost nothing to protect their bodies. They had gloves that resembled the sort of thing people wear on ski hills, and leg pads similar to those of a cricket wicket-keeper. And, of course, their faces were completely unprotected. But goalies were sane enough to at least get their heads out of the target zone: using a "stand-up" style, the goalie elevated his head above the crossbar, rarely going down. (The top bar of a hockey net is four feet high.) For decades, this style is what every goalie was taught.

Goaltenders told their coaches, who were usually former defencemen or forwards, that using this style was the best way to prevent goals. And their coaches believed them. But the goalies were only passing on the ways and reasons of another time. With a well-protected head, the more efficient way to block the goal area actually involves bringing one's head down, while flaring the arms and hips to the sides—in "butterfly" position, as it is called—as modern goalies do.

THE FATEFUL 1959 GAME had taken place on November 1, prompting a journalist to mock Plante: "Halloween's over now, Jacques." Everyone assumed the Canadiens goalie would remove the mask as soon as his face healed. Following his initial opposition, Blake didn't press the issue: he assumed Plante's performance would suffer because of his limited visibility—and that the goalie himself would abandon it after letting in a flurry of easy goals.

Instead, the Canadiens—who had been on an eight-game winning streak—went unbeaten in ten more. Blake was left without anything to say. Plante never played a single game without a mask again.

Five weeks later, Don Simmons of Boston wore a mask, recording a shutout against the Rangers. But then he gave it up. It took three years before another goalie, Terry Sawchuk of the Detroit Red Wings, put on a mask and kept it on for good. Yet by the time the 1960s were over, a maskless goalie would be a curiosity. Andy Bathgate's slapshot to Plante's face set in motion a chain of events that (quite literally) changed the face of hockey goaltending.

Plante was the ideal forerunner. He never minded bucking the received wisdom—if he thought the received wisdom was wrong. It was Plante, for instance, who first began wandering outside his crease in an era when few goalies dared do so. To venture behind one's own net, or to flush a puck out of the corner—these were things that just weren't done by goalies in the 1950s. The image of a wide-open net was disturbing to one's teammates, coaches, and fans. It was craziness, they argued.

It's not craziness if I have the puck, Plante argued back.

Plante had seen that times had changed. For decades, players had rushed up the ice stickhandling the puck into an opponent's zone, an offensive tactic that offered no rationale for a goalie to leave his crease. But when teams learned to jam up the centre zone defensively, offensive players began simply dumping and chasing. Locked to their crossbars by decades of tradition, goalies watched as opponents won the race for the puck and gained avoidable chances to score. Why, Plante wondered, couldn't *he* get to the puck first after it was dumped in, then control it, and pass it to a teammate?

Plante's decision to wear a mask was, likewise, a response to a changed game. As sticks grew lighter, slapshots became harder and more common. Players increasingly crowded the front of the net, looking to produce deflections, seize on rebounds, and screen the goalie. To go maskless amid this mess seemed more reckless than brave.

Yet everyone knew you couldn't be a goalie unless you were fearless, and if you wore a mask, you weren't fearless so you couldn't be a goalie. Besides, wearing a mask was an affront to a goalie's pride. A goalie is willing to do what few in the world are willing to do. Teammates may play through smashed mouths and carved-up faces, losing barely a minute of action; but a goalie is the toughest of all, and teammates know it. This wasn't a medal one wanted to give up.

But Plante, who by this time had broken his cheekbone and nose—both more than once—as well as his jaw, didn't think he had to prove his toughness to anybody. He saw no purpose in getting hurt. He also had a slightly different way of looking at what he did. Like other goalies, he was a competitor. His job was to help his team win. But on a deeper level, he played to a different standard.

He saw goaltending as an art, and himself as an artist. Others pushed themselves onto the ice sick or injured even if they couldn't give their best performance, because even playing at 70 per cent of their capability, they were better than their replacement at 100—because this wasn't about them, it was about the team. So they played hurt. Plante, on the other hand, sometimes chose not to. (Only one goalie since Plante's retirement has played with that same ethic. Not Patrick Roy or Martin Brodeur, not me, but Dominik Hašek.)

For Plante, that attitude caused periodic bouts of distrust among his teammates throughout his entire career. The media and fans, too, sometimes sensed that he seemed more interested in his own goals-against-average than in winning. (During my own career with the Montreal Canadiens, I had one particular teammate who was very talented. But even minor aches and pains caused him to miss games. He joked that he was a thoroughbred, that he had to feel just right to play. He didn't understand that even thoroughbreds have to exhibit a plough horse mentality if they want to earn their teammates' respect and trust. His role on the team became increasingly marginal, and he never reached his true potential.)

Plante's own love of the game outlasted his career with the Canadiens by more than a decade. In 1963, he was traded to New York, where he had a disappointing season, got sent down to the farm team in Baltimore, and retired. But then a few years later, the NHL expanded from six to twelve teams, and Plante was offered a fresh chance, and a lucrative new contract, in St. Louis. As a forty-year-old, in a goaltending tandem with fellow great Glenn Hall, he could play fewer games, often against lesser opponents (this allocation of assignments was something his teammates noticed), and he enjoyed new success.

As Nureyev aged, he couldn't leap as high. As Sinatra got older, his vocal range shrank. But both adapted and found new ways to express their art. In sports, however, such graceful adaptations are impossible—because opponents will always play to your weakness. So it was with Plante. He could no longer meet the test of the best teams. To try and fail would mean to fail his art. Only against lesser opponents could he could leap as high and sing as many notes as he needed to, and still look artful.

After St. Louis, he went to Toronto, then briefly to Boston for the end of the 1973 season. Then came a second retirement, followed by one final anti-climactic year with the Edmonton Oilers of the World Hockey Association. In 1975, having won seven Vezina Trophies, one Hart Trophy, and six Stanley Cups, and with every goalie in the NHL now wearing a mask, Plante retired for the third and final time. He was forty-six.

IN PLANTE'S TIME, almost every mask was constructed by hand, out of fibreglass, from a cast of the goalie's face. These were very low-tech pieces of equipment: Plante's original fibreglass mask from 1959, for instance, looks like something a middle-school student might have made out of papier mâché in art class.

These masks rested flush against the skin of a goalie's face, on the bony ridges of his eyebrows and cheekbones. Some goalies added foam pads to the inside of the mask. But these had to be extremely thin: a mask that extended more than a few millimetres from a goalie's face would narrow his field of vision at the eyeholes, preventing him from seeing a puck at his feet.

With only a quarter-inch of fibreglass between a goalie and the outside world, the puck still hurt. It might split your skin, or leave you with a bruising headache. So goalies still tried their best not to get hit in the head. They continued to use a stand-up style, their head above the bar. Having played this way for so long, it seemed the only way to do the job. In practices, goalies still yelled at their teammates to keep their shots lower, and coaches did the same.

But by the early 1970s, most European goalies were embracing a second technological revolution, donning "birdcage" masks made with thin metal bars that arced away from the face. A goalie wearing one of these could see the puck at his feet through the mask's many large holes. And with the mask resting an inch or two off the face, the goalie no longer feared headshots.

Still, North American goalies resisted these transatlantic imports. If Canadian goalies were the best *by far*, and we were, why would we follow what our lesser counterparts did? (At the time, Vladislav Tretiak was the only European goalie whom we acknowledged as our equal.) It was also because we liked the snug fit of a moulded fibreglass mask.

The goalie's mask came into its truly modern form when netminders realized they could create hybrid head protection that combined the best of both worlds: a goalie's ears, outer jaw, and the top of his head could remain inside a frame of moulded fibreglass, while eyes would peek out from inside an arced cage. For goalies, the Plante mask was a blessing; the hybrid mask was a miracle.

The protection offered by the hybrid product is nearly perfect. Struck by a shot to the head these days, a goalie barely blinks. Once the player most vulnerable to a serious injury, a goalie has become the *least* vulnerable. Who's crazy now?

It took several years, but goalies eventually came to realize the tactical implications of this new technology. The long-dominant stand-up style had been a compromise between (a) the goalie's mission to keep pucks out of his net and (b) his biologically rooted desire to keep pucks away from his head. With the new mask, no compromise was necessary. A goalie could bring his head and shoulders below the bar and cover more net. He could crouch lower—spreading his feet to each corner in a permanent butterfly style.

Around the same time, goalies realized that leg pads and gloves didn't need to be so heavy. They could be made of nylon, plastic, and foam—instead of medieval holdovers such as leather and animal hair.

And if the equipment became lighter, it could become bigger, too. There were rules governing the maximum width of leg pads, but not their length, and no regulations on torso pads or gloves at all. Goalies ballooned to Brobdingnagian proportions, causing the exposed areas of the net to shrink. Shooters became frustrated. Many just gave up aiming, and shot blindly instead, hoping for good luck or a deflection.

Even the hole between a goalie's legs as he spread them out toward the net's corners began to close: with his long leg pads left loose, a goalie in butterfly position could cause his (intentionally) unbuckled leg pads to flop down and cover the "five-hole." The purpose of the equipment is now not only to protect the body but to protect the net.

With these developments, goals became harder to score. But teams still needed to score them. So they began drafting quicker players with "good hands" and passing skills, who were rugged enough to take on turf-protecting defencemen yet adept enough to shoot into whatever vanishingly small spaces still presented themselves. Dedicated tough guys now had a much harder time making the roster.

Follow the chain of causality from the innovation in goalie equipment design, to the frustration and ultimate transformation of goal-scorers, to the changing face of hockey rosters, to the decline of the goon, and you find that, decades after Plante played his last game, his influence on hockey continues to be felt in all sorts of direct and indirect ways.

PLANTE WAS PART OF the golden age of hockey in Quebec. It was a time so spectacularly fruitful that many hockey fans—even those within the province—assume that conditions were always thus. But they weren't. Before 1950, few great teams or players had emerged from Quebec. The Montreal Wanderers folded in 1918, as did the Maroons in 1938. From their founding in 1909 until the 1950s, the Canadiens won only six Stanley Cups—fewer than the Maple Leafs or the Boston Bruins.

Hockey's nineteenth-century origins were in Quebec. Yet its first players were anglophones, rugby players at McGill. Even into the 1950s, most Canadiens players were English speaking, including their first great star, Howie Morenz from Ontario. Not until the advent of Rocket Richard would Quebec generate its first big star. Eventually, other great French players joined him. It would be the remarkable Québécois "Class of '31," named for the year of their birth, who joined the Canadiens in the early 1950s and created history: Jean Béliveau, Boom Boom Geoffrion, and Dickie Moore.

The outdoor game was now moving indoors. The season could go longer, fewer games would get weathered out, and more kids could play, which in turn meant more prospects for the new farm system being built by Canadiens general manager Frank Selke. He recruited young players with names such as Talbot and Provost, and later Tremblay, Rousseau, Laperrière, Cournoyer, Savard, and Lemaire. Games that had been broadcast on radio were now on TV. Heroes could be *seen*. And with the Stanley Cup victories piling up, the reality that Quebeckers saw was as good as the fantasy.

To those outside Quebec, the Canadiens were "the Flying Frenchmen." They skated faster. They played with unmatched finesse and flair. They were the Cirque du Soleil of their time. And they had a need to win. "Like an army on ice we march south every winter and return in the spring the conquerors," Rick Salutin wrote in his play *Les Canadiens*. Was this need because of Richard or Blake? Was it something about being a Québécois? Who but the Rocket would attack a referee? Who but a Canadiens fan would tear-gas a game and trash Sainte Catherine Street?

Players on other teams put everything into a game. Canadiens players put in more. Other teams won sometimes, the Canadiens won all the time. Everything about this game, this team, these players seemed to matter more in Quebec. To us outside the province, the Canadiens were a mystery. Quebec was a mystery.

Okay: Béliveau we understood. Tall, graceful, he played like we did, only better. Richard, dangerous, Plante, a cartoon, were unknowable.

And what we didn't understand, we imagined. We drew on stereotypes, then blew them up to mythical dimensions: Quebeckers play as they do because of a different kind of love for a team and a game. Or because of an anger and resentment at living in an English world. Or out of desperation: *This is my chance to truly make it, to earn money, to be adored. To enter the realm of myth in Quebec.*

We think of sport as connecting the unconnected. Sport puts players from different worlds on the same field of play and makes their cultures seem less foreign. But in the 1950s and 1960s, before the advent of sports channels and TV games every night, almost nobody outside Quebec ever saw a Canadiens game with their own eyes. The team became the stuff of legend, not of reality, and so did Quebec. In this way, ironically, the Canadiens made the divide wider, the solitudes deeper.

It is different now. The Canadiens haven't won a Stanley Cup in twenty-three years, and have only won twice since 1979. Yet because of the great teams that won fifteen Stanley Cups between 1956 and 1979, the impact of the Canadiens on the NHL and on hockey itself remains profound. When the game was getting slower in the 1960s, the Canadiens opened it up. When the Philadelphia Flyers bullied their way to two straight Cups in the mid-1970s, the Canadiens were tough enough to stand up to them, and fast enough to sweep them in four straight games in the 1976 finals. The game, and the Canadiens, never looked back. Fifty-six years after his last game, it's Richard, not Gretzky, Howe, or Orr, who remains the enduring symbol of drive, desire, and the need to win. It's Plante, not his close rivals Sawchuk or Hall, who is remembered. The others were merely great. Plante was important. And now, in a time when teams are worth hundreds of millions of dollars or more, when they have become a central asset to a rich owner (and not just a beloved hobby), when teams have to be run as businesses, the Canadiens still seem like a team whose first purpose is to win. The Canadiens are hockey's most important team.

THE NUMBERS, HOWEVER, are beginning to tell another story. Quebec now has 23 per cent of Canada's population. But it is the birthplace of just 12 per cent of Canada's players in the NHL. Ontario has 39 per cent of the population and 43 per cent of its players. Alberta stands at 12 and 14 per cent; B.C., at 13 and 11. Saskatchewan, at 3 and 8, has one-eighth of Quebec's population and three-quarters of its number of players. Of all the provinces, only New Brunswick has fewer players per capita in the NHL than Quebec.

Look at today's NHL: Vincent Lecavalier, Alex Tanguay, Patrice Bergeron, Antoine Vermette, Kris Letang, Marc-André Fleury—they are the best francophone players from Quebec now in the league. Not one of them is a star; not one is even close. In junior leagues, not one Québécois great is on the horizon. The last Québécois star was a goalie, Martin Brodeur. Before him, it was Mario Lemieux, who, except for brief comeback attempts, retired in 2003, as did Patrick Roy; Ray Bourque retired in 2001. Then it's a long time back to the last wave of stars, to Guy Lafleur, Mike Bossy, Marcel Dionne, and Gilbert Perreault, whose final years were in the 1980s. Now, after the aging, and then retirement of Roy and Brodeur, Quebec no longer develops the NHL's best goalies (Carey Price, Jonathan Quick, Henrik Lundqvist, Pekka Rinne), nor the most (Ontario).

The best Canadian NHL players today—Sidney Crosby (Nova Scotia), Jonathan Toews (Manitoba), Carey Price (B.C.), Steven Stamkos (Ontario), John Tavares (Ontario), Drew Doughty (Ontario), Ryan Getzlaf (Saskatchewan), Shea Weber (B.C.), Claude Giroux (Ontario)—are not from Quebec. Nor is the best young NHL player, Connor McDavid (Ontario). The Canadiens' roster, which in the 1950s included Richard, Béliveau, and Plante, and in the 1970s, Lafleur, Cournoyer, and Savard, today has only three players from Quebec, none of them household names: David Desharnais, Torrey Mitchell, and Mark Barberio.

Before every hockey World Cup, someone will argue that a team should be included from Quebec. After all, Scotland, Wales, and Northern Ireland compete in soccer's top event. But today, if there were a Team Quebec, it might not finish in the top six. And if teams from other Canadian provinces were also included, the Quebec team might not finish in the top eight. Some have said that the Canadiens should have many more francophone Quebeckers on their roster. But today, if the Canadiens had a *full* roster of francophone Quebeckers taken from the entire NHL talent pool, they might not make the playoffs.

How did this happen?

Players from Quebec were always known for their quickness and skill. They were often smaller, but they were tough, in mind and body, because they needed to win. Players from the rest of Canada were bigger, less creative, more predictable in how they played. They were the solid, reliable defenders, able to play more varied roles in more varied situations in a game. Quebeckers were the scorers.

Things have changed for three major reasons:

First, European players began to arrive in the NHL in the 1970s; many more came during the following decade, and more still in the 1990s after the Berlin Wall came down. They too were known for their quickness and skill—some were small, many were big—but not for their toughness. In the years since, however, they have added toughness to their skill set. In many ways, European players do now what Quebec players once did.

Second, players from the rest of Canada have added finesse to their strength and reliability. Players from outside Quebec are now the scorers, so where do Quebec players fit in?

Lastly, Quebec's competitive advantage once came from its natural resources of cold, ice, and time alone. Now hockey has moved indoors, and it is organized around sophisticated teaching systems instead of individual play. Quebec's inherent advantage has therefore been lost.

No province, no place in the world, has had a greater impact on hockey than Quebec. The game was born in Quebec. Its greatest team and deepest passions reside there. Perhaps two of the five most outstanding players in NHL history, Richard and Lemieux (along with Howe, Orr, and Gretzky), and its two greatest goalies, Plante and Roy, are from Quebec. No province has shaped the game so powerfully. But now I ask: What is Quebec's next great hockey act? Who is the next Jacques Plante?

anxi
ner wild da
ed into that and
did the explaining.
stank. I found out
truck. Freddy always
about things. He
go!"

DENI ELLIS BÉCHARD

JACK KEROUAC

THE REAL-LIFE BACKSTORY of Jack Kerouac's unpublished novel is classic Beat Generation. It's December 1952, and tensions are running high as Jack and his friend Neal Cassady—the inspiration for the character of Dean Moriarty in *On the Road*—drive from San Francisco to Mexico City. Just before their departure, Neal's wife, Carolyn, threatened to leave him for Jack, whom she'd already taken on as a lover (albeit with Neal's approval). To secure her permission for the trip, Neal had to promise she could join Jack later for a Mexican vacation.

Whereas Neal is looking for adventure and a chance to stock up on weed, Jack is in a difficult period. His first novel, *The Town and the City*, published under the name John Kerouac in 1950, met with lukewarm reviews and poor sales. In April 1951, he wrote *On the Road* on a (now famous) 120-foot-long scroll, but wasn't able to find a publisher (nor would he for another six years). He was thirty, and had been laid off by the railroad after a bout of phlebitis in his leg.

Kerouac decided to convalesce in Mexico City with William Burroughs, who would later author *Naked Lunch*. Three months earlier, Burroughs had performed a William Tell act with his wife, Joan, while they were drunk, and had accidentally shot her in the head, killing her.

Shortly after Kerouac's arrival, Burroughs skipped bail and fled the country. Neal Cassady went home. Carolyn decided not to visit Jack, and Neal kept Jack's last paycheque rather than forward it on. Alone, living in a rooftop apartment in Mexico City, Jack wrote a short novel over the course of five days.

The first line reads: *Dans l'moi d'Octobre, 1935, (dans la nuit de nos vra vie bardasseuze) y'arriva une machine du West, de Denver, sur le chemin pour New York.* Written in Kerouac's childhood language, a French-Canadian patois then commonly spoken in parts of New England, the line has an epic, North American ring. Kerouac would later translate it: "In the month of October, 1935, in the night of our real restless lives, a car came from the West, from Denver, on the road for New York."

The novel's title is *Sur le chemin*—"On the Road." But it is not the *On the Road* we all know (which would be translated in France as *Sur la route*). It was the *On the Road* of Kerouac's vernacular—*chemin* being used in the title as both "path" and "road." (My own family in Quebec often uses the same expression, asking, "Tu prends le chemin?" to say, "Are you hitting the road?")

Over the course of his literary career, Kerouac did so much to redefine the archetype of the American man, and has since become so integral to American culture, that his identity as an immigrant writer often is forgotten. He was born in 1922 as Jean-Louis Lebris de Kérouac to parents from Quebec. He spoke French at home and grew up in the French-Canadian community of Lowell, Massachusetts. In one of his letters, he wrote, "The English language is a tool lately found . . . so late (I never spoke English before I was six or seven). At 21, I was still somewhat awkward and illiterate sounding in my [English] speech and writings."

In 1954, Kerouac would list everything he had written, and include *Sur le chemin* among his "completed novels"—even though it would remain in his archives for more than sixty years before publication was arranged. *Sur le chemin* and his other French writings provide a key to unlocking his more famous works, showing him as obsessed with the difficulty of living between two languages as he was with his better-known spiritual quests.

In particular, they help explain the path—*le chemin*—he took as he developed his influential style, which fundamentally changed the way writers throughout the world have thought about prose. To this day, Kerouac remains one of the most translated writers, and one of the few whose work is widely shared across generations. His unpublished French works shine a light on how the voice and ideas of an iconic American figure emerged from the experiences of French-Canadian immigrants—a group whose language and culture remain largely unknown to mainstream America.

⚜ ⚜ ⚜ ⚜

IN 1760, WHEN THE BRITISH conquered Quebec—then called New France—they initially repressed the Catholic Church, in keeping with the sectarian antipathies they'd brought over from Europe. But with the uprisings in the Thirteen Colonies and the beginning of the American War of Independence in 1775, the British began to view Catholics—whose notions of divine order were naturally hostile to democracy—as potential allies. In exchange for the Church using the power of the pulpit to discourage the French from making common cause with American rebels, the British agreed not to interfere in how the priests managed the daily lives of their people.

What began as an agreement necessary for the Church's survival in Quebec became a mandate to preserve a doctrinaire form of Catholicism. In 1789, when revolutionaries in France defied religion—destroying churches and desecrating Christian symbols—exiled conservative priests fled to Quebec and imposed even stricter controls over people's lives. They encouraged the formation of large families, with priests often refusing to let women say confession unless they had a child every two years. A society that was poor, uneducated, and agrarian did not have the means or knowledge to rise up against the forces of theocracy. Families commonly had more than a dozen children, and French Canadians became one of the fastest-growing populations in recorded history, absorbing Irish and Scottish immigrants, as well as Aboriginals.

Over time, some French Canadians headed south in search of land or work, or fled there after failed attempts to overthrow British colonial rule in the Rebellions of 1837. Stories made it back of the more temperate winters in the United States, and the abundant employment and good pay in New England's textile, paper, and leather mills. Though Quebec's cultural cohesion—reflecting French Catholic solidarity within a largely Anglo-Saxon and Protestant continent—has historically given it the greatest rate of population retention of any Canadian province, daily life during this particular period was becoming increasingly difficult.

Between 1784 and 1844, Quebec's population increased 400 per cent while available agricultural land grew by only 275 per cent. By 1840, the most fertile areas already had been developed. Land scarcity, compounded with repeated crop failures, the short growing season, and a lack of industrialization, led to the exodus of approximately nine hundred thousand French Canadians between 1840 and 1930—a group now described as the Quebec Diaspora. Thousands set out for the Canadian west and the American Midwest. But the majority—nearly half the population of Quebec—went to New England's mill towns. Fall River, Rhode Island, would, at one point, constitute the third-largest francophone city in North America.

Among immigrant groups, the French Canadians were low on New England's social ladder, and often were looked down on—especially by the Irish, who competed with them for jobs and control of the Catholic Church. Franco-American author Clark Blaise writes that these newcomers to New England were "one of the first immigrant people in the United States to challenge the myth of the Melting Pot"—and so were in some ways analogous to "today's Latin Americans."

Blaise cites a *New York Times* editorial from 1892 that warned against the French Canadians' "singular tenacity as a race and their extreme devotion to their religion," and that describes their migration as a "priestly scheme" to bring "New England under the control of the Roman Catholic faith." The editorial accuses the *curé*, the parish priest, of blocking the assimilation to American ways: "It is next to impossible to penetrate this mass of protected and secluded humanity with modern ideas. . . . No other people, except the Indians, are so persistent in repeating themselves."

In the 1930s, with the onset of the Great Depression, the U.S. government made immigration more difficult, imposing strict border controls. States implemented policies that forced French Canadians to assimilate, no longer allowing them to study exclusively at French parochial schools. Franco-Americans recall being spat at and insulted as "frogs," "pea-soupers," and "dumb Canucks," or told to "speak white." To avoid racism and assimilate more easily, many changed their names.

Kerouac grew up in Lowell during this period. It was a time when decades of relative prosperity and hope had turned to hardship, when dislike of French Canadians intensified. In his memoir *American Ghosts*, Franco-American author David Plante recalls his mother discussing how French Canadians often were dismissed as "white niggers." (The phrase later would be co-opted by Quebec nationalists. In 1968, for instance, Québécois author and activist Pierre Vallière produced a book called *White Niggers of America*, which argued that the oppression of French Canadians was analogous to that suffered by African-Americans.) In a similar vein, Clark Blaise recounts how American nativists feared the "rodent-like rapidity" of French reproduction cycles, and described the prevailing hatred as "a sexual terror, a racist, white-nigger terror." (Though the adoption of the word *nigger* to describe French Canadians highlights the prejudices they faced, the racially justified enslavement and savagery inflicted on generations of African-Americans has no true parallel in the continent's history.)

Kerouac's first novel, *The Town and the City*, while deeply autobiographical, largely masked his French-Canadian upbringing. In a review in *Le Travailleur*, a French-language newspaper published in Worchester, Mass., the Franco-American critic Yvonne LeMaître asked whether Kerouac might be avoiding the genre of the immigrant novel. LeMaître pointed out that although Kerouac's family were known *survivants*—a term denoting those who sustained the "survival" of the French identity—he failed to plant human roots in his writing.

Kerouac responded in September 1950 with a passionate letter to LeMaître, in which he betrayed how unsettled he felt about his identity: "I cannot write my native language and have no native home any more, and am amazed by that horrible homelessness all French-Canadians abroad in America have. . . . Someday, Madame, I shall write a French-Canadian novel, with the setting in New England, in French. It will be the simplest and the most rudimentary French. . . . All my knowledge rests in my 'French-Canadianness' and nowhere else. . . . Isn't it true that French-Canadians everywhere tend to hide their real sources. Believe me, I'll never hide it again; as once I did, say in high school, when I first began 'Englishizing myself.'"

Jean-Christophe Cloutier, the translator of Kerouac's soon-to-be-published French writings, and the editor of a forthcoming volume of collected French texts, notes that in the period following this exchange between Kerouac and LeMaître, "French begins to [re-] infiltrate Kerouac's thoughts, and he comments [in his journal] on how the assimilative pressures of the U.S. have forced him to 'pass' as an American for years."

In 1951—a year before he wrote his only complete French novel, the aforementioned *Sur le chemin*—Kerouac penned a novella, *La nuit est ma femme* ("The Night Is My Woman"). Subtitled *The Labors of Michel Bretagne*, it is more simply written than many of Kerouac's works, its tone distinctly confessional. As the subtitle suggests, it describes the jobs that he had held (under the alter ego Michel Bretagne), and the hardships of a workingman's life.

"*Je suis Canadien Français*—I am French Canadian, born in New England," he wrote. "When I am angry I often curse in French. When I dream I often dream in French. When I cry I always cry in French, and I say: 'I don't like it, I don't like it!' It's my life in the world that I don't want."

Cloutier points out that Kerouac often uses English words to describe work, embedding them in the French language. The linguistic interruptions evoke his sense of cultural subjugation, with English being the language of the system that immigrants must adopt to survive. Kerouac's narrative suggests how the private voice—the confessional, Catholic voice—struggles within a society that delivered a livelihood to dispersed French Canadians while also gradually erasing their culture.

Within this bilingual coming-of-age story, Kerouac also implicitly explores the overarching question of how he creates literature—a subject that he had touched on in his letter to LeMaître, in which he wrote: "The reason I handle English words so easily is because it is not my own language. I refashion it to fit French images." In *La nuit est ma femme*, he addresses the same issue in another way: "I dreamed for too long that I was a great writer. . . . At first I used big 'fancy' words, big forms, 'styles' that had nothing to do with me. When I was a child in New England I ate my supper at the table and wiped my mouth with the dishrag—done, and gone. Why the big words, the grand lyrics, to express life?" And then Kerouac supplies this astonishing line: "I never had a language of my own. French patois until 6 years old, and after that the English of the guys on the corner. And after that—the big forms, the lofty expressions, of poets, philosophers, prophets. With all that today I'm all mixed up in my noggin."

These thoughts help chart Kerouac's transition between *The Town and the City* and *On the Road*—between the more conventional narrative of that early time and the rhythmic, free writing that Kerouac invented to express himself authentically—and that generations of young readers have come to associate with his name. He had to bridge not only two worlds, but two ways of speaking of these worlds. One was a private patois, the voice of a community that used its language to communicate solidarity. The other was public and assimilative.

And though English would all but extinguish French usage in the United States, it was the language of the literature Kerouac loved, the literature that introduced him to the world outside his community and forged his intellectual bonds with Allen Ginsberg, Gary Snyder, Neal Cassady, William Burroughs, and numerous childhood friends. These included boys from other ethnic backgrounds—such as Sebastian Sampas, a son of Greek immigrants, who died in World War II (and whose sister Kerouac eventually would marry).

Accordingly, Kerouac's life embraced two visions of identity and sainthood. The first was embodied in Neal Cassady—a neo-pioneer whose workingman knowledge of life compelled him to reject the strictures of mainstream society, even as he embodied the virile, masculine purity of the "archetypal West, the energy of the frontier" (in Gary Snyder's words). The second vision was that of the individual who lived and suffered for his community, and who at times faced America with the watchful, wary disposition that Kerouac attributed to himself.

⚜ ⚜ ⚜ ⚜

WHEN BURROUGHS SAID that Kerouac "sold a trillion Levi's, a million espresso coffee machines, and also sent countless kids on the road," he was referring to the influence of *On the Road*, the book that forged the image of the Beat Generation and Kerouac as its rambling, all-American pied piper. He was no longer Jean-Louis or even John, but Jack. A more American-sounding name could hardly be imagined.

The style of *On the Road*—with its illusion of natural, uninhibited, stream-of-consciousness composition—presented an aesthetic that many readers saw as the very embodiment of Beat attitude. Yet few readers who've taken inspiration from *On the Road* understood its relationship to the French language. Even among scholars, little attention has been given to how the book's distinctive style emerged from Kerouac's struggle with questions of voice and belonging.

I first read the as-yet-unpublished *Sur le chemin* at the New York Public Library's Kerouac archives, in two small worn Mexican school notebooks that Kerouac carried in his backpack for years, along with the rest of his works in progress. Though Kerouac announced his intention to translate and publish the novel in a 1953 letter to Neal and

Carolyn Cassady (he describes it as the "solution to the *On the Road* plots"), the archives contain only an unfinished typescript translation—which he entitled *Old Bull in the Bowery*.

Cloutier, while transcribing the notebooks, marked several points where Kerouac indicated insertions. The thought that the notebooks were part of a larger project haunted Cloutier. And so, over several years, he returned to the Kerouac archives, where, with the permission of Kerouac's executor, he was able to identify and consolidate sections of narrative that had been scattered in the voluminous files.

In its fully assembled form, *Sur le chemin* is more wholly representative of Kerouac's world view than any other novel in his oeuvre, bringing together as it does many of the other novels' themes and characters. Some sections are in French, some are in English. In both languages, there are traces of the other.

Sur le chemin begins with nine-year-old Dean Pomeray Jr. on his way to New York. He is the embodiment of Neal Cassady, but this time as a child. Kerouac is indecisive in naming him, first calling him Dean McGee and then crossing out "McGee." (Such are the forensic benefits of reading a manuscript in its original form.) At times thereafter, the author refers to him as "Neal." Whether or not this indecision may have been the effect of too much Benzedrine, Kerouac did settle firmly on "Pomeray," a French name that presents a departure from Cassady's own Irish roots.

Travelling with Dean Jr. is his father, the wino Dean Pomeray, and his half-brother Rolfe Glendiver, a cowboy. With America mired in the Great Depression, Rolfe is driving them all to New York so they can start over in an apartment belonging to relatives in Massachusetts. Their main contact is Guillaume Berniér, nicknamed Old Bull, the Quebec-born brother of Rolfe and Dean Jr.'s dead mother. Leo Duluoz, Old Bull's nephew, is on his way from Boston with his own son, the thirteen-year-old Ti Jean (Kerouac's actual childhood nickname—"Lil John"), and the keys to the apartment.

Like *On the Road*, *Sur le chemin* unites Neal and Jack under different names, along with other characters who appear in Kerouac's novels, such as Pictorial Review Jackson and his older brother Slim, a jazz musician. These they meet in the gambling room of a Chinese-American man, Ching Boy, who is there with his own son. The narrative loops in long passages through these characters' backstories, and then returns to junctures where their lives intersect.

Sur le chemin has the feel of a classic American text of its era, almost Faulkneresque with its driving language and changing points of view, full of sudden digressions rich with descriptions of the United States. It moves from Rolfe's life in the West as a cowboy—"he castrated bulls and rode the long fences with shears and pliers, eyes half closed in the wind . . . . He was the tragic son of broken marriage and death of both parents, he was all alone among the aunts of eternity in a big house full of incomprehensible bustle with doors that opened on the mountains of snow and rock, the Rockies, and the great dun bleak land of Denver plain"—to descriptions of dangerous, hardscrabble travels in search of work.

"Huge prairie clouds massed and marched above the indescribable anxiety of the earth's surface where men lived as their car belittled itself in immensity, crawled eastward like a potato bug over roads that led to nothing," Kerouac wrote, in a section of the book describing Old Bull and Dean Pomeray Sr.'s efforts as door-to-door salesmen, peddling handmade flyswatters they've constructed from wire, screen, and cloth. "[Little Dean] sat in the rattly back seat counting the lonely pole-by-pole throb of telegraph lines spanning sad America."

And then the narrative shifts to Leo Duluoz and Ti Jean. As they drive west from Boston, Kerouac details their French-Canadian ancestry in biblical cadence, listing which Duluoz "begat" which. Of Ernest Duluoz, he writes "there never was an American white garage putterer with tools and hobbies like the original Canuck with his miserly cold dead calm." Joseph Duluoz "was sick all his life, cried, gasped all the time; from asthma, sadness; a grocer built like a pickle barrel, 230 pounds, bilious sufferings made his face gray like doom . . . he had the soul of a harassed saint."

The story gradually returns to Rolfe, who, in New York now, sets out to find the apartment where Dean and his son will live. When Rolfe arrives at the window, he sees a man inside with two women, but can't discern the man clearly enough to recognize him as his friend Omer Leclerc.

Rolfe is outraged by the scene—a failed, drugged-out threesome. In the process, he experiences a reverse discovery from that described in *On the Road*: not the expansive American west, but the cramped, confusing, filthy industrial east. Recoiling from the debauchery, Rolfe decides this is no place for a family. He leaves, taking Dean and his father back to Denver. Indeed, all the individuals who briefly came together set out again, back to Boston or, in the case of Slim Jackson, to Chicago, to play in a jazz band.

The presence of the black musician evokes the novel's order—the precarious balance of jazz itself, the narrative improvising in cultural solos across the landscape. Through the rhythmic juxtaposition of voices and narratives, Kerouac captures the feeling of the jazz he loved so much, his hybrid language an expression of confusion and cultural collision like the music itself.

Though *Sur le chemin* continues Kerouac's exploration of masculine American strength and inventiveness, he embodies it this time not in the character of *On the Road*'s Dean Moriarty, but in Rolfe, an offshoot of the French-Canadian Diaspora. Rather than rewriting his characters to be more American—as in *On the Road*—he puts their Frenchness at the heart of their American identity. He writes his history into the most recognizable American figure: the cowboy.

KEROUAC WOULD GO ON to write two sets of novels: his so-called "Lowell novels"—such as *Maggie Cassidy* and *Visions of Gerard*—which describe growing up in Massachusetts and in which he would further explore his French roots, albeit almost entirely in English; and his better-known "Beat novels," which say little about his French-Canadian identity, or even efface it entirely.

In *On the Road*, by pegging its narrator as Italian-American—a more established and recognizable immigrant archetype—Kerouac increased the book's chance of success. But though the narrative focuses on Moriarty as Cassady's alter ego—a man with a primal sex drive, the creative intuition of a frontiersman, and "the tremendous energy of a new kind of American saint"—there are moments that do point to the larger questions of identity haunting Kerouac (who exists within the book as narrator Sal Paradise). At one point, he compares himself to a Mexican. Later, infamously, he tells readers that he wishes he were black.

In the former instance, Paradise is shacking up with Terry, a Mexican woman living in a California migrant labour camp. When a group of "Okie" migrants beats a man, he worries for his own safety: "From then on I carried a big stick with me in the tent in case they got the idea we Mexicans were fouling up their trailer camp. They thought I was a Mexican, of course; and in a way I am." (In the original, unedited manuscript version of the book, Sal and his Italian-American heritage are nowhere to be found. Instead, the narrator is Jack himself, openly French Canadian. In the trailer camp scene, tellingly, he drops "in a way," and writes: "They thought I was a Mexican, of course; and I am.")

These glancing allusions to the author's feeling of otherness are nothing compared to the theme of immigrant identity conveyed explicitly in Kerouac's Lowell novels. Take, for instance, *Visions of Gerard*'s description of the "particular bleak gray jowled pale eyed sneaky fearful French Canadian quality of man, with his black store, his bags of produce, his bottomless mean and secret cellar, his herrings in a barrel, his hidden gold rings, his wife and daughter jongling in another dumb room, his dirty broom in the corner, his piousness, his cold hands, his hot bowels, his well-used whip, his easy greeting and hard opinion." There is a strong sense of cultural self-loathing here. Kerouac even concludes that description with a rejection of French Canadianness unto death: "Lay me down in sweet India or old Tahiti, I don't want to be buried in their cemetery."

This same sense of cultural insecurity is evoked, rather ineptly, in the aforementioned scene in *On the Road*, in which the narrator expresses a desire to be black: "At lilac evening I walked with every muscle aching among the lights of 27th and Welton in the Denver colored section, wishing I were a Negro, feeling that the best the white world had offered was not enough ecstasy for me, not enough life, joy, kicks, darkness, music, not enough night. I stopped at a little shack where a man sold hot red chili in paper containers; I bought some and ate it, strolling in the dark mysterious streets. I wished I were a Denver Mexican, or even a poor overworked Jap, anything but what I was so drearily, a 'white man' disillusioned. All my life I'd had white ambitions; that was why I'd abandoned a good woman like Terry in the San Joaquin Valley."

It's a controversial passage, one that African-American author James Baldwin correctly dismissed as "offensive nonsense." Kerouac co-opts the black community as a semantic indicator, an arrow pointing home, reducing blacks to props for his nostalgia. A contemporary reader is likely to cringe at the naive romanticizing of a people who suffered enslavement and centuries of marginalization, dehumanization, and brutality. While Kerouac's desire to belong to a culturally authentic close-knit community is genuine, this section of *On the Road* smacks of navel-gazing, and of self-pity for the fact that he can so easily hide his immigrant past behind his whiteness.

As well as selling Levi's and espressos, Kerouac encouraged a very real counterculture. And as much as his perceptions were a symptom of his belonging to that group of white men who, as Baldwin writes, "believe the world is theirs and who, albeit unconsciously, expect the world to help them in the achievement of their identity," Kerouac also attempted to reveal the ways that boundaries and the divisions between people could be crossed.

His Lowell novels do so repeatedly, showing children from different ethnic backgrounds coming together. And his Beat novels suggest a desire to tear down status quo America and make a place for everyone. He attempts to do this in *Sur le chemin*, showing the various faces of the country in one room: black, Irish, Chinese, and French Canadian—the adults and even one child from each group occupying the same space, recognized for their American journeys.

READ AS A PROUSTIAN MEMOIR, a *roman-fleuve*, or, in his own words, "one vast book," Kerouac's combined writings suggest something complicated: a lifelong identity crisis and a search for spiritual and cultural belonging. Even as he fabricated the persona and voice of the American Jack Kerouac, he was concocting alternate legends for his own identity, by turns claiming both Iroquois and European aristocratic heritage.

One of his most sustained and beloved myths was that his lineage was Breton "as far back as anybody could remember, one hundred percent through." The claim is questionable, Quebec being a highly miscegenated society: Normans, Bretons, Acadians, Channel Islanders, and others of French descent mixing with Irish, Scots, and Aboriginals. In *Satori in Paris*, published only three years before Kerouac drank himself to death at the age of forty-seven, the author offers up a specious etymology for "Kerouac," claiming that *ker* derives from "house," and *ouac* from "field." (He builds the comparison by analogy to *bivouac*—"tent" and "field"—a word most likely from the Swiss German *Bîwacht*.) In a *Paris Review* interview with Ted Berrigan, Kerouac supplies a different derivation, saying *ouac* means "language of," and *ker*, "water," in the Cornish tongue.

These conflicting narratives suggest that Kerouac's search for meaning had an anxious, desperate quality. He was trying to legitimize his heritage by rooting it in European history—just as he once had by housing it in archetypal American characters—while also universalizing his experience, showing himself to be one of the *fellaheen* (Arabic for "tiller of the soil,"), a word Kerouac used often to reference the great mass of working people to whom he belonged. And yet his questionable Celtic Breton past connected with the Celtic

Irish-American lineage of Dean—bypassing his very real French-Canadian heritage entirely.

Though a critic such as LeMaître could conclude that Kerouac's debut was "in no way a Franco-American novel," his rejection of his identity, even as he struggled to validate it, speaks more clearly to the immigrant experience of not having one's language or culture valued than any topical treatment ever could.

Sur le chemin and *La nuit est ma femme*, both written in Kerouac's regional French and mixed with English, are of tremendous historical value—even apart from what they tell us about their author. Virtually no other enduring texts from that time show us the cultural collision then taking place in New England, nor the Franco-Americans' contribution to America in a voice that was authentically theirs. In the way Kerouac merges the two languages, in the phonetic renderings of French words he knew by sound but struggled to reproduce on paper, the ebbing of the French-Canadian experience in New England is powerfully felt.

In Quebec, the equivalent use of popular, idiomatic language wasn't observed in literature and theatre until 1968, with the stage production of Michel Tremblay's *Les Belles soeurs*, sixteen years after Kerouac wrote *Sur le chemin*. The play's focus on the real lives of plain-spoken working-class women scandalized the conservative, deeply religious society, and started a revolution in Québécois literature. Until then, the voices of the poor and uneducated, the vernacular of the working class, hadn't been represented in books or on stage.

That way of speaking is still called *joual*, a name originally used to refer to the slang spoken in Montreal's East End. (The word derives from the way "horse"—*cheval*—is spoken by joual speakers.) Kerouac's language differs from that in *Les Belles soeurs*, though it does share an embrace of the real patterns and idioms of the French spoken by ordinary people in a particular part of North America.

The distinctive rhythms of Kerouac's patois come through in this excerpt from *Sur le chemin*, in which the author describes how Dean's wino father sees the world:

Y'eta un ti Catolique, de sa mêre, il chanta des ti cantons des fils d'hotels, les ti gars de cœurs, dans les t'a d foin salopri de les chwals de Nebraska, y'attenda dans le vent pour le toot toot d'l'engineer du chain gang freight avant d'embarquez de se montez des corps entre les trackes pour embarquez un gondola. Il voya les etoiles de montagne dans le ciel; les arbres cria apra eux autres contre les fleus, les grosses rous rolla entour d'eux autre comme des gros benanguez evarouillez d'peur marchant a leux bras a leux guêle poussant dans la blanchesses de la brume les éporduante monstre passeur de steal qui cria sur la tracke avec un 'squee squee'—c'eta le chien de leux asseye-someil dans les coats dans la nuit, tête accottez sur le fer.

Kerouac's translation reads as follows:

He was a Catholic, from his mother, he sang little altar boy songs, little heart-boy songs, in the haystacks dirtied by the horses of Nebraska; he waited in the wind praying for the toot toot of the engineer of the chain gang freight before rising from the barrels of the tracks to climb a gondola. He saw the mountain stars in the sky; trees yelled at him and his father near creeks; malignantly crashing from every leaf; the great wheels rolled underneath them like gigantic beasts haggard with fright walking arm-to-mouth pushing in the whitenesses of the fog the empowdering monstrous weights of steel that screamed on the track with a "squee squee"—it was the dog of their try-sleep in coats in the night, heads on iron.

The patois version gives the impression of a passage from James Joyce's *Finnegans Wake* (a book Kerouac admired), of multiple languages hybridized, inhabiting the same lines and words. Even in Kerouac's English version, the shadow presence of another language is evident. The writing offered a new sound, an original, fresh, and challenging presentation of an American experience.

Kerouac writes in this passage of "*les* chwals *de Nebraska*"—"the horses of Nebraska"—*chwal* being the New England variant (or at least Kerouac's) of *joual*. The term, spelled this way, frequently appears in

Louisianan and Haitian Creole, evoking not only the long history of the French colonial presence, but the peasant language of the people who carried it around the world. Elsewhere in his writing, Kerouac spells the word *shwal*, a more American variant—as Jean-Christophe Cloutier points out—because of the Anglicized "sh" rather than the French "ch" (though they sound the same). Cloutier and I, over the course of our many conversations as he was reconstructing and translating *Sur le chemin*, searched for a shorthand to describe this Franco-American patois—for a term that would crystallize that historical moment in relationship to its language, to its roots in Quebec, and to the larger North American francophone experience.

We finally settled on *shwal*.

WHILE THE EXPERIENCE OF being an immigrant writer does not uniquely define Kerouac's body of work, it helps make sense of his conflicting impulses: an attachment to traditional values and an old community, alongside the desire to succeed in a new one; a dislike of the cultural garments being donned, despite the urgency to get them on; the need to attack what he was becoming, even as he was becoming it.

But Kerouac did find moments of equilibrium in his novels. These tended to come when the project of shaping himself to American ways led to a more radical process of self-creation. The bliss he felt in his Catholic faith became mirrored in drug-fuelled mysticism and Buddhist meditations, in his poetry and bebop prose, which expressed his love of experience and his awe before the vast beauty of America. His vitality in these instances reminds us of how much minorities and immigrants have enriched the fabric of North American life, forging countercultures that have profoundly transformed not only the arts but the very concept of identity.

As discussed above, Kerouac is rightly credited with inspiring the great countercultural movement of the 1960s, which encouraged young people born into the mainstream to search for identity in escape or even rebellion. But today, his influence is difficult to measure—in part because many of his ideas and narratives became indistinguishable from the now-dominant North American obsessions with authenticity and individualism. Todd Tietchen, a Kerouac scholar and the editor of his posthumously published works, writes that Kerouac's "readership seems to be growing as time goes on, despite being dismissed with so much vitriol by his peers such as [Truman] Capote and [Norman] Mailer, both of whom seem to be read less and less." Tietchen argues that Kerouac continues to connect with readers because of his honesty, vulnerability, and lack of guile—as well as a "sprawling memory aesthetic" that foreshadowed the confessional self-narration of social media.

Meanwhile, widespread disillusionment with our economic system and with traditional goals built around career and family have given more resonance to Kerouac's quest to fully live in the moment. Among millennials, the emphasis on experience over materialism has become a defining feature of youth culture—with the mantras of yolo ("You only live once") and fomo ("Fear of missing out") reflecting a desire to reject an uncertain future in favour of a concrete present. Just as the Beat Generation grew up with devastating war, economic uncertainty, and rising social conservatism, today's youth have been raised in the age of terror, with low-grade Forever Wars raging around the world, a global recession, and a resurgence of reactionary ideologies. Many of today's youth would agree with Kerouac's passionate and urgent vision for how to live.

In his novels, the characters are on their own, meeting outside of institutions; working together to create solutions; and embarking on sexual, intellectual, and spiritual exploration. In an age when distrust of all large institutions is high, these narratives have retained their relevance—for they supply a basis for optimism. As Ralph Gleason wrote in 1958, "not once in *On the Road*, no matter how sordid the situation nor how miserable the people, is there no hope."

Kerouac's influence can also be seen in the American tradition of working-class and immigrant literature, which has attempted to capture the authentic voices and experiences of the downtrodden and marginalized. His work drove attention away from the white elite, and focused it on the lives of ordinary Americans. As the Hispanic theorist Jose De La Isla writes, "Sometimes, it takes a novelist's hitchhiking sociology and the psychology at truck stops to capture a mood that gets left out of a nation's story."

Jean-Christophe Cloutier teaches Kerouac in both graduate and undergraduate courses at the University of Pennsylvania, and has kept an eye on Kerouac's ongoing global influence. As of this writing, he notes, a "Jack Kerouac" Wikipedia entry exists in sixty-two languages. Just last year, *The Dharma Bums* was translated into Farsi.

While some American cultural elitists will dismiss Kerouac, echoing criticisms first supplied by Capote and Baldwin, the fact remains that all of Kerouac's books are still in print. His influence is on display in the work of musicians such as Patti Smith, Tom Waits, and Bob Dylan; Quebec writers Victor-Levy Beaulieu and Jacques Poulin; and Mexico's La Onda movement. A German student has even turned *On the Road* into a series of navigable GPS directions, so that young people anywhere can set out in his footsteps.

ALMOST AS SOON AS Kerouac rose to fame in the late 1950s, he became torn between the Beat culture he'd elevated and his traditional Catholic values. His 1962 novel *Big Sur* captures this conflict a few years after the publication of *On the Road*. In his private life, he lived with his mother in Florida, and missed her and their cats each time he ventured out among friends. This domesticity was very much at odds with the myth of Kerouac, which presented him as being in a constant state of creative rebellion. The alter-ego protagonist of *Big Sur* (Jack Duluoz) sums this up when he says of a young Beatnik admirer: "the poor kid actually believes that there's something noble and idealistic and kind about all this beat stuff, and I'm supposed to be the King of the Beatniks according to the newspapers, so but at the same time I'm sick and tired of all the endless enthusiasms."

The author's travels have changed, too—though he seems to take no pleasure in the upgrades: "all so easy and dreamlike compared to my old harsh hitch hikings before I made enough money to take transcontinental trains (all over America highschool and college kids thinking 'Jack Duluoz is 26 years old and on the road all the time hitch hiking' while there I am almost 40 years old, bored and jaded in a roomette bunk)."

In one of the more striking passages in *Big Sur*, Duluoz suffers from the DTs in a cabin on the coast, and can no longer maintain his facade. He begins praying to God in French: "*O mon Dieux, pourquoi Tu m'laisse faire malade comme ça—Papa Papa aide mué—Au j'ai mal au coeur—J'envie d'aller à toilette 'pi ça m'interesse pas—Aw 'shu malade—Owaowaowao . . .*" He then notices that the aforementioned Beat fan is sitting outside the window with a book.

Briefly, the two Kerouacs occupy the same space: the Beat hero, and the son of French-Canadian immigrants who prays to medallions of the Virgin Mary and speaks in *shwal*. Scarcely has he called out to God than he has judged himself, concerned about what his young admirer might say: "I wonder now what he told people about this later, it must have sounded horrible."

The image is beautiful and strangely biblical: the prophet of a generation calling out for salvation only to judge what is truest in himself. Kerouac's honesty here exemplifies his enduring appeal. He shows himself suffering, drunk, confused, lonely, missing his mother and cats—and yet also desiring admiration. He is the aging writer, the devout Catholic, the Beat, the American man, and the French-Canadian immigrant.

If someday the English-speaking world outlives its romance with the simple, exuberant Beat Kerouac, there may be space to free him from myth, to humanize him and place him back in a history no less American for its being French-Canadian as well. Maybe then this conflicted, kneeling Kerouac can be remembered: his story as much an inspiration as a warning, a record of loss—and, in this way, far more American than most of us know it to be.

JONATHAN KAY

AFTERWORD

I TOOK ON THE JOB *of co-editing this book because I wanted to change the way my fellow English Canadians think about their country. Specifically, I believed—and continue to believe—that Anglos would exhibit more respect for the Québécois if we took stock of all the ways in which the French have contributed to modern Canada in the domains of politics, social values, literature, and even sports.*

I will confess to my own ignorance in these areas. Though I grew up in Quebec, my knowledge of many of the protagonists discussed in this book was shallow—in some cases, non-existent—until I took up this project.

It's not something I'm proud of. But I believe my experiences growing up as a Quebec Anglo, described below, may help explain why so much work remains to be done in repairing relations between English and French.

THAT PLACE ON THE LAKE where you go on weekends with the family. In Toronto, it's called a cottage. In Newfoundland, a cabin. In New Brunswick, camp. In the Montreal of my childhood, Anglos called them country houses.

The term was accurate in a literal sense. Yet the two words also came with the unspoken Victorian residue of duck decoys and after-dinner sherry. Which suited many of us just fine. This was the 1970s. René Lévesque's separatist PQ was rewriting the province's language laws. In this climate, the maintenance of old-stock English affectation was a point of pride.

My own family's "country house"—situated in the Laurentian hamlet of Ivry-sur-le-Lac, an hour's drive north of Montreal—was shabbier than most. Ants and larger creatures left their calling cards everywhere. (I have a distinct memory of my father catching a bat in the attic using a butterfly net. The bat bit his thumb as he tried to remove the thing from the netting, and we had to go to the hospital so he could get rabies tests.) The power went out often—once famously resulting in my mother arriving to a freezer full of rotted chicken after a long absence. It was so putrid, she claims, that the stench bore permanently into the metalwork of the appliance itself.

The cable companies hadn't wired up the Laurentians yet, which meant the only English-language channel that came in clearly was CBC. (Naturally, my sister and I memorized the local programming schedule. *Star Trek* on Sunday at 10 a.m. was the weekend highlight.)

Over the summer and winter holidays, my family would go to Ivry for weeks at a time. The absence of other children aggravated my penchant for weirdness. I was fond of building the evening fire—patiently watching the flame jump and catch from newspaper to kindling to logs. I imagined that there were whole communities of tiny invisible people living on these items, fleeing from one to the next until they finally ran out of the fireplace entirely.

Ivry was a place for books. In the summer of my ninth year, mom read me *The Hobbit* chapter by chapter, from start to finish, on a scratchy green sofa covered in dog hair. The section in which Bilbo Baggins escapes Gollum's subterranean lair ranks as the most powerful, and formative, literary experience of my entire life.

I would claim to my wealthier friends at private school—more on them later—that our country home was situated on a "small lake." The truth is that it was more of a pond—a tiny downstream adjunct to massive Lake Manitou. Mosquitoes loved the weak current—and my father and I would spend evenings hurling weighted insecticide capsules into the dense swampy areas on the far shore. On sunny days, I spent my time prowling the rocks piled on the shore with a net, catching frogs, tadpoles, minnows, perch, crayfish.

I'd pick wild blueberries, and my mother would make pies. I'd find hornet's nests, throw rocks at them, get stung, wonder at the stupidity of man and the burden of freedom, then do it all again, this time imagining the sadistic folly as an act of righteous vengeance against the insect kingdom.

In our city house, the business of plumbing and electricity hummed along unseen behind drywall. Not so in Ivry, where breakers, fuses, pipes, pumps—the true guts of a home—lay in open view, or peeked out from behind roughly laid insulation. The basement, in particular, always felt like an active construction site.

After a big storm or a harsh cold snap, something would break down. The septic tank would fail. A pipe would freeze. A circuit would fry. If the fix was simple, my dad would do the job himself. But when things got more complicated, he'd pick up the phone and call Léo Cadieux.

Léo could fix anything. He also happened to be the only francophone who was ever regularly invited into our house.

My dad would speak to Léo in a respectful but awkward mix of pidgin English and plain-awful French. Léo would respond in kind, and the two would go back and forth like this for a while. Eventually, silence would descend, as the expert handyman took out his tools and got the job done. In this way did Léo keep our house, and every country house in the neighbourhood, from collapsing into its foundations.

Léo lived near us, but not among us. As country house owners, we decorated our lawn with dirt-filled tires in bloom with begonias, hammocks strung between shaved-at-the-waist pine trees, a Wiffle ball diamond (my dad and I were fanatics), hobby gardens happily surrendered to rabbits, beached rowboats, and canoes with funny names painted on the side. Not so with Léo—whose house sat on the inland side of the water. His property was full of band saws, wheelbarrows, piles of gravel and sand.

As my father would drive me to play tennis with our local country house friends—the Steinbergs, the Lewiteses, the Perlmans, the Robinsons, the Ptacks, the Millers, the Decklebaums—I sometimes would pass the Cadieux house and lock eyes with Léo's children and other younger relatives, some not so much older than me, as they fed tree branches into a shredder or helped their father unload cargo from a pickup.

That was our two solitudes, of English and French. And until too late in life, I never questioned why it should be so.

It's embarrassing to admit this—but I saw that world, that division of labour between French and English, as the natural order of things. My father was then a stockbroker. Henry Steinberg was a judge. Richard Deckelbaum was a doctor. These were not people who knew their way around a pile driver or snowplow. Who else but Léo was going to keep our little enclave clean and functional?

We had our own troubles anyway. As the names above attest, we weren't just Anglos, but also Jews—a minority within a minority. The most sought-after homes in our part of Ivry existed on a Manitou lakefront road christened with a Yiddish name—Losmira Lane, *Losmira* meaning "Leave me alone." Water ski from one end to the other, and you'd be hard pressed to find a single Gentile, let alone a francophone.

This was still the 1970s, the decade of the Munich Massacre and the Yom Kippur War. Much of Montreal's Jewish community consisted of Holocaust survivors and their children. Discrimination was something that happened to *us*.

Even among my non-Jewish friends, a sense of Anglo victimhood was on the rise. Under Lévesque, the Parti Québécois created a massive bureaucracy aimed at promoting French—largely by suppressing English. New laws limited the use of English on road and commercial signage, and severely restricted access to English-language public schooling. The Régie de la langue française set up a snitch line, and unleashed a legion of clipboard-wielding language gendarmes. At times, it really did go too far. Even many francophones came to believe as much.

In the Montreal-area anglophone bastions of Town of Mount Royal, Hampstead, Notre Dame de Grace, the West Island, Baie D'Urfé, Hudson, and Westmount—especially Westmount—our panic was expressed in the form of rectangular lawn signs, marked *For Sale / À Vendre*. Real estate values plunged. A Montreal diaspora, which I eventually joined, sprang up in Toronto.

But my parents, proud Montrealers, stuck it out—to this day, in fact—refusing to join the exodus. My breadwinning dad was sufficiently established in business that he could run out the professional clock as a unilingual.

That trick doesn't work any more. Léo's generation of Quebec francophones might have been content with the inland side of the road. But not those who came after. In a hundred different ways, Jean Lesage's 1960s-era dream of *maîtres chez nous* began to take definitive form in front of our anxious Anglo eyes. Quebec's French majority finally began to shake off its second-class status.

I would be proud to report that we young Anglos of the era grew to champion this movement for social justice in Quebec—much in the way that straight high school and college students would help further the campaign for gay rights in the 1990s, and white students marched for Black Lives Matter after the tragic disgrace of Ferguson in 2015. But I am ashamed to report that the opposite happened: among my friends, francophone culture was something we defensively mocked as vulgar. When we'd smoke, we'd buy Players, Craven A, and other local brands, then shove the packs up into the shoulders of too-tight T-shirts—a send-up of the street-corner French tough who existed as a stock figure of Anglo mockery.

Other elements of the stereotype: the fuzzy, adolescent moustache; the wardrobe dominated by low-end heavy-metal leatherwork; the Nova SS with *J'aime Ma Femme* mudflaps, Offenbach in the cassette deck, and fuzzy dice hanging from the rear-view mirror. At my suit-and-tie Anglo boys school, Selwyn House, we brats thought this was all so hilarious.

By this time, Montreal's wealthy WASP core was so hollowed out that the patrician Brahmins of upper Westmount took their Anglo allies where they could find them. (They needed *someone* to buy their neighbours' evacuated homes.) We Jewish *parvenus* repaid the favour by taking on the Anglo establishment identity as our own—at least as regards the language question.

In hindsight, I realize that, at a school such as Selwyn House, it was more socially difficult to be a francophone than a Jew (or perhaps even a visible minority). I remember one particular French classmate who drove in every day from an outlying francophone community forty-five minutes away. Never mind that his father was a bilingual, Shakespeare-quoting doctor who sacrificed much so that his son could learn proper English—my language—at a fine school. We called this classmate a "Pepper" to his face, roughly the equivalent of "wop" to an Italian, or "kyke" to a Jew.

We read Molière in French class, and so knew full well that the language was as rich and refined as our own. But in our narrow Victorian-holdover bigotry, that was forgotten. And Fred's Frenchness became wrapped up in the mortifying issue of class. We were bullies. There's no other word for it.

A few years ago, Selwyn House invited me back for Career Day. I got up at the podium and spoke to the school about the joys of journalism—trying to be casual and funny, but really desperately anxious to show my old teachers that yesterday's schoolyard wise-ass had made a success of himself in middle age.

It was the first time I'd been back among Selwyn House students since the day I'd graduated in 1985, and I was shocked by the transformation. In the cafeteria, the wartime-cookbook-era British fare of shepherd's pie and boiled Brussels sprouts had been replaced by a modern menu designed by nutritionists. No one sang "God Save the Queen" at assembly anymore. The terrifying cane, which a sadistic middle-school teacher had used to discipline wayward students in my era, was gone. The student body, once lily-white, now was a multicultural reflection of Montreal.

And I heard as much French in the hallways as English. Queen Victoria, it seemed, had left the building. As a former Montreal Anglo brat, I now had the maturity to say: good riddance.

⚜ ⚜ ⚜ ⚜

FROM MY HOME IN TORONTO, I still travel to Quebec often. The experience always fills me with regret at what could have been. Surrounded by French for the first twenty-four years of my life, I still never bothered to learn it properly. I told myself that I was bad with languages. But the truth is that I believed, on some level, that there would always be an Anglo bubble of wealth and safety for me to call home—and that the only time I'd really need French would be when the pipes froze at my country house.

French cinema, music, theatre, literature—I was a complete stranger to all of it while living at the heart of the second-largest French-speaking city of the world. I could have grown up bilingual. Instead, I'm an English fellow from Quebec who speaks French as if he learned it at an American high school.

Thankfully, people like me aren't created anymore: it's become virtually impossible to grow up in the province without learning at least reasonably fluent conversational French. Most twenty- or thirty-something Quebeckers I meet are comfortable in both languages—studying or working in French, say, while taking in their Netflix and Twitter in English.

To an outsider, this may look a lot like true closure—a great coming-together of the two solitudes embedded within the Quebec of my youth. But not so. Because the modern relationship between English and French in Quebec was never one of true colonial subjugation or brutality, neither side felt the need for any sort of formal reconciliation process between language groups. And so the language wars between French and English ended not with a period but an ellipsis.

In the run-up to the last Quebec provincial election, the then premier, Pauline Marois, and her language lieutenant, Bernard Drainville, tried to continue to play the language card—along with a series of ugly ethno-religious gambits—as part of a nationalist-themed campaign for re-election. Anglo Quebeckers, backed up by pundits in the rest of the country, attacked the Marois phenomenon as a stain on the province itself. From my days as a newspaper editor, I can attest that the topic of Quebec often brings out the worst instincts among English readers. Stereotypes of Quebeckers as lazy, entitled socialists living off the fruits of Anglo industry still abound.

I hope that readers of the essays in this volume will agree with me that the whole basis of this tribalism between French and English is not only destructive but nonsensical—because the influence of great French women and men is reflected in every aspect of our Canadian culture, political legacy, and national institutions.

Deni Béchard explains how Jack Kerouac's *On the Road*—which inspired not only generations of young people but a whole literary movement that remains well read to this day—emerged from the experience of French working-class people displaced from Quebec to New England. As Margaret Atwood argues, many of the accomplishments of modern feminism can be traced to the brilliance of Gabrielle Roy. Ken Dryden shows us how Jacques Plante changed the way hockey, our defining sporting passion, is played, from one end of the ice to the other.

North American Anglos have been parading in negative stereotypes about French speakers since the European settlement of this continent. In some cases, the invective has descended into hate speech as vile as anything said about Jews in the twentieth century, or Muslims in the twenty-first.

Béchard's essay, for instance, references a *New York Times* editorial from 1892 that described French Canadians as a dangerously fecund people who exhibit a "singular tenacity as a race and . . . extreme devotion to their religion," and that denounced their migration to the

United States as a "priestly scheme" to bring "New England under the control of the Roman Catholic faith." No respectable person talks in such a nakedly bigoted way in 2016, of course. But one still hears shades of this attitude—as with the Anglo agitation against Pauline Marois and her charter of secular values in 2014 and 2015. According to the most extreme form of this critique, Marois's disgrace bespoke not just an ugly and unsuccessful political gambit but an inveterate streak of insularity and xenophobia lodged within the French-Canadian character itself.

To rebut this group libel, one need only read Jeremy Kinsman's beautiful essay on Georges Vanier, also contained within this volume. As Kinsman notes, it was the francophone Vanier—not his well-heeled anglophone nemesis Vincent Massey—who fought for the Canadian admission of Jewish refugees in the aftermath of World War II, and who forged in the crucible of wartime suffering a humanist creed that foreshadowed modern Canadian multiculturalism.

Or examine Philip Marchand's fine profile of Pierre Gaultier de Varennes, sieur de La Vérendrye—a French Canadian explorer who forged a trail deep into the Canadian wilderness by building respectful alliances with First Nations people. While the settler communities of New England were waging a war of extermination against surrounding Indigenous peoples, La Vérendrye was trading, negotiating, learning, teaching—setting a rough model for the nation-to-nation relations that modern tribes seek in their negotiations with the federal government.

In its parts, this book is just a collection of biographical essays. But in its whole, it is something more than that—a wake-up call for those anglophones who imagine that the French contribution to this country can be geographically circumscribed by the contours of Quebec on a map.

The French legacy lives within all of us. That is a truth that seems obvious to me now, following on the long and fulfilling task of co-editing this volume. For the sake of Léo, Fred, and all the other francophones to whom I once disgracefully condescended, it is a truth that I wish I had learned earlier in life.

ACKNOWLEDGEMENTS

The publishers would like to thank the following people for their work on this project: André Pratte and Jonathan Kay; Caroline Jamet and Yves Bellefleur; Michael Gilson; Tara Tovell; and Francis Léveillée. Especially appreciated is Michael Levine, whose original vision for this book—a creative partnership between French and English writers, editors, and publishers to celebrate the contributions of French Canadians—and hard work in assembling the various pieces, made it all possible. And, of course, the writers! Rarely in Canadian publishing history has such an eclectic and brilliant group of authors, in both official languages, come together for a common cause: to promote nationalism and bring to life a group of French Canadians that have shaped our shared history.

SOURCES

FOREWORD

Bédard, Éric. *Recours aux sources—Essais sur notre rapport au passé.* Montreal: Les Éditions du Boréal, 2011.

Bouchard, Gérard. *Genèse des nations et cultures du nouveau monde—Essai d'histoire comparée.* Montreal: Les Éditions du Boréal, 2000.

Couture, Claude. *Le Mythe de la modernisation du Québec: Des années 1930 à la Révolution tranquille.* Montreal: Éditions du Méridien, 1991.

Wade, Mason. *The French Canadians.* New York: Macmillan, 1955.

PIERRE DE LA VÉRENDRYE

Benham, Mary Lile. *La Vérendrye.* Toronto: Fitzhenry & Whiteside, 1983.

Champagne, Antoine. *Les La Vérendryes et le Poste de l'Ouest.* Quebec: Presses de l'Université Laval, 1968.

_______. *Nouvelle etudes sur les La Vérendryes et le Poste de l'Ouest.* Quebec: Presses de l'Université Laval, 1971.

Combet, Denis. *In Search of the Western Sea: Selected Journals of La Vérendrye.* Winnipeg: Great Plains Publications, 2001.

Crouse, Nellis M. *La Vérendrye: Fur Trader and Explorer.* New York: Kennikat Press, 1956 (rev. 1972).

Dictionary of Canadian Biography, vol. 2. University of Toronto/Université Laval, 1969 (rev. 1982).

_______, vol. 3. University of Toronto/Université Laval, 1974.

_______, vol. 4. University of Toronto/Université Laval, 1979.

Parkman, Francis. *A Half-Century of Conflict*, vol. 2. New York: Little, Brown, 1897.

ALBERT LACOMBE

Bouchard, Serge and Marie-Christine Lévesque. *Ils ont couru l'Amérique: De remarquables oubliés*, Tome 2. Montreal: Lux Éditeur, 2014.

Dictionary of Canadian Biography, vol. 14. University of Toronto/Université Laval, 1998.

Huel, Raymond J.A. *Proclaiming the Gospel to the Indians and the Métis: The Missionary Oblates of Mary Immaculate in Western Canada, 1845–1945*. Edmonton: University of Alberta Press, 1999.

Hughes, Katherine. *Father Lacombe, the Black-Robe Voyageur*. Toronto: William Briggs, 1911.

Lacombe, Albert. *"l'homme au bon coeur" d'après ses mémoires et souvenirs, recueillis par une soeur de la Providence*. Montreal: Le Devoir, 1916.

Legal, Émile. *Short Sketches of the History of the Catholic Churches and Missions in Central Alberta*. Winnipeg: West Canada Publishing Co., 1914.

Levasseur, Donat. *Les oblats de Marie-Immaculée dans l'Ouest et le Nord du Canada, 1845–1967*. Edmonton: University of Alberta Press, 1995.

MacGregor, J.G. *Father Lacombe*. Edmonton: Hurtig, 1975.

PRUDENT BEAUDRY

Bancroft, Hubert Howe. *History of the Pacific States of North America*, vol. XIX: *California*, vol. VII, 1860–1890. San Francisco: The History Company, Publishers, 1890.

Dictionary of Canadian Biography, vol. 7. University of Toronto/Université Laval, 2003.

_______, vol. 11. University of Toronto/Université Laval, 1998.

_______, vol. 14. University of Toronto/Université Laval, 1998.

Rudin, Ronald. *Banking en français: The French Banks of Quebec 1835–1925*. Toronto: University of Toronto Press, 1985.

Warner, J.J. *An Illustrated History of Los Angeles County, California*. Chicago: Lewis Publishing Co., 1889.

SIR GEORGE-ÉTIENNE CARTIER

Dictionary of Canadian Biography, vol. 10. University of Toronto/Université Laval, 1972.

Lacoursière, Jacques, Jean Provencher, and Denis Vaugeois. *Canada–Québec, 1534–2015*. Quebec: Septentrion, 2015.

Young, Brian J. *George-Étienne Cartier: Montreal Bourgeois*. Montreal and Kingston: McGill-Queen's University Press, 1981.

HENRI BOURASSA

Angers, François-Albert and Patrick Allen (eds.). *La pensée de Henri Bourassa*. Montreal: L'Action nationale, 1954.

Bélanger, Réal. *Henri Bourassa: Le fascinant destin d'un homme libre*. Quebec: Presses de l'Université Laval, 2013.
Bock, Michel. *A Nation Beyond Borders: Lionel Groulx on French-Canadian Minorities*, tr. Ferdinanda Van Gennip. Ottawa: University of Ottawa Press, 2014.
Bourassa, Henri. *Mémoires*, 1943.
Cardinal, Mario. *Pourquoi j'ai fondé* Le Devoir. Montreal: Libre Expression, 2010.
Dictionary of Canadian Biography, vol. 15. University of Toronto/Université Laval, 2005.
_______, vol. 18, University of Toronto/Université Laval, 2009.
Groulx, Lionel. *Mes Mémoires*, vol. II. Montreal: Éditions Fides, 1970.
Hommage à Henri Bourassa. Montreal: Imprimerie Populaire, 1952.
Levitt, Joseph. *Henri Bourassa and the Golden Calf: The Social Program of the Nationalists of Quebec, 1900–1914*. Ottawa: University of Ottawa Press, 1972.
_______. *Henri Bourassa on Imperialism and Bi-culturalism, 1900–1918*. Toronto: Copp Clark, 1970.
O'Connell, Martin. *Henri Bourassa and Canadian Nationalism*, Ph.D. thesis. University of Toronto, 1954.
Pratte, André. *Extraordinary Canadians: Wilfrid Laurier*. Toronto: Penguin Books, 2011.
Rumilly, Robert. *Henri Bourassa: la vie publique d'un grand Canadien*. Montreal: Éditions Chantecler, 1953.
Wade, Mason. *Essais sur le Québec contemporain / Essays on Contemporary Quebec*, Jean-Charles Falardeau, (ed.). Sainte-Foy: Les Presses de l'Université Laval, 1953.

THOMAS-LOUIS TREMBLAY

Ferland, Raphaël Dallaire (tr.). "Patriotism and Allegiances of the 22nd (French Canadian) Battalion, 1914–1918," *Canadian Military Journal*, vol. 13, 2012.
Keelan, Geoff. "'Il a bien merité de la Patrie': The 22nd Battalion and the Memory of Courcelette," *Canadian Military History*, vol. 19, 2015.
Tremblay, Thomas-Louis. *Journal de guerre, 1915–1918: Texte inédit, établit et annoté par Marcelle Cinq-Mars*. Montreal: Athéna, 2006.

GEORGES VANIER

Arabella, Irving and Harold Troper. *None Is Too Many: Canada and the Jews of Europe 1933–1948*. Toronto: Lester & Orpen Dennys, 1986.
Bissell, Claude. *The Imperial Canadian: Vincent Massey in Office*. Toronto: University of Toronto Press, 1986.

Burns, James McGregor. *Roosevelt, The Soldier of Freedom: 1940–1945*. New York: History Book Club, 2006.

Courteaux, Olivier. *Canada Between Vichy and Free France, 1940–1945*. Toronto: University of Toronto Press, 2013.

De Gaulle, Charles. *The Complete War Memoirs of Charles de Gaulle*, tr. Richard Howard. New York: Caroll & Graf Publishers, 1998.

Donaghy, Greg and Stéphane Roussel (eds.). *Mission Paris: Les Ambassadeurs du Canada en France et le triangle*. Montreal: Les Éditions Hurtubise, 2001.

Duguay, Gilles. *Le Triangle Québec–Ottawa–Paris*. Quebec: Septentrion, 2010.

Gildea, Robert. *Fighters in the Shadows: A New History of the French Resistance*. Boston: Belknap Press, 2015.

Granatstein, J.L. *A Man of Influence: Norman A. Robertson*. Ottawa: Deneau Publishers, 1981.

Paxton, Robert. *Vichy France*. New York: W.W. Norton & Co., 1975.

Ritchie, Charles. *Diplomatic Passport: More Undiplomatic Diaries, 1946–1962*. Toronto: Macmillan, 1981.

Speaight, Robert. *Vanier: Soldier, Diplomat and Governor General*. London: Collins, 1970.

THÉRÈSE CASGRAIN

Forget, Nicolle. *Thérèse Casgrain: la gauchiste en collier de perles*. Anjou: Groupe Fides, 2013.

Casgrain, Thérèse. *A Woman in a Man's World*. Toronto: McClelland and Stewart, 1972.

PAUL DAVID

Anne-Marie (Nellie Maillard-David). *L'aube de la joie*. Montreal: Le Cercle du livre de France, 1959.

Bensaïd, Norbert. *La consultation: le dialogue médecin/malade*. Paris: Bibliothèque Méditations, 1974.

David, Laurent-Olivier. *Les Patriotes de 1837–1838*. Montreal: Eusèbe Senécal & fils, 1884.

David, Paul. "À l'aube de l'assurance maladie," *L'Hôpital d'aujourd'hui*, vol. 22(1), January 1970.

Linteau, Paul-André, René Durocher, François Ricard, and Jean-Claude Robert. *Histoire du Québec contemporain, vol. 2: Le Québec depuis 1930*. Montreal: Les Éditions du Boréal, 1989.

Mercure, Philippe. "Des chercheurs montréalais partent à la chasse aux gènes," *La Presse*, May 13, 2015.

Tomatis, Alfred. *Écouter l'univers. Du Big Bang à Mozart: à la découverte de l'univers où tout est son*. Paris: Robert Laffont, 1996.

GABRIELLE ROY

Dictionary of Canadian Biography, vol. 21. University of Toronto/Université Laval, 2005 (rev. 2016).

Roy, Gabrielle. *Street of Riches*. Toronto: McClelland & Stewart, 2008.

_______, *The Tin Flute*. Toronto: McClelland & Stewart, 2009.

JEHANE BENOÎT

Benoît, Jehane. Revised and translated as *My Grandmother's Kitchen*. Toronto: McGraw-Hill Ryerson, 1981.

Driver, Elizabeth. *Culinary Landmarks: A Bibliography of Canadian Cookbooks, 1825–1949*. Toronto: University of Toronto Press, 2006.

The Encyclopedia of Canadian Cuisine, published under the auspices of *Canadian Homes Magazine*. Montreal: Southam Printing, 1964.

Lambert, Michel. "Retour aux sources," *Continuité*, no. 130, Fall 2011.

JACQUES PLANTE

Sources various.

JACK KEROUAC

Baldwin, James. *Nobody Knows My Name*. New York: Vintage, reprint edition, 1992.

Blaise, Clark. *I Had a Father: A Post-Modern Autobiography*. Boston: Addison-Wesley, 1993.

Charters, Ann. *Kerouac: A Biography*. New York: St. Martin's Griffin, 1994.

Kerouac, Jack. *Big Sur*. Toronto: Penguin Books, reprint edition, 2011.

_______ and Jean-Christophe Cloutier (ed.). *La vie est d'hommage*. Montreal: Les Éditions du Boréal, 2016.

_______. *On the Road*. Toronto: Penguin Books, reprint edition, 1999.

_______. *On the Road: The Original Scroll*. Toronto: Penguin Classics, 2008.

_______. *Satori in Paris & Pic*. New York: Grove Press, 1988.

_______ and Ann Charters (ed.). *Selected Letters: vol. 1, 1940–1956*. Penguin Books, 1996.

_______ and Todd Tietchen (ed.). *The Unknown Kerouac: Rare, Unpublished & Newly Translated Writings*, tr. Jean-Christophe Cloutier. New York: The Library of America, 2016.

_______ *Visions of Gerard*. Toronto: Penguin Books, reprint edition, 1991.

Plante, David. *American Ghosts*. Boston: Beacon Press, 2006.
Review of *The Town and the City*. Yvonne LeMaître, *Le Travailleur*, March 23, 1950.

AFTERWORD

Sources various.

INDEX